Allan Pinkerton

**Mississippi Outlaws and the Detectives**

Allan Pinkerton

**Mississippi Outlaws and the Detectives**

ISBN/EAN: 9783337341251

Printed in Europe, USA, Canada, Australia, Japan

Cover: Foto ©Suzi / pixelio.de

More available books at **www.hansebooks.com**

# MISSISSIPPI OUTLAWS

AND THE

# DETECTIVES.

## DON PEDRO AND THE DETECTIVES.

## POISONER AND THE DETECTIVES.

BY

ALLAN PINKERTON,

AUTHOR OF

"THE EXPRESSMAN AND THE DETECTIVE," "THE MODEL TOWN AND THE DETECTIVES," "THE SPIRITUALISTS AND THE DETECTIVES," "THE MOLLIE MAGUIRES AND THE DETECTIVES," "STRIKERS, COMMUNISTS, TRAMPS AND DETECTIVES,"
ETC., ETC., ETC.

 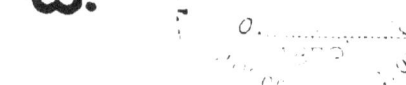

NEW YORK:

*G. W. Carleton & Co., Publishers.*

LONDON: S. LOW, SON & CO.

MDCCCLXXIX.

COPYRIGHT
BY
ALLAN PINKERTON,
1879.

SAMUEL STODDER,
STEREOTYPER,
90 ANN STREET, N. Y.

TROW
PRINTING AND BOOK BINDING
N. Y.

# CHARLES DICKENS' WORKS.

### A New Edition.

Among the many editions of the works of this greatest of English Novelists, there has not been until now one that entirely satisfies the public demand.—Without exception, they each have some strong distinctive objection,—either the form and dimensions of the volumes are unhandy—or, the type is small and indistinct— or, the illustrations are unsatisfactory—or, the binding is poor—or, the price is too high.

An entirely new edition is *now*, however, published by G. W. Carleton & Co. of New York, which, it is believed, will, in every respect, completely satisfy the popular demand.—It is known as

### "Carleton's New Illustrated Edition."
COMPLETE IN 15 VOLUMES.

The size and form is most convenient for holding,—the type is entirely new, and of a clear and open character that has received the approval of the reading community in other popular works.

The illustrations are by the original artists chosen by Charles Dickens himself—and the paper, printing, and binding are of an attractive and substantial character.

This beautiful new edition is complete in 15 volumes—at the extremely reasonable price of $1.50 per volume, as follows:—

    1.—PICKWICK PAPERS AND CATALOGUE.
    2.—OLIVER TWIST.—UNCOMMERCIAL TRAVELLER.
    3.—DAVID COPPERFIELD.
    4.—GREAT EXPECTATIONS.—ITALY AND AMERICA.
    5.—DOMBEY AND SON.
    6.—BARNABY RUDGE AND EDWIN DROOD.
    7.—NICHOLAS NICKLEBY.
    8.—CURIOSITY SHOP AND MISCELLANEOUS.
    9.—BLEAK HOUSE.
    10.—LITTLE DORRIT.
    11.—MARTIN CHUZZLEWIT.
    12.—OUR MUTUAL FRIEND.
    13.—CHRISTMAS BOOKS.—TALE OF TWO CITIES.
    4.—SKETCHES BY BOZ AND HARD TIMES.
    15.—CHILD'S ENGLAND AND MISCELLANEOUS.

The first volume—Pickwick Papers—contains an alphabetical catalogue of all of Charles Dickens' writings, with their positions in the volumes.

This edition is sold by Booksellers, everywhere—and single specimen copies will be forwarded by mail, *postage free*, on receipt of price, $1.50, by

**G. W. CARLETON & CO., Publishers,**
Madison Square, New York.

# MRS. MARY J. HOLMES' WORKS.

TEMPEST AND SUNSHINE.
ENGLISH ORPHANS.
HOMESTEAD ON HILLSIDE.
'LENA RIVERS.
MEADOW BROOK.
DORA DEANE.
COUSIN MAUDE.
MARIAN GREY.
EDITH LYLE.
DAISY THORNTON. *(New)*.

DARKNESS AND DAYLIGHT.
HUGH WORTHINGTON.
CAMERON PRIDE.
ROSE MATHER.
ETHELYN'S MISTAKE.
MILLBANK.
EDNA BROWNING.
WEST LAWN.
MILDRED.

## OPINIONS OF THE PRESS.

"Mrs. Holmes' stories are universally read. Her admirers are numberless. She is in many respects without a rival in the world of fiction. Her characters are always life-like, and she makes them talk and act like human beings, subject to the same emotions, swayed by the same passions, and actuated by the same motives which are common among men and women of every day existence. Mrs. Holmes is very happy in portraying domestic life. Old and young peruse her stories with great delight, for she writes in a style that all can comprehend."—*New York Weekly.*

The North American Review, vol. 81, page 557, says of Mrs. Mary J. Holmes' novel, "English Orphans":—"With this novel of Mrs. Holmes' we have been charmed, and so have a pretty numerous circle of discriminating readers to whom we have lent it. The characterization is exquisite, especially so far as concerns rural and village life, of which there are some pictures that deserve to be hung up in perpetual memory of types of humanity fast becoming extinct. The dialogues are generally brief, pointed, and appropriate. The plot seems simple, so easily and naturally is it developed and consummated. Moreover, the story thus gracefully constructed and written, inculcates without obtruding, not only pure Christian morality in general, but, with especial point and power, the dependence of true success on character, and of true respectability on merit."

"Mrs. Holmes' stories are all of a domestic character, and their interest, therefore, is not so intense as if they were more highly seasoned with sensationalism, but it is of a healthy and abiding character. Almost any new book which her publisher might choose to announce from her pen would get an immediate and general reading. The interest in her tales begins at once, and is maintained to the close. Her sentiments are so sound, her sympathies so warm and ready, and her knowledge of manners, character, and the varied incidents of ordinary life is so thorough, that she would find it difficult to write any other than an excellent tale if she were to try it."—*Boston Banner.*

☞ The volumes are all handsomely printed and bound in cloth, sold everywhere, and sent by mail, *postage free*, on receipt of price [$1.50 each], by

G. W. CARLETON & CO., Publishers,
*Madison Square, New York.*

# CONTENTS.

## MISSISSIPPI OUTLAWS AND THE DETECTIVES.

### CHAPTER I.
A daring Express Robbery.—Mr. Pinkerton appealed to.—Cane-brakes and cane-fed People.—Annoying delays and Amateur Detectives............ 9

### CHAPTER II.
Difficulties.—Blind Trails and False Scents.—A Series of Illustrations showing the Number of Officious People and Confidence Men that often seek Notoriety and Profit through important Detective Operations............ 21

### CHAPTER III.
"Old Hicks," a drunken Planter, is entertained by a Hunting-Party.—Lester's Landing.—Its Grocery-Store and Mysterious Merchants.—A dangerous Situation.—The unfortunate Escape of Two of the Robbers........ 32

### CHAPTER IV.
The Captured Ruffians are desired for Guides, but dare not join in the Search for the Outlaws.—One of the Robbers is Taken, but subsequently Escapes from the Amateur Detectives.—Another Clue suddenly fails.... 44

### CHAPTER V.
A Rich Lead Struck at Last....................................................... 50

### CHAPTER VI.
The Mother of the Farringtons, being arrested, boasts that her Sons "Will never be taken Alive."—Another Unfortunate Blunder by Amateur Detectives.—An interesting Fate intended for the Detectives.—William A. Pinkerton captures the Murderer of a Negro in Union City, proving "a very good Fellow—for a Yankee."............................................ 56

### CHAPTER VII.
The Scene of Action transferred to Missouri.—The Chase becoming Hot..... 68

### CHAPTER VIII.
A determined Party of Horsemen.—The Outlaws surrounded and the Birds caged.—A Parley.—The burning Cabin.—Its Occupants finally surrender. 80

### CHAPTER IX.
Barton's Confession.—The Express Robberies, and the Outlaw's subsequent Experiences fully set forth therein.—A Clue that had been suddenly dropped taken up with so much Profit............................................ 91

### CHAPTER X.
A terrible Struggle for Life or Death upon the Transfer-boat "Illinois."—"Overboard!"—One less Desperado.—Fourth and Last Robber taken... 104

### CHAPTER XI.
The last Scene in the Drama approaching.—A new Character appears.—The Citizens of Union City suddenly seem to have important business on hand.—The Vigilantes and their Work.—The End...................... 114

## DON PEDRO AND THE DETECTIVES.

### CHAPTER I.
A fraudulent Scheme contemplated.—A dashing Peruvian Don and Donna.—A regal Forger.—Mr. Pinkerton engaged by Senator Muirhead to unvail the mystery of his Life...................................................... 125

### CHAPTER II.
Madame Sevier, Widow, of Chicago, and Monsieur Lesparre, of Bordeaux, also arrive at Gloster.—Mr. Pinkerton, as a Laborer, anxious for a Job, inspects the Morita Mansion................................................. 143

### CHAPTER III.

Monsieur Lesparre, having a retentive memory, becomes serviceable to Don Pedro.—Diamond fields and droll Americans.—A pompous Judge in an unfortunate Predicament.—The grand Reception closes with a happy Arrangement that the gay Señor and Señora shall dine with Mr. Pinkerton's Detectives on the next evening.................................................... 159

### CHAPTER IV.

Madame Sevier and Her Work.—Unaccountable Coquettishness between Man and Wife.—A Startling Scheme, Illustrating the Rashness of American Business Men and the Supreme Assurance of Don Pedro...... 170

### CHAPTER V.

The third Detective is made welcome at Don Pedro's.—The Señor is paid the first half-million dollars from the great Diamond Company.—How Don Pedro is "working" his diamond mines.................................................. 189

### CHAPTER VI.

An unexpected Meeting and a startling Recognition. An old friend somewhat disturbs the Equanimity of Don Pedro. The Detectives fix their Attention upon Pietro Bernardi........................................... 205

### CHAPTER VII.

Pietro Bernardi and the Detective become warm Friends.—A Tête-à-tête worth one thousand dollars............................................... 219

### CHAPTER VIII.

Don Pedro anxious for Pietro Bernardi's absence.—"Coppering the Jack and playing the Ace and Queen open."—Bernardi Quieted, and he subsequently departs richer by five thousand dollars......................... 232

### CHAPTER IX.

Important Information from the Peruvian Government.—Arrival in Gloster of the Peruvian Minister and Consul.—In Consultation.—"Robbing Peter to pay Paul."—Mr. Pinkerton's Card is presented.—Juan Sanchez, I arrest you, and you are my Prisoner.—Mr. Pinkerton not "For Sale."........ 249

### CHAPTER X.

The Fête Champêtre.—A grand Carnival.—The disappointed married Lover.—A vain Request.—Unmasked!—An indignant Deacon.—Don Pedro taken to Peru in a man-of-war, where he is convicted and sentenced to fifteen years Imprisonment................................................... 265

## THE POISONER AND THE DETECTIVES.

### CHAPTER I.

Mr. Pinkerton at a Water-cure becomes interested in a Couple, one of whom subsequently causes the Detective Operation from which this Story is written.—A wealthy ship-owner and his son.—The son "Found dead."—Mr. Pinkerton secured to solve the Mystery.—Chicago after the Fire..... 283

### CHAPTER II.

The Detectives at work.—Mrs. Sanford described.—Charlie, the Policeman.—Mrs. Sanford develops Interest in Government Bonds.—Chicago Relief and Aid Benefits.—Mrs. Sanford's Story of Trafton's Death.......... 298

### CHAPTER III.

The dangerous Side of the Woman's Character.—Robert A. Pinkerton as Adamson, the drunken, but wealthy Stranger, has a violent Struggle to escape from Mrs. Sanford, and is afterwards robbed.—Detective Ingham arrested, but very shortly liberated....................................... 319

### CHAPTER IV.

Connecting Links.—Mrs. Sanford's Ability as an Imitator of Actors.—One Detective tears himself away from her, and another takes his Place.—Mrs. Sanford's mind frequently burdened with the subject of Murder... 340

### CHAPTER V.

A moneyed young Texan becomes one of Mrs. Sanford's Lodgers.—The bonds are seen and their Numbers taken by the Detectives.—Mrs. Sanford arrested.—She is found guilty of "Involuntary Manslaughter," and sentenced to the Illinois Penitentiary for five years.—Mr. Pinkerton's Theory of the Manner in which Trafton was murdered................... 356

# PREFACE.

In presenting to the public another volume of my detective stories, I would call the attention of the reader to the fact, that these stories are literally written from facts and incidents which have come under my own observation, or been worked up by officers acting directly under my instructions.

The Mississippi River has for many years—more especially since the close of the war—been infested by a class of men who never would try to get an honest living, but would prey upon their neighbors or attack the property of southern railroads and express companies; these marauders could be seen any day prowling along the banks of the Mississippi, in fact, the shores and immediate neighborhood were peopled by just such a class, who cared not how they obtained a living; for the crimes they committed, they often suffered infinitely worse punishment, more so than any suffering which could have been entailed on them from leading a poor but honest life.

The story of the "MISSISSIPPI OUTLAWS AND THE DETECTIVES" is written to illustrate incidents which took place in the southern section of the country at no very remote date.

"DON PEDRO AND THE DETECTIVES" is another story of detective experience, which came under my own observation and management; it is a truthful narrative, and shows that some men are worse than known criminals, and can squander the money they have obtained by false pretenses, in a very lavish manner.

"THE POISONER AND THE DETECTIVES" is a well-known bit of detective experience, which, when read, will be recognized by any one who ever takes an interest in crime, and the bringing to justice its perpetrators.

The reader must remember that fictitious names are used in all of these stories, otherwise the facts are plainly and truthfully told as they occurred.

ALLAN PINKERTON.

*April*, 1879.

# THE MISSISSIPPI OUTLAWS

AND

## THE DETECTIVES.

―――◆―――

### CHAPTER I.

*A daring Express Robbery.—Mr. Pinkerton appealed to.—Cane-brakes and cane-fed People.—Annoying Delays and Amateur Detectives.*

THE southern and border states, since the close of the war of the rebellion, have been the frequent scenes of extensive and audacious robberies. This has been largely owing to the sparsely-settled condition of certain districts, to the disorder and lawlessness generated by the war, and to the temptations offered by the carelessness of many persons having large sums intrusted to their care in transit through lonely and desolate localities.

The express companies have always been favorite objects of attack by thieves of every grade, from the embezzling cashier to the petty sneakthief, and some of the operations connected with the detection of this class of criminals are among the most difficult and dangerous that have ever been intrusted to me. Probably a no more reckless and desperate body of men were ever banded together in a civilized community than those who were brought to my attention in 1871 by the Southern Express Company's officers in Memphis; and I consider the successful termination of my efforts in this case as of the greatest value to the people of the South and West. The whole affair was conducted with such a limited force, and under such adverse circumstances, that I take pride in here recording the history of the affair and my connection with it. Though I maintained a general supervision of the operation, my eldest son, William A. Pinkerton, was the person having immediate charge of the matter, and to his energy, perseverance, and sagacity is mainly attributable our success.

Some time in the latter part of July, 1871, an express messenger on the Mobile and Ohio Railroad was overpowered by three men at Moscow, Kentucky, and his safe was robbed of about sixteen hundred dollars. The manner of effecting the robbery was a very bold one, showing the presence of men of experience in crime. The loss was not heavy, but the company made every effort to discover the robbers, in the hope of bringing them to a severe punishment as a warning to other criminals. In spite, however, of the efforts of two of my men, who were immediately sent to the scene of the robbery, the guilty parties escaped into the almost impenetrable swamps along the Mississippi River, and the chase was reluctantly abandoned, as it was impossible to tell where they would come out or cross the river. The amount stolen was not sufficiently large to warrant the expenditure of much time or money in the pursuit of the thieves, and my men were soon wholly withdrawn from the operation. In order, however, to guard against a repetition of such a raid, an extra man was placed in each express car to act as guard to the regular messenger. It was considered that two men, well armed, ought to be surely able to protect the company against further loss, and everything ran smoothly until October 21, 1871. At this time, the money shipments by express were very heavy, as a rule, and orders were given that special care should be exercised by all the employés having money packages in charge.

The northern-bound train on the Mobile and Ohio Railroad was due at Union City, Tennessee, about half-past seven o'clock in the evening. At this point the northern and southern-bound trains usually passed each other, and stopped long enough for supper, the train arriving first being the one to take the side track ready to pull out. Saturday evening, October 21st, the northern-bound train arrived on time, stopped at the station long enough to let the passengers go to supper, and then took the side track to await the arrival of the train bound south. As soon as the side track was reached the conductor, engineer, fireman, brakeman, and express messenger went to supper, leaving the train deserted except by the express guard, named George Thompson, and a few passengers. The local express agent came up at this moment, gave his packages to Thompson, receiving his receipt therefor, and returned to the station. This action was directly contrary to the rules of the company, which forbade the messenger to leave the car during his whole run, or to go to sleep; also, the guard was forbidden to transact any business, or to have possession of the safe key. Martin Crowley, the messenger, had given his key to Thompson, however, to enable him to attend to the business of the local agent while Crowley was away at supper. In accordance with Thompson's request, Crowley sent a negro porter to the express car with Thompson's supper on a tray, and the porter, after handing the tray to Thompson, turned to walk away. As he did so, he saw two men spring into the partly open door of the express car, and, almost immediately, the train began to back. The negro knew that something was wrong, and he hurried to the station to give the alarm. By the time he arrived there, however, the train was backing at a moderate speed, and was well beyond the reach of pursuit on foot.

Meantime, the guard, having received his supper from the negro porter, turned his back to the door to set the tray down. Before reaching the desk, he heard a noise at the door, and turning, he was confronted by two men, one of whom held a revolver at his head, while the other seized his throat. Thompson was a young man, and, not being accustomed to meet such hard characters, he was badly frightened. He immediately gave up the safe key and helped one of the men to unlock the safe. Having taken all the money out of the safe, one of the robbers took also the contents of Thompson's pocket-book; but here the other man interfered, insisting that the guard's money be returned to him, which was done. No conversation took place, but when the safe had been carefully examined and all the money it contained taken, one of the men stepped to the door and swung a lantern once or twice. The train, which had been backing at a moderate rate of speed, now stopped, and the two men jumped off, telling Thompson to stay where he was and keep quiet. When the conductor, engineer, and other persons, whom the porter had alarmed, reached the train, they found everything in order except the safe, into which poor Thompson was vainly peering in the hope of discovering that some portion of the funds might have been overlooked. The men had disappeared in the thick woods, and no trace of them was found except a small carpet-bag containing potatoes and bread. The amount missing from the safe was about six thousand dollars in currency.

Although the robbery was at once reported to Mr. M. J. O'Brien, the General Superintendent, by telegraph, no action seems to have been taken until the following Wednesday—four days later—when Mr. O'Brien sent me a brief telegram announcing the robbery, and requesting me to come to Union City in person, if possible, and if not, to send my eldest son, William A. Pinkerton. The telegraph was used freely for the next two days, and while my son was gathering clues and making his preparations, we learned most of the facts by letter. William arrived in Union City on Saturday, just one week after the robbery had been committed, and he instantly began to gather information from every available source. Except the statements of the negro porter and Thompson, the guard, as condensed in the account heretofore given, little information could be obtained, as so few persons were about the train when it began to move off. While two or three had seen the men who had entered the car, no one had seen who had run the locomotive, and there was, therefore, no certainty as to the number of persons engaged in the job. One passenger had seen two men walking toward the engine in a suspicious manner, and, as his description of these two was entirely different from that given of the men who had entered the car, it was fair to presume that they had been a part of the gang. Still, no one had seen them get on the engine, and it was not certain that they had had anything to do with the affair. At the end of three days, however, William had collected sufficient information to satisfy himself that either four or five men had been at work together; and, by collating the various descriptions he received, he obtained a pretty fair idea of the party.

The first thing which struck him was the similarity of this robbery to the one which had occurred exactly three months before at Moscow, Kentucky. The appearance of the men and their actions had been precisely like those of the Moscow party, and it was evident that they had been emboldened to a second venture by the ease with which they had carried through their former scheme. One thing was imperative: the capture of the whole gang would be necessary to insure the safety of the express company's property in the future. Indeed, it was a mere piece of good fortune that the loss in this instance was not irreparable, for the amount of money carried on the southern-bound train was eighty thousand dollars, and the robbers would have obtained this large amount if the southern-bound train had chanced to arrive first. The robbery was clearly one which no common tramp or sneak-thief would have dared to attempt, and William saw immediately the difficulties of his work. Before proceeding with the incidents of the operation, I must give some idea of the country and the people living there, since no one would otherwise comprehend one-half of the obstacles and dangers which were involved in a search for the criminals in that vicinity.

The southwestern part of Kentucky and the northwestern part of Tennessee are about as desolate portions of the world as are inhabited by a civilized people. There seems to have been some convulsion of the earth at this point, which is sunk so far below the general level of the whole country as to make it a perpetual swamp. The annual overflow of the Ohio and Mississippi lays the country under water for a distance of many miles, while even in the dryest season, the morasses, sunken lakes, and dense cane-brakes, render it almost impassable, except for people who have been thoroughly acquainted with the locality for years.

The sunken lakes are natural curiosities in themselves, and, although they have attracted considerable attention from scientific men, no satisfactory explanation of their causes and phenomena has been found. The country is full of game and the water is alive with fish, so that the necessities of life are easily obtainable. The cane-brakes are wonderful growths of bamboo cane, and they sometimes cover strips of country as much as seventy miles long. In the spring-time, the water rises to such a height that a skiff can navigate freely above and through the tops of the cane; but in dry weather, the stalks grow so closely together that the brake becomes impenetrable to man or beast, except by winding tortuously around the clumps through the comparatively thin portions of the undergrowth. To search for any one wishing to remain concealed therein is like the proverbial attempt to look for a needle in a hay-stack, since a man can pass within ten yards of another without seeing him or being aware of his presence. The only roads which traverse these places are mere cattle paths, which begin at no place and run nowhere; and, unless a man be thoroughly acquainted with the country, he can never tell where any given path will lead him.

The people around the towns, such as Hickman, Union City, Dyersburg, and Moscow, are a highly respectable and well-educated class; but in the low, swampy country, in the cane brake and along the river, they are not, as a rule, a very agreeable class to live among. Of course, here, as in all other places, there are many intelligent, reliable, honorable men, but the great mass of the canebrake population are ignorant and brutal. The term which they apply to their stock is also eminently appropriate to designate the people : they are "cane-fed." It is the custom to turn the cattle into the cane to feed when it is young and tender, and, as the amount of nutriment thus obtained is not very large, the "cane-fed" animals bear about the same relation to grain-fed stock that the people in that vicinity bear to the residents of healthy, prosperous, and educated communities. The larger portion of the population may be classed as "poor whites," and they constitute a peculiar variety of the human species. The men are tall, loose-jointed, and dyspeptic; they bear a marked resemblance to the vegetable productions of the vicinity, being rapid of growth, prolific, and generally worthless. Their education consists mainly of woodcraft and rifle-shooting; their proficiency in both of these branches is sometimes astonishing, and it is frequently said of their most expert hunters that they seem to have been born shot-gun or rifle in hand. Accomplishments they have none, except the rare instances where a few tunes upon the banjo have been learned from the negroes. Their tastes are few and simple,—whisky, snuff, hog, and hominy being the necessities and luxuries of life; that is, whisky and snuff are the necessities, all other things being secondary considerations. In their sober moods, they are frank, rough, and courageous; yet, even then, there is little about them to excite other feelings than those of pity and aversion. When full of bad whisky, however, they are apt to become quarrelsome and brutal, so that no man can feel sure of his safety in their company. An affront, real or imaginary, will then be apt to cause bloodshed, even if the insulted party has to bushwhack his enemy from a secure covert on the roadside as he is returning to his home. Every man goes armed, and, though fair fights in broad daylight are rare, cold-blooded murders are not infrequent. The law is seldom invoked to settle private differences, and, in fact, the functions of the legal officials are practically very limited in their influence. If a coroner ever sits upon a corpse, it is understood that he has done his whole duty by recording a verdict that "the deceased came to his death at the hands of some person or persons unknown."

The women, like the men, are tall, thin, and round-shouldered. Up to the age of sixteen they sometimes are quite pretty, though sallow and lifeless always; after that period, they become gaunt, emaciated, and yellow. Whisky hath charms for them, also, but their favorite dissipation is snuff-dipping. They marry very early and bear children nearly every year, so that the size of many of these West Tennessee families is often enormous. The father exercises patriarchal control over his whole household until the daughters are married and the sons old enough and strong enough to defy the parental authority as enforced by a hickory rod. The wife never escapes the application of this potent instrument of marital discipline; and, indeed, should a husband fail to make frequent use of it for the correction of his better half, he would probably soon learn that his dutiful spouse could find a use for it on his own person.

Throughout this whole district, the people suffer from fever and ague for nine months of the year, and dyspepsia seems hereditary. Their physicians, however, usually require no further education than is requisite to attend fractured limbs and gun-shot wounds, the whole school of medicine being limited to three specifics: quinine, calomel, and whisky.

As before stated, it should be understood that the foregoing description applies to the majority of the inhabitants of the low swamp lands only, and not to the residents in and about the towns; even in the cane country itself are to be found occasionally men of education, ability, and good character, and to several of them William was largely indebted for assistance and information.

There was one redeeming feature also to the character of the "cane-fed" population; in the main they were honest, and they would do all in their power to break up a thieving gang, even if they had to hang a few of its members as a warning to the rest. I was thus able to trust them to a certain extent, though the fear which they had of this band of desperadoes rather kept their naturally honest impulses in check for a time.

William was thoroughly acquainted with the character of the people, and he knew what a difficult task had been set before him, especially as he was allowed no other detectives of my force to assist him, the express company being desirous of conducting the operation as economically as possible. Among the large number of men employed directly by the company were two or three good men, but the majority were even worse than useless, and the expense of the affair was finally much greater than as if only my own men had been employed. Besides the fact that William was thus continually working with strange men, he was harassed by large numbers of amateur detectives, to whose stories the company's officers too often lent a ready ear. Indeed, every express agent in Tennessee, Kentucky, and Missouri seemed impressed with the idea that he was a naturally gifted detective, and many were the annoying delays which resulted from their interference.

## CHAPTER II.

*Difficulties.—Blind Trails and False Scents.—A Series of Illustrations showing the Number of Officious People and Confidence Men that often seek Notoriety and Profit through important Detective Operations.*

THE art of detecting crime cannot be learned in a day, nor can the man of business understand, without previous experience in the habits of criminals, the expedients which the boldest class of law-breakers adopt; hence none but skilled detectives can hope to cope with them. Yet often my clients insist on some certain method of procedure wholly contrary to my judgment and experience, until the total failure of their plan convinces them that there can be but one thoroughly successful mode of detection, namely, to submit the case to a skilled detective of character and standing, and allow him to act according to his judgment.

The range of investigation in such a case as this robbery will often extend from New York to San Francisco, and unless one mind gathers up the clues, classifies the information, and determines the general plan, there will be continual error and delay. Such a state of affairs frequently occurred during this operation, and much time and money were spent upon matters too trifling even for consideration.

The principal of a detective agency, from his long experience with criminals, learns the ear-marks of different classes of men, and he is often able to determine the name of the guilty party in any given robbery by the manner in which the job was done. He can readily see whether a novice in crime was engaged, and also whether any collusion existed between the parties robbed and the criminals; and so, when he sees the traces of a bold, skillful, and experienced man, he knows that it is useless to track down some insignificant sneak-thief, simply because the latter happens to have been in the vicinity. Yet, neither will he slight the smallest clue if there is a bare chance that any valuable fact may be obtained from it. But the *sine quâ non* is that he, and he alone, shall direct the whole affair. A divided responsibility simply doubles the criminal's opportunities for escape.

Among the many difficulties of the detective's work, none are more embarrassing than the early development of false clues. In the stories heretofore published, the direct steps leading to the detection and arrest of the criminals have been related, without referring to the innumerable other investigations, which were progressing simultaneously, and which, though involving the expenditure of much thought, time, and money, proved after all to be of no value whatever in developing any evidence in the case. In this operation, such instances were of frequent occurrence, and I propose to mention a few of them to show how wide is the range of the detective's inquiries, and also the annoying delays to which he is often subjected by the inconsiderate zeal and interference of outside parties. These latter may be—indeed, they generally are—well meaning people, anxious to serve the cause of justice; though, on the other hand, they are sometimes spiteful meddlers, striving to fix suspicion upon some personal enemy.

The plan of detection which alone can insure success, must be one which neither forgets nor neglects anything. In investigating any alleged crime, the first questions to be considered are: 1. Has any crime been perpetrated, and, if so, what? 2. What was the object sought thereby?

The matter of time, place, and means employed must then be carefully noted, and finally we come to consider: 1. Who are the criminals? 2. Where are they now? 3. How can they be taken?

The fact that a crime has been committed is generally apparent, though there have been cases in which the determination of that point requires as much skill as the whole remainder of the operation. Such was the case in the detection of Mrs. Pattmore's murder, related in my story of "The Murderer and the Fortune Teller." The object of a crime is also sometimes obscure, and, where such are the circumstances, the detection of the criminal is apt to be one of the most difficult of all operations. Having once solved these two difficulties satisfactorily, however, and having observed the relative bearings of time, place, and means to the crime itself, the question of individuals is the important one to be determined. It often happens that there is no concealment of identity, the problem to be solved being simply the way to catch the guilty parties; but, on the other hand, the greatest skill, experience, patience, and perseverance are sometimes required to discover, first of all, the persons engaged in the crime. Indeed, an operation is often divisible into two distinct methods of action, the first being to find out the identity of the criminals, the second to follow up and capture them.

In the course of a blind trail, such as we were obliged to travel in the case of this express robbery, it was impossible to know whence the men had come or whither they had gone; hence, I was forced to take up every trifling clue and follow it to the end. Even after I was satisfied in my own mind of the identity of the criminals, the agents and officers of the express company were continually finding mares' nests which they wished investigated, and the operation was sometimes greatly hindered on this account. As an example of the number of discouragements which the detective must always expect to encounter, I propose to mention some of the false scents which we were forced to follow during this operation.

Three or four days after William's arrival in Union City, he was informed by the superintendent of the express company having charge of the operation, that there was a young man in Moscow who could give important information relative to the first robbery at that place. This young man, Thomas Carr by name, was a lawyer who had once had fine prospects, but he had become very dissipated, and he finally had been taken seriously ill, so that he had lost his practice. On recovering his health he had reformed his habits, but he had found great difficulty in winning back clients, and his income was hardly enough to support him. On learning that this impecunious lawyer had valuable information, William strongly suspected that it would amount to little more than a good lie, invented to obtain money from the express company; nevertheless, he sent for the young man and heard his story.

According to Carr, a man named John Witherspoon had visited him about six weeks before, and had asked him whether he would like to get a large sum of money. Carr replied affirmatively, of course, and wished to know how it could be obtained. Witherspoon had said that the express company could be robbed very easily by boarding a train at any water-tank, overpowering the messenger, and making him open the safe. Witherspoon also had said that he and several others had robbed a train at Moscow some weeks before, and that they had got only sixteen hundred dollars, but that they should do better next time. He had asked Carr to go to Cairo and find out when there would be a large shipment of money to the South; then Carr was to take the same train and give a signal to the rest of the party on arriving at the designated spot.

On hearing Carr's story, William sent him back to Moscow with instructions to renew his intimacy with Witherspoon, and to report any news he might learn at once; in case it should prove to be of any value, the company would pay him well for his services. It is hardly necessary to add that Mr. Carr, having failed to get, as he had hoped, a roving commission as detective at the company's expense, was not heard from again, his bonanza of news having run out very quickly on discovering that no money was to be paid in advance.

The next case was a more plausible one, and William began its investigation with the feeling that something might be developed therefrom. It was learned that a former express messenger named Robert Trunnion, who had been discharged several months before, had been hanging around Columbus, Kentucky, ever since. While in conversation with the clerk of a second-class hotel, Trunnion had spoken of the ease with which a few determined men could board an express car, throw a blanket over the messenger's head, and then rob the safe. The clerk said that Trunnion had made the suggestion to him twice, and the second time he had given Trunnion a piece of his mind for making such a proposition. Trunnion had then said he was only fooling, and that he did not mean anything by it. William learned that Trunnion was then engaged in selling trees for a nursery at Clinton, Kentucky, and that he was regarded as a half-cracked, boasting fool, who might be anything bad, if he were influenced by bold, unscrupulous men. William therefore paid a visit to Mr. Trunnion, whom he found to be a very high-toned youth, too fiery-tempered and sensitive to submit to any questioning as to his words or actions. In a very brief space of time, however, his lordly tone came down to a very humble acknowledgment that he had used the language attributed to him; but he protested that he had meant nothing; in short, his confession was not only complete, but exceedingly candid; he admitted that he was a gas-bag and a fool, without discretion enough to keep his tongue from getting him into trouble continually; and, having clearly shown that he was nowhere in the vicinity of either robbery, he asked humbly not to be held responsible for being a born idiot. William was satisfied that the fellow had told the truth, and, after scaring him out of all his high-toned pride, he let him go, with a severe lecture on the danger of talking too much.

On the nineteenth of November, when the identity of the robbers had been fully established, William was called away to Iuka, Mississippi, on information received from Mr. O'Brien, the general superintendent of the express company, that a man named Santon had seen the leader of the party in that place, just a week before. Santon represented that he knew the man well, having been acquainted with him for years in Cairo, and that he could not be mistaken, as he had spoken with him on the day mentioned. William found that the man Santon was a natural liar, who could not tell the truth even when it was for his interest to do so. The descriptions of the various robbers had been scattered broadcast everywhere, and none of them were represented as over thirty-five years of age; yet Santon said that his man was over fifty years old, and that he had been a pilot on the Mississippi for years. This was a case—not an infrequent one, either—where people talk and lie about a crime for the sole purpose of getting a little temporary notoriety. Owing to various accidents and railway detentions, William lost three days in going to hunt up this lying fellow's testimony.

Perhaps the most impudent of all the stories brought to the express company's officers was that of a man named Swing, living at Columbus, Kentucky. He sent a friend to Union City to tell them that he could give them a valuable clue to the identity of the robbers, and William accompanied this friend back to Columbus. On the way, William drew out all that Swing's friend knew about the matter, and satisfied himself that Swing's sole object in sending word to the officers of the company was to get them to do a piece of detective work for him. It appeared that his nephew had stolen one of his horses just after the robbery, and he intended to tell the company's officers that this nephew had been engaged in the robbery; then if the company captured the nephew, Swing hoped to get back his horse. A truly brilliant scheme it was, but, unfortunately for his expectations, William could not be misled by his plausible story; and, if he ever recovered his horse, he did so without the assistance of the express company. Nevertheless, he took William away from his work for nearly a whole day, at a time when his presence was almost indispensable.

Another peculiar phase of a detective's experience is, that while following up one set of criminals, he may accidentally unearth the evidences of some other crime; occasionally it happens that he is able to arrest the criminals thus unexpectedly discovered, but too often they take the alarm and escape before the interested parties can be put in possession of the facts. About two weeks after the Union City robbery, in the course of my extended inquiries by telegraph, I came across a pair of suspicious characters in Kansas City, Missouri. I learned that two fine-looking women had arrived in that city with about eight thousand dollars in five, ten, and twenty dollar bills, which they were trying to exchange for bills of a larger denomination. The women were well dressed, but they were evidently of loose character, and the possession of so much money by two females of that class excited suspicion instantly in the minds of the bankers to whom they applied, and they could not make the desired exchange. One of the women was a blonde and the other was a brunette. They were about of the same height, and they dressed in such marked contrast as to set each other off to the best advantage; indeed, their dresses seemed to have attracted so much attention that I could gain very little acquaintance with their personal appearance. I could not connect them in any way with the robbery at Union City, nor with any other recent crime, though I had little doubt that the money they had with them was the proceeds of some criminal transaction; still, having my hands full at that time, it would have been impossible for me to look after them, even had I thought best to do so. As it is my practice to undertake investigations only when engaged for the purpose by some responsible person, I did not waste any time in endeavoring to discover the source whence these women obtained their money; though, of course, had I learned enough about them to suspect them of complicity in any specific crime, I should have reported my suspicions to the parties interested, to enable them to take such action as they might have seen fit.

The most important of all the false clues brought out in this investigation was presented by a noted confidence man and horse-thief named Charles Lavalle, *alias* Hildebrand. I call it the most important, not because I considered it of any value at the time, but because it illustrates one of the most profitable forms of confidence operation, and because the express company, by refusing to accept my advice in the matter, were put to a large expense with no possibility of a return.

Very shortly after the Union City robbery, a letter was received from a man in Kansas City, calling himself Charles Lavalle. The writer claimed that he had been with the gang who had robbed the train, but that they had refused to divide with him, and so, out of revenge, he was anxious to bring them to punishment. He claimed further that he was then in the confidence of another party, who were soon going to make another raid upon the express company somewhere between New Orleans and Mobile.

The plausibility of his story was such that he obtained quite a large sum from the express company to enable him to follow up and remain with the gang of thieves with whom he professed to be associated. No news was received from him, however, and at length I was requested to put a "shadow" upon his track. My operative followed him to St. Joseph, Missouri, and thence to Quincy, Illinois, but, during two weeks of close investigation, no trace of the villains in Lavalle's company could be found, and he was never seen in the society of any known burglars or thieves. It was soon evident that he was playing upon the express company a well-worn confidence game, which has been attempted probably every time a large robbery has occurred in the last fifteen years. He became very importunate for more money while in Quincy, as he stated that the gang to which he belonged were ready to start for New Orleans; but, finding that his appeals were useless, and that no more money would be advanced until some of his party were actually discovered and trapped through his agency, he soon ceased writing.

The foregoing are only a few of the instances in which our attention was diverted from the real criminals; and, although the efforts of my operatives were rarely misdirected in any one affair for any length of time, still these false alarms were always a source of great annoyance and embarrassment.

## CHAPTER III.

"*Old Hicks*," *a drunken Planter, is entertained by a Hunting-party.—Lester's Landing.—Its Grocery-store and Mysterious Merchants.—A dangerous Situation and a desperate Encounter.—The unfortunate Escape of Two of the Robbers.*

ONE of the most direct sources of information relative to the party was found in the person of an old planter, named Hicks, who lived some distance down the track of the railroad. He was in the habit of visiting Union City very frequently, and he usually rounded off his day's pleasure by becoming jovially drunk, in which condition he would start for his home, walking down the railroad track. He had been in Union City all of Friday before the robbery, and about ten o'clock in the evening he was in a state of happy inebriety, ready to "hail fellow, well met," with any person he might encounter.

On his way home, about three-quarters of a mile west of Union City, he saw a camp-fire burning a short distance from the track, and around it were gathered five men. They hailed him, and asked him to take a drink; and as this was an invitation which Hicks could not refuse, even from the devil himself, he joined them, drank with them, and danced a hornpipe for their edification. Hicks acknowledged in his account of meeting them, that by the time they had made him dance for them, he was heartily frightened at their looks and talk. He heard one of them say that they wanted ten thousand at least, but he could not tell what the remark referred to. He asked them why they were camping out, and one, who seemed to be the leader of the party, said they were out hunting.

"Yes," continued another one, "I am out hunting for somebody's girl, and when I find her we are going to run away together."

At this, they all laughed, as if there was some hidden meaning in his words.

Hicks described all of the men, three of them quite minutely; but the fourth was evidently the same as the second, and the fifth was lying down asleep all the time, so that Hicks could not tell much about him. They were armed with large navy revolvers, which they wore in belts, and their clothing was quite good. The tall man, who seemed to be the leader, related an account of a deer-hunt in which he had participated, in Fayette county, Illinois, on the Kaskaskia river, and when he mentioned the place, the others scowled and winked at him, as if to stop him. Hicks said that they seemed to be familiar with Cincinnati,

Louisville, Evansville, and other northern cities, and that they talked somewhat like Yankees. He remained with them until about midnight, when a negro came down the track. Hicks and the negro then went on together to Hicks's house, leaving the five men still camped in the woods.

Other persons reported having seen the same party in the same vicinity several times before the night of the robbery, though some had seen only two, others three and four; but no one, except Hicks, had seen five. The accounts given by the persons near the train when the robbery occurred did not show the presence of more than three persons, though possibly there might have been a fourth. The descriptions of the suspected parties were quite varied in some respects; yet the general tenor of them was to the same effect, and, as no one knew who these persons were, it was quite certain that this quartette of strangers had committed the robbery.

In the case of the Moscow robbery, we had strongly suspected two notorious thieves, named Jack Nelson and Miles Ogle, so that my first action, on learning of this second affair in the same vicinity, was to telegraph to my correspondents and agents throughout the country, to learn whether either of these men had been seen lately. I could gain no news whatever, except from St. Louis, whence an answer was returned to the effect that Nelson was said to be stopping somewhere in the country back of Hickman, Kentucky. Ogle's wife was in St. Louis, and she had been seen by a detective walking and talking earnestly with a strange man a short time previous. The information about Nelson was important, since, if true, it showed that he was in the immediate neighborhood of the points where the robberies had occurred. The man seen with Mrs. Ogle might have been one of the party, sent by her husband to appoint a future rendezvous. The description of the tall, dark man, mentioned by Hicks and others, tallied very closely with Ogle's appearance. My son, William, was well advised of these facts, and, as soon as he had obtained the statements of every one acquainted with any of the occurrences at the time of the robbery, he was ready for action.

His first inquiries were directed toward discovering where Nelson was staying near Hickman, and he learned in a very short time that this rumor had no truth in it. While making search for Nelson, however, he heard of a low grocery-store at Lester's Landing, about twelve miles below Hickman on the Mississippi River. The store was situated four miles from any other house in a sparsely settled country, where the amount of legitimate trade would hardly amount to twelve hundred dollars per year. It was said to be the resort of a very low class of men, and the proprietors passed for river gamblers.

On William's return to Union City from Hickman, he decided to make a visit to this grocery-store to learn something about the men who frequented it. Having none of his own men with him, he chose one of the express company's detectives, named Patrick Connell, to accompany him, and, on the last day of October, they started on horseback, with an old resident named Bledsoe for a guide. On arriving at the house of a well-to-do planter, named Wilson Merrick, they obtained considerable information about the men who kept the store and the people who visited it.

Mr. Merrick said that a man named John Wesley Lester kept a wood-yard on the Mississippi, and the spot was called Lester's Landing. About three or four months before, three men arrived there and obtained leave from Lester to put up a store, which they stocked with groceries and whisky. The men gave their names as J. H. Clark, Ed. J. Russell, and William Barton, and they seemed to have some means, as the store did only a limited business, except in whisky. They were all men of ability and determination, and, as they were always well armed, the people of the cane-brake country were rather afraid of them. Nothing positive was known against them, but it was suspected from their looks and actions that they were Northern desperadoes lying quiet for a time. They seemed to be well acquainted in Cincinnati, Louisville, St. Louis, Memphis, Vicksburg, and New Orleans, but they were careful never to give any hint of their previous place of residence in the hearing of strangers. Mr. Merrick had, however, heard Russell say that he had once run a stationary engine in Missouri, and from occasional expressions by

Barton it would appear that the latter had once worked on a railroad in some capacity. They dressed quite well, and treated strangers politely, though not cordially. Although they were all three rather hard drinkers, they never became intoxicated, and they seemed to understand each other well enough not to quarrel among themselves. Clark was the oldest of the party, but Russell seemed to be the leader, Barton being apparently quite a young man. They stated that they intended to exchange groceries for fish and game, and ship the latter articles to St. Louis and Memphis.

From the description of the men, William began to suspect that they formed a portion of the party of robbers, and he determined to push on at once. He induced a young man named Gordon to go with him as guide and to assist in making the arrest of these men, if he should deem it advisable. By hard riding they succeeded in reaching Lester's Landing before nightfall, but the twilight was fast fading as they came out of the dense underbrush and cane-brake into the clearing around Lester's log-cabin.

The spot was dreary and forlorn in the extreme. The river was then nearly at low water, and its muddy current skirted one side of the clearing at a distance of about thirty yards from the house. The wood-yard and landing at the water's level were some ten or fifteen feet below the rising ground upon which the house stood. The store was a shanty of rough pine boards with one door and one window, and it stood at the head of the diagonal path leading from the landing to the high ground. A short distance back was a rail fence surrounding Lester's house and corn-field, and back of this clearing, about one hundred yards from the house, was a dense cane-brake. The corn-stalks had never been cut, and, as they grew very high and thick within twenty feet of the house, they offered a good cover to any one approaching or retreating through them. A rough log barn stood a short distance inside the rail fence, and, like the house, it was raised several feet above the ground, on account of the annual overflow of the whole tract. The house was a rather large building built of logs, the chinks being partly filled with mud, but it was in a dilapidated condition, the roof being leaky and the sides partly open, where the mud had fallen out from between the timbers.

On entering the clearing, William's party rode up to the store and tried to enter, but, finding the door locked, they approached the house. At the rail fence, William and Connell dismounted, leaving Gordon and Bledsoe to hold their horses. Up to this time, they had seen no signs of life about the place, and they began to think that the birds had flown. The quiet and the absence of men about the clearing did not prevent William from exercising his usual caution in approaching the house; but he did consider it unnecessary to take any stronger force into an apparently unoccupied log-cabin, where at most he had only vague suspicions of finding the objects of his search; hence, he left Gordon and Bledsoe behind. Knowing the general construction of this class of houses to be the same, he sent Connell to the rear, while he entered the front door. A wide hall divided the house through the center, and the occupants of the house were in the room on the right. William's door leading into the room opened from this hall, while Connell's was a direct entrance from the back porch, and there were no other doors to the room.

As the two strangers entered simultaneously, five men, a woman, and a girl started to their feet and demanded what they wanted. The situation was evidently one of great danger to the detectives; one glance at the men, coupled with the fierce tones of their inquiries, showed William that he had entered a den of snakes without adequate force; but it was too late to retreat, and he replied that they were strangers who, having lost their way, desired information.

The scene was a striking one, and it remains as vividly in William's mind to-day, as if it had occurred but yesterday. In the center of the room, opposite him, was a broad fireplace, in which the smouldering logs feebly burned and gave forth the only light in the room. In one corner stood several shot-guns, and in another, four or five heavy axes. Grouped about near the fire, in different attitudes of surprise, defiance, and alarm, were the occupants of the cabin, while to the left, in the half-open door, stood

Connell. The flickering flame of the rotten wood gave a most unsatisfactory light, in which they all seemed nearly as dark as negroes, so that William asked the woman to light a candle. She replied that they had none, and at the same moment a young fellow tried to slip by Connell, but he was promptly stopped. Another large, powerful man, whose name afterward proved to be Burtine, again demanded, with several oaths, what their business was.

"I've told you once that I want some information," replied William, "and now I intend to have you stop here until I can take a look at your faces."

While William was making them stand up in line against the wall, one of the largest drew a navy revolver quickly and fired straight at William's stomach, the ball just cutting the flesh on his left side. At the same instant, the young fellow previously mentioned, darted out the door, Connell having sprang to William's side, thinking him seriously wounded. Connell's approach prevented William from returning the fire of the tall man, who had jumped for the door also the moment he had fired. William fired two shots at him through the doorway, and Connell followed him instantly, on seeing that William was unhurt. Once outside, the tall fellow sprang behind a large cottonwood tree and fired back at Connell and William, who were in full view on the porch. The second shot struck Connell in the pit of the stomach, and he fell backward. At this moment,

*The fight at Lester's Landing.—Page —*

the powerful ruffian, Burtine, seized William from behind and tried to drag him down, at the same time calling for a shot-gun "to finish the Yankee —— —— ——." Turning suddenly upon his assailant, William raised his revolver, a heavy Tranter, and brought it down twice, with all his force, upon Burtine's head. The man staggered at the first blow and fell at the second, so that, by leveling his revolver at the other two, William was able to cow them into submission. The affray had passed so quickly that it was wholly over before Gordon and Bledsoe could reach the house, though they had sprung from their horses on hearing the first shot.

The two men had escaped by this time into the dense cane-brake back of the house, and it was necessary to attend to those who had been secured, and to examine the injuries of Connell and Burtine. The latter's head was in a pretty bad condition, though no serious results were likely to follow, while Connell had escaped a mortal wound by the merest hair's breadth. He was dressed in a heavy suit of Kentucky jeans, with large iron buttons down the front of the coat. The ball had struck one of these buttons, and, instead of passing straight through his vitals, it had glanced around his side, cutting a deep flesh furrow nearly to the small of his back, where it had gone out. The shock of the blow had stunned him somewhat, the button having been forced edgewise some distance into the flesh, but his wound was very trifling, and he was able to go on with the search with very little inconvenience. Having captured three out of the five inmates of the cabin, William felt as though he had done as much as could have been expected of two men under such circumstances, and he then began a search of the premises to see whether any evidence of their connection with the robbery could be found. Absolutely no clue whatever was obtained in the cabin and barn, nor did the store afford any better results so far as the robbery was concerned, but on this point William was already satisfied, and he was anxious to get all information possible about these so-called storekeepers. In the store, he found bills and invoices showing that the stock of goods had been purchased in Evansville, but there was no other writing of any character except some scribbling, apparently done in an idle moment, upon some fragments of paper in a drawer. On one was written: "Mrs. Kate Graham, Farmington, Ill."; and on another, amid many repetitions of the name, "Kate Graham," were the words, "My dear cousin."

Having found very little of value, the party returned to the three prisoners and closely examined them. To William's intense chagrin, he found that these men were, undoubtedly, mere wood-choppers living with Lester and having no connection with the proprietors of the store. Although desperate, brutal, and reckless, ready for a fight at all times, as shown in this affray, they were clearly not the train robbers, while it was equally evident that the two who had escaped were the guilty parties.

William learned that the young man who had first slipped out was Barton, and the man who had done the shooting was Russell. Clark, they said, had taken the steamer for Cape Girardeau, Missouri, two days before, accompanied by a married woman, named Slaughter. The description of the train robbers tallied so well with the appearance of Barton and Russell, that, taking their actions into consideration, there could no longer be any doubt of their complicity in the affair, and it was highly provoking that these two should have escaped. Still, it was an accident which could hardly have been avoided. The fact that the express company would not consent to the employment of a larger force of detectives was the principal cause of this misfortune, for it could have been prevented easily, had William been accompanied by two more good men of my force.

As it was, two detectives, dropping unexpectedly upon a nest of five villainous-looking men in the dark, could have hardly hoped to do better than to secure three of them. It could not have been supposed that they would know which were the important ones to capture, especially as they could not distinguish one from another in the uncertain light. Indeed, as afterward appeared, they were fortunate in having escaped alive, for the close approach to fatal wounds, which they both received, showed how deadly had been the intentions of the man Russell, while Burtine had evidently intended that they should never leave the house alive.

It may be supposed that the shooting on both sides was none of the best, but it must be remembered that it began without warning, and was over in two minutes. It cannot be expected that snap-shooting, even at close quarters, should be very accurate; yet it was afterward learned that Russell's escape had been about as narrow as William's, two balls having passed through his clothes and grazed his flesh.

## CHAPTER IV.

*The Captured Ruffians are desired for Guides, but dare not join in the Search for the Outlaws.— One of the Robbers is Taken, but subsequently Escapes from the Amateur Detectives.—Another Clue suddenly Fails.*

HAVING searched the whole place, and satisfied himself that the men captured had had no connection with the robbery or the robbers, William offered them one hundred dollars to act as guides through the cane-brake to arrest Barton and Russell. They said they could not if they would, since no man could find his way there in broad daylight, much less at night. They further admitted that they dare not attempt it, as Russell would kill them if they learned of their action. It was now pitch dark, and after a vain attempt to beat through the cane in search of the fugitives, William decided to return to Mr. Merrick's until next day.

The next morning at daybreak he started back for Lester's, accompanied by a number of the cane-brake population, all of whom were anxious to secure the one hundred dollars reward. They had long suspected the men at the store of being desperadoes, but they had had a wholesome fear of them on account of their fierce ways and their reckless habit of drawing their revolvers on slight provocation.

On arriving at Lester's, the party found that Lester had returned from Hickman during the night. He was a treacherous-looking scoundrel, and his reputation was bad, although he had never been caught in any crime in that vicinity. His name, John Wesley Lester, showed that he must have once belonged to a pious Methodist family, and, indeed, he claimed to have once been a Methodist preacher himself. He had sunken eyes, milky white, and his hair was lank and long; his complexion was dark, cheeks hollow, chin pointed, and forehead low. His manner was fawning and obsequious to those above him, and he looked and acted like a second "Uriah Heap." He pretended to know nothing of Russell, Clark, and Barton, except that they had come to his place in July, built the store there, and had been around the landing more or less ever since. He said that he knew nothing against them, except that they were gamblers, and that they often went off on gambling excursions, during one of which, according to their own statements, they had killed a man in a quarrel.

William learned from Lester's daughter that Barton had returned during the night to get a shawl, blanket, and two shot-guns. He had told her that Russell was hurt pretty badly, but that they intended to take the first packet down the river. From other parties William learned that the packet Julia had passed down during the night, and had stopped at a point about seven miles below, having been hailed from the bank. He did not place much faith in the theory that the men had taken passage by the Julia, for the reason that Lester's girl was too anxious to tell the story of the route Barton proposed taking. He discovered that Barton had been paying lover-like attentions to the girl, and he believed that Barton had instructed her to say that he intended taking the next packet, in order to give them a false scent. Having set the men of the neighborhood at work searching for Russell and Barton, William returned to Union City.

From Hickman Connell was sent to Cape Girardeau, Missouri, to capture Clark, who was said to have gone there three days before.

On the arrival of William in Union City, the superintendent telegraphed to me the result of William's visit to Lester's Landing, and authorized me to send an operative to Farmington, Illinois, to hunt up Mrs. Kate Graham, and learn what she could tell about Russell, Clark, and Barton. A man was sent there the next day, and he had no difficulty in finding Mrs. Graham, who proved to be the wife of a highly respectable business man. She was a member of the church, and was held in high esteem by every one acquainted with her. My agent, therefore, called upon her without any circumlocution or deception, and asked to see her on business. She was confined to her room by illness, but she saw him for a few minutes, and answered his questions so frankly that there was no doubt she was telling the truth. She stated that she was not acquainted with any one living at Lester's Landing; that she did not know, nor ever had known, any persons of the names given (Russell, Clark, and Barton); and that she knew no one who would answer to their descriptions. This clue seemed to come to an end very quickly, yet it afterward proved to be the means by which we captured one of the gang, and it was a striking instance of the necessity for the most careful and minute inquiry upon every point of news obtained, especially upon those received directly from the criminals themselves.

On the 3d of November, Connell went with a constable to the house of Mrs. Gully, the mother of Clark's companion, Mrs. Slaughter, and there he found them both. Clark was surprised by the officers, but he made a bold fight, and was overpowered with difficulty. When finally handcuffed and searched, a navy revolver and fifty dollars in money were taken from him; he was then taken nine miles on horseback to Cape Girardeau, where Connell obtained a light wagon to drive sixteen miles to Allenville, on the railroad leading to Hickman. On this trip Connell made the mistake of trusting to handcuffs alone, instead of securely fastening his prisoner's feet with rope. The idea that one man in handcuffs could escape from two active, unimpeded men did not, however, occur to Connell, and so the constable drove the horse, while Clark and Connell occupied the back seat. In justice to Connell, it should be stated that he had been constantly in the saddle for several days in raw and rainy weather, and had had very little sleep for two nights previous.

About nine o'clock in the evening, when only a mile from Allenville, Clark suddenly made a leap out of the wagon. The horse was jogging along at a good trot, and, though Connell sprang after his prisoner instantly, it was a couple of minutes before the constable could follow. As he ran, Connell fired at the dim figure disappearing in the thick brush; but the next instant he pitched headlong into a deep mud-hole, and, by the time he got out, the cylinder of his revolver was choked with mud, and Clark was far in advance. The chase was kept up as long as the pursuers were able to distinguish the direction of his flight, but, in the darkness of the gloomy woods, it was impossible to follow an athletic fellow like Clark with any hope of success. Connell returned to

Union City very much crestfallen, and reported his misfortune. My first feeling, on learning the news, was one of deep regret and anxiety at the loss of one of the leaders of the gang; my second thought was one of profound thankfulness that my men were in no way responsible for it. The situation was an illustration of the disappointments and difficulties which are so often met in a detective's experience; and, though I felt somewhat discouraged, I was more than ever determined that none of these men should eventually escape, even though it should be necessary to follow them for months.

The desire of the express company to employ as few as possible of my operatives embarrassed me exceedingly, for William was obliged to depend upon strangers, and he had little confidence in their ability or discretion. He was now satisfied of the identity of the parties he was in search of, and all that he needed was a small force of experienced and reliable men.

Had I been limited and interfered with in the Maroney case, described in "The Expressman and the Detective," as I was in this, there is no doubt that I might have failed to capture the criminal; but the cordial coöperation and support of the Adams Express Company gave me a fair opportunity to work to good advantage, and victory was the result.

## CHAPTER V.

*A Rich Lead Struck at Last.*

WILLIAM was quite sure, from the reputation and actions of Russell, Clark, and Barton, that they had been the leaders in the robbery, and he believed that Lester could give important information about them; he therefore caused Lester to be brought to Union City, and, on November 5, he succeeded in getting a statement of the doings of these men since Lester had known them. The important points developed were as follows :

They came to Lester's Landing in the middle of July, and built their store. They were rarely there together, as they would go off for two or three weeks at a time, leaving Barton or Clark in charge, and sometimes putting Lester in as storekeeper during the absence of all three. On one occasion, Russell showed him a pocket-book containing nearly one thousand dollars, which he thought he had lost, but which he found under a rail fence where he had hidden it; the other men, also, seemed to have plenty of money. About the middle of October, the three storekeepers went away, and were gone until October 24, three days after the robbery, on which day Lester met Clark and Barton walking toward his house, on the way from Hickman. They seemed quite excited, and said that they had been engaged in a difficulty, but they did not state what it was. They asked him whether he had seen Russell recently, and also whether there was a skiff at his landing; both questions were answered negatively, and they passed on toward the store, while Lester continued his walk to Hickman. On his return at night, he found that Clark and Barton had been across the river all day, scouting the Missouri shore for Russell, and that shortly after their return, Russell had come across the river in a skiff. Russell said that he had been shot, but that he was not much hurt, and he did not seem to act as if he had been hurt at all. Sunday morning, October 29, Clark took passage in a steamer for Cape Girardeau, having Mrs. Slaughter in company, and it was understood that he was going with Mrs. Slaughter to the house of her mother, nine miles from the Cape. Tuesday evening, William and Connell arrived at Lester's, the fight took place, and Barton and Russell escaped. After the detectives had gone back to Campbell's, Barton returned to the house and obtained a shawl, blanket, and two shot-guns; he said that they would never be taken alive, but that Russell had been badly wounded by one of the detectives. William had left two men at the landing the next day to capture the men if they returned, but they were afraid to attempt it, although they had a good opportunity that night. Russell came into the house alone, showing no signs of having been wounded, and said that he and Barton had joined four friends, who were outside waiting for him ; that they were all well mounted and armed, and that they intended to kill any one who should betray them or attempt their capture. He added that they intended to make their way on horseback to Alabama, and that they were strong enough to fight their way through, if necessary. Of course, Russell's object was to frighten the detectives and others who were searching for him, as he had no one with him except Barton.

Among other points of value in Lester's statement, was some incidental information relative to the men, which he had learned during the time they boarded with him. He had heard Clark say that his mother lived sixty miles back of Nashville, and Russell had once run a stationary engine in Missouri. Lester was shown the satchel found on the engine after the robbery, and he recognized it as having been left at his house once by a wood-chopper named Bill Taylor, who lived in the cane-brake, some distance below him. He said that the three men each carried a navy revolver and a derringer, while Russell had also a new, large-sized Smith & Wesson revolver.

Meantime, the telegraph had been used constantly to learn something about the three men, Russell, Clark, and Barton, from whatever source information could be obtained. Barton was well known in Nashville, New Madrid, and Union City. He was quite young, but he had been involved in a stabbing affray in Nashville, and was regarded as a desperate character. He had been respectably brought up by Major Landis, General Agent of the Nashville and Northwestern Railroad, and had been given a place in the employ of that road, with good prospects for promotion. Having become dissipated and hardened, he had been discharged from his position, and Major Landis had cast him off; thenceforward, his career had been rapid in the downward direction.

With regard to the other two men, little could be learned, until a rich lead was struck on the seventh of November. The corrected descriptions of the different parties having been sent to all the agents of the express company, Mr. Charles Pink, agent at Cairo, recognized Russell as a man who had sent eight hundred dollars in currency from Cairo to Mrs. M. Farrington, Gillem Station, Tennessee, on the eleventh of September, and who had then started, according to his own statement, for his home in Illinois. Mr. Pink also stated that the chief of police in Cairo claimed to know Russell, and to be able to find him—for a sufficient consideration. Not having any use for the services of this disinterested officer, his offer was politely declined.

The superintendent of the express company was strongly impressed with the belief that Russell and Barton were lurking around Lester's, and so, while William went to Nashville to see what could be learned about Barton and his companions, a number of men were hired to scour the country, hunt through the brake, and guard the

Mississippi ferries, while Connell and Crowley, the express messenger, were placed on the Missouri bank, to scout that side of the river. I may say here, *en passant*, that, with the exception of the two named, these men were a source not only of great unnecessary expense to the company, but of vexation and hindrance to William. In most cases, their scouting consisted in riding the high-roads from one tavern to another, and in order to have something to show for their work, they would bring in every species of wild and foolish rumor that they could discover or invent. As the superintendent frequently desired that these reports should be investigated, much valuable time was thus wasted. These men were not only employed without my advice, but they were retained long after I had urgently requested the discharge of the whole party, and I had great difficulty in obtaining their discharge, even after I was positively sure that the robbers had crossed the Mississippi and escaped into Missouri.

William spent one day in Nashville, and then went to Gillem Station, where he learned that Mrs. Farrington, to whom Russell had sent eight hundred dollars from Cairo, lived on an old, worn-out farm, and passed for a rich widow. She had three sons—Hillary, Levi, and Peter, the latter being quite young. Hillary and Levi Farrington bore a very bad reputation, having been mixed up in all kinds of fights and quarrels for a number of years. They were suspected of horse-stealing and counterfeiting; but most people were afraid of them, and they had never been arrested in that vicinity. William here learned, also, that Barton had been a frequent visitor at the Farringtons', and that he was as bad as the others. While at Gillem Station, William met Pete Farrington, the youngest of the three brothers, and his resemblance to Russell, whose face William had seen by the dim firelight and the flash of his pistol in the cabin at Lester's Landing, caused a sudden possibility to flash across his mind. He reasoned out the connection of the different facts about as follows:

"Russell was, undoubtedly, one of the Moscow and Union City robbers, and he obtained a considerable share of the plunder; two months after the first robbery, I find that he sent eight hundred dollars to Mrs. Farrington; this establishes the connection of those two persons. Barton was one of the actors in both robberies, also, and I find that he was formerly intimate with Mrs. Farrington and her sons; another link. Pete Farrington bears a strong resemblance to Russell, their peculiar Roman noses, with a lump in the middle, being exactly alike, and this creates a strong presumption that they belong to the same family. Now, Russell and Clark were so similar in their general appearance, that many people who have seen them together believe them to have been brothers. Hillary and Levi Farrington, I am told, also closely resemble each other, and they have not been seen about here for some months, they being, according to their mother's account, in Texas. The chain of evidence is very complete; what if Russell and Clark should prove to be the Farrington brothers!"

## CHAPTER VI.

*The Mother of the Farringtons, being arrested, boasts that her Sons " Will never be taken Alive."—Another Unfortunate Blunder by Amateur Detectives.—An interesting Fate intended for the Detectives.— William A. Pinkerton captures the Murderer of a Negro in Union City, proving " a very good Fellow—for a Yankee."—An Unfortunate Publication. —Nigger-Wool Swamp and its Outlaws.*

THE more William thought about it, the more convinced he became that his theory was correct, and he took steps to verify his suspicions by placing a watch upon Mrs. Farrington's movements. He also made arrangements to get possession of any letters that might come for her, and then, being hastily recalled by the superintendent of the express company, he hurried back to Union City.

He there learned that, during his absence, Clark had talked with both Lester and his wife. The latter had warned him of his danger, and he had then disappeared in the cane-brake. The men stationed at Lester's for the express purpose of arresting any of the robbers who might come there, had been either unaware of Clark's visit, or else they had been afraid to attempt his capture, and he had escaped again when almost within our grasp. William had, therefore, been called back by telegraph to take charge of the men engaged in beating through the cane-brake, as it had been clearly demonstrated that, without a determined leader, these men were no more useful than a flock of sheep. The hunt went on for several days with no results whatever, while at the same time scouts patroled the highways, and other men kept watch upon the ferries and fords for many miles around.

While this was going on, the express agent at Gillem Station was keeping a close watch upon Mrs. Farrington, when suddenly she announced her intention of going to join her sons in Texas. Instead of sending word to William at once, the agent began operations on his own account, and when Mrs. Farrington arrived at Waverly, Tennessee, he caused her arrest. She had started with two new wagons and a complete outfit for an overland journey of some length, so that her progress could not have been very rapid, and nothing would have been lost by waiting for instructions ; but the insane desire to play detective seemed to overpower all other considerations in the minds of the company's agents, and she was arrested by the sheriff and a *posse* of citizens. Her salutation to the officer who stopped her settled the question of identity at once, for, on being told that she would be obliged to let him search her wagons for certain men, she replied :

"Oh! yes; I know what you want. You would like to find my two sons and Barton for the express robbery; but you will never catch them, for they are not now in this country, and they will never be taken alive."

This piece of information led the express agent to take the only sensible step of his whole proceeding. Mrs. Farrington had two negro families with her, some of whom had belonged to her before the war; and, with the personal attachment noticeable in many of the colored people, they were now desirous of going West with her. It occurred to the agent that some of them, from their confidential relations to the family, might be able to give some information as to the whereabouts of the boys. The negroes were, therefore, taken separately and closely examined, until one of the men was urgently persuaded to reveal what he knew. He said that Levi, Hillary, and Barton had committed the robbery, and that they had since been at Mrs. Farrington's together. According to an agreement between the mother and her sons, she was to start for Texas, passing through Nigger-Wool Swamp, on the west side of the Mississippi, and the two eldest sons were to meet her in the swamp, when they would determine where to go.

The agent also learned that the men had arrived at their mother's house Friday evening, November 10, and that a man who had gone there to sell her a wagon had been met by Hillary Farrington with a shot-gun; on seeing that it was a neighbor, however, Hillary had lowered his gun and allowed him to come in. It was also learned that the three desperadoes had been seen at the house of the Farringtons' uncle, named Douglas, on Hurricane Creek, about ten miles from Waverly; again, on Monday, they had been noticed at Hurricane Mills, making their way to Fowler's Landing, on the Tennessee River between Florence and Johnsonville, fourteen miles from the last-named place. It was evident that they intended to strike across the country below Reel's Foot Lake, and cross the Mississippi at some point between Columbus and Memphis. The men were all well mounted and armed, and they had changed their personal appearance somewhat by altering the arrangement of their hair, whiskers, and beards.

The arrest of Mrs. Farrington was a most unfortunate blunder, since it disclosed to the criminals how close had been their pursuit, while little really important information was obtained. It was a good illustration of the danger of taking any decided step in a criminal investigation before knowing to a certainty that some good result would be obtained. The parties thus learned that we were not only aware of their identity, but also that we were very close upon their track, and the danger, as well as the difficulty, of the case was largely increased. These men were desperadoes of the most reckless type, and they would not have hesitated a moment to lie in ambush and kill their pursuers, if they had found it possible to do so.

In order to intercept the fugitives before reaching the swampy country near the Mississippi, the number of scouts and patrolling parties was increased by the superintendent of the express company, and two men, named Ball and Bledsoe, were engaged to follow Mrs. Farrington on horseback until her sons should join her in Nigger-Wool Swamp. This would have been a sensible and necessary move if the right kind of men had been employed; but the selection of untrained men for the delicate and important work of "shadowing" such an experienced gang of villains was risky in the extreme. Had they ever met Barton and the Farringtons, the latter would have undoubtedly murdered both of them without scruple; but there was no danger of such a meeting, since the robbers, and Mrs. Farrington also, were perfectly aware of the presence of their pursuers from the start. Indeed, they afterward stated that it had been their intention to have led the detectives on as far as the wild, unsettled country of Western Missouri, and to have then hanged them in some unfrequented spot, placing the inscription "Horse-thief" upon each of the bodies. Subsequent events prevented them from carrying out this plan, but there was no doubt that they would have taken that or some other equally daring means of ridding themselves of pursuit. The manner in which Ball and Bledsoe exposed their intentions wherever they went showed the inexperience of both men in such work; for, along the whole route over which

## ANOTHER UNFORTUNATE BLUNDER. 61

they passed, they were known as officers tracking a band of thieves ; and we afterward learned that, while they were innocently and unsuspectingly following Mrs. Farrington, two of the men, Barton and Clark, were almost continually watching them. However, they had been started on their mission by the superintendent before William could make any other arrangements, as he was away at Lester's Landing when the chase began.

From William's reports to me, I saw the uselessness of maintaining such a body of men in the work of scouting, watching ferries, and beating the cane-brake, for the reason that no good could come of it. I knew that if the robbers could escape from Lester's Landing and make their way to Gillem Station once, they could do it again. Clark (or Hillary Farrington) had been at Lester's early Thursday morning, while guards were stationed all about ; yet, on Saturday morning he was at his mother's farm, and no one had even seen him on the way. This convinced me that they had such a knowledge of the country as to make it impossible to stop them by any system of guards or patrols, and I therefore wrote several letters asking that the superintendent discharge this expensive force at once, and allow me to manage the whole operation by my own plans and with my own men. While William, therefore, was at work with indefatigable energy and perseverance, scouting and following up all the reports brought in by the vast army of volunteer detectives in the company's employ, we were both satisfied that the method adopted was useless, and that even the ferry guards would discover nothing. Knowing the character of the three desperadoes, I had no doubt of their sagacity in avoiding observation and pursuit; they would never try to cross without knowing positively whether the ferry was guarded, and if there should be any real danger, they would undoubtedly steal a skiff and make their horses swim across the river, a feat of no great risk in the then low condition of the water.

About this time an incident occurred which added greatly to William's popularity in Union City, and gained for him the respect and kindly feeling of the community. On Sunday two roughs, having drank enough bad whisky to be absolutely fiendish, began to beat an old and inoffensive negro whom they happened to meet. A merchant, named Blakemore, who was passing at the time, stopped to remonstrate with the ruffians, when one of them turned and plunged a knife into his stomach, inflicting a wound which caused his death next day. The murderer was the terror of the town, and so great was the fear of him that he would have probably escaped had not William appeared on the street as he rushed away flourishing his bloody knife and threatening to kill any one who should stand in his way. The sight of William's heavy revolver leveled at his head, backed by the certainty which he saw in William's face that death or surrender was his only alternative, caused him to choose the latter, and he was lodged in jail to await his trial for murder. The people of the town were quite enthusiastic over the way in which William had brought the fellow to bay, and then compelled his surrender; and they even went so far as to say that he was "a good fellow, a very good fellow indeed—for a Yankee."

On the twentieth of November an unfortunate publicity was given to our operations by the publication in the Union City *Journal* of a long history of the Farringtons, showing their whole career of crime, and terminating with an account of their latest exploit, as developed by our investigations in and about Union City. It is unnecessary to state the source whence this information was derived, further than to say that it was not obtained from any member of my force. It was a very dangerous piece of news to be published, since it might have wholly overthrown all our plans, besides involving the death of two or three men engaged in the operation; fortunately, the robbers were undoubtedly across the Mississippi by that time, and beyond the reach of newspapers for some weeks at least.

On the same day that this matter was published, Mrs. Farrington crossed the Mississippi River at Bird's Point, opposite Cairo, and the fact was reported to William and to me by telegraph. We had previously learned that Mrs. Farrington had relatives in Springfield, Missouri, and in Dade County, in the same State, and the probabilities were that, instead of going to Texas, she was going to visit in one of these places. Meanwhile, though my opinion was that her sons intended to rejoin her somewhere, either in Nigger-Wool Swamp or at her place of destination, I had no certainty that such was their intention; and, bearing in mind the warning they had received by her arrest at Waverly (and possibly by reading the newspaper article previously mentioned), I felt that every clue must be carefully traced, even though it might lead in an exactly opposite direction from that in which our previous suspicions had caused us to look. My correspondents and agents in Louisville, Cincinnati, St. Louis, and New Orleans were, therefore, kept on the alert to capture the men if they should venture into those cities, while I held three determined men ready to go at once in pursuit of Mrs. Farrington, in case she should take the route through Nigger-Wool Swamp.

It will be remembered that one of the negroes accompanying Mrs. Farrington had stated that her sons were to join her in that swamp; now, there were three possibilities about this statement: first, the negro might have lied; second, he might have been so informed by the old lady on purpose to give a false scent in case he should be questioned; and, third, while their intention might have been to meet there, subsequent events might have altered their plans. Still, thinking the subject over carefully, I decided that she would not take so difficult a course unless she really intended to meet her sons there. My reasons for so thinking were based upon the nature of the place, and, to comprehend my solicitude about Nigger-Wool Swamp, a description of it will be necessary.

The swamp is more than seventy miles long by about thirty-five miles wide, and, as a piece of bottomless ooze, its superior cannot be found in the United States. There are just two roads crossing it, one running from Hall's Ferry, at Point Pleasant, Missouri, and the other from Mitchell's Ferry, thirty-five miles below. These roads are mere bog-paths in themselves, being heavily overlaid with underbrush and corduroy logs, yet they afford the only means of crossing this vast morass. The period of the annual overflow turns it into a turbid, sluggish lake, the roads being then deeply buried under water; but even in the dryest seasons the greater portion of the swamp is a bottomless slime of mud and putrefying vegetation. Large tracts of thickly-wooded land are contained within the limits of the swamp, and these constitute a semi-substantial basis for the two roads which run through them; but even these clumps are impassable at most seasons, except along the artificially-constructed roads. Sometimes, for miles and miles, nothing but the rankest of swamp-vegetation is seen, growing in wild profusion and covering the treacherous ooze with a close network of leaves and branches, until the surface looks firm enough to be taken for solid ground; but should any unfortunate traveler venture to cross such a spot, his limbs would be clogged by these clinging water-plants, his feet would find no secure resting-place, and, sinking rapidly deeper and deeper into the mire, his bones would find a sepulcher where nothing but a general natural convulsion would ever disturb them.

Still, there are occasional islands of firm ground through this section, and these have become the resort of lawless characters of every nationality and degree of crime. Over the entrance to Nigger-Wool Swamp might be placed, with perfect truthfulness, the motto: "Who enters here leaves hope behind." Each man is a law unto himself, and he must maintain his rights by the strong arm and the ready shot-gun. In one thing only are the dwellers of the swamp united, namely: a bitter and deadly resistance to the law. No officer of justice ventures therein to perform any of the duties of his office; unless backed by a powerful body of determined men, he would never return alive, and, if so accompanied, he would never succeed in catching a glimpse of any criminal whom he might be seeking.

About the middle of the swamp, the two roads cross each other at a spot called "The Gates," and every person traveling through either way must pass this place. Knowing this fact, I felt sure that Mrs. Farrington would await the arrival of her sons at "The Gates," in case she entered the swamp, and I determined that, in such an event,

I should try to capture them there. I was fully aware of the danger of such an attempt, but I knew that to take the bull by the horns is sometimes the safest means of overpowering him. To send officers to that point with the avowed purpose of arresting any one, would be equivalent to sending them to their certain death, and I had no intention of doing anything of the kind; but I had men of my force who could visit Nigger-Wool Swamp for the professed purpose of hiding there from pursuit for alleged crimes, and, when the moment came for action, I did not doubt that they would bring out their men before the neighboring outlaws could discover their object.

Everything depended upon the course Mrs. Farrington should take on leaving the Mississippi River, since by striking north from the point where she crossed, she could skirt the edge of the swamp, while if she turned south toward Point Pleasant, I should know that she intended to carry out her original programme. This question was quickly settled, however, not only by the reports of the scouts, Ball and Bledsoe, who were following Mrs. Farrington, but also by an unexpected piece of intelligence from Gillem Station. Mrs. Farrington moved about twenty or twenty-five miles each day, and, from the fact that she went north to Fredericktown, there was no doubt that she had changed her plan of meeting her sons in Nigger-Wool Swamp.

## CHAPTER VII.

*The Scene of Action transferred to Missouri.—The Chase becoming Hot.*

ON the twenty-second of November, William learned that a letter had arrived at Gillem Station, postmarked Verona, Missouri, November 13, and he immediately took measures to obtain this letter. Three days later he learned its contents, which were of such an important character as to give a new direction to our efforts. The letter read as follows:

"VERONA, MO., Nov. 13, 1871.
" MY DEAR COUSIN:

" I seat myself to answer your kind letter, which came to hand last evening, and was glad to hear from you, and hear you was well and doing well. I have nothing new to write, only that we are all well at present, hoping that when these few lines come to hand they may find you well and doing well as ever, as you say you have been doing very well. It must be a good thing if it could stay so. Sometimes it was well and sometimes it wasn't, but I hope it will stay so, as you say it is a soft thing—as soft as things gets to be. I would like to see something like that, you bet. You talk like it can't be beat. That is the thing to take in. I think, and I know you think it, for I saw your name. I guess I did see you. You know Mr. Crapmel? He is a great fellow; you bet it is so. I have nothing more to write at present, as you said you are going to start out here. You said you was coming by here. Cousin, if you do come by, we don't live where we did when you were here; we live two miles nearer Verona. Come the same road. We live now half mile off the road on John Ellis' place. You can find out where we live anywhere. Come out the same road you did when you came before. John Timothy has just come out here; has been out here about three weeks. He is well satisfied here. So I will close for this time.

"From your cousin,
"J. M. DURHAM.

"M. F. sends her love to all of the family. Excuse my bad writing and bad spelling."

It was evident that Mrs. Farrington had previously written to her cousin informing him of her intention to visit him soon, and this letter was intended to direct her to the new location. The allusions in the letter to the "good thing" in which she was engaged showed that the writer had been made aware of the Farringtons' success as express robbers, and that he quite approved of their operations.

On reading this letter, William sent a copy to me immediately, and suggested that one or two good men be sent to Verona to get work near this man Durham, and to get into the confidence of the family, so that, when Mrs. Farrington should arrive, she would not be likely to suspect any one who had come before her. I fully approved of William's plan, and, on the last day of November, Detectives George W. Cottrell and Arthur C. Marriott started for Verona. I inferred that the people in that vicinity were rather lawless and desperate characters, from the fact that Durham spoke of "John Timothy" being well satisfied there. On the principle that "birds of a feather flock together," I judged the Farringtons, the Durhams, and this fellow Timothy to belong to the same type of people; hence, I concluded that, if Durham and Timothy were satisfied with the country, the people living there must be congenial spirits, especially since Mrs. Farrington was about to make a place of refuge in that vicinity.

My two men were detained a day in St. Louis, and they did not arrive in Verona until the second of December. The first thing they noticed about the town was the total absence of liquor saloons, and a few minutes' conversation with one or two of the citizens convinced them that no more orderly, honest, law-abiding community existed in Missouri than the population of Lawrence County. This discovery made a marked change in their plans necessary, as my instructions to them had been based upon the supposition that they would find a number of robbers, horse-thieves, and counterfeiters around Verona, and that they would be easily able to get Durham's confidence by appearing as reckless and desperate as any one. They had each prepared a choice autobiography for use among the residents, and, according to their own intended accounts of themselves, two greater scoundrels never went unhung.

All this was necessarily useless in the changed circumstances surrounding them. To attempt the *rôle* of criminal characters, hiding from justice, would quickly cause their banishment from the place, or possibly their arrest, and a new plan was essential. Their instructions had been that they should not put any confidence in any one, and they were obliged to invent a plausible reason for their presence there; also to have some business which would enable them to ride about the country, making inquiries and scouting for Mrs. Farrington and her sons.

Finding that the railroad company had a land agent in Verona, Cottrell decided to represent themselves as would-be purchasers of land. This would give them an excuse for going all over the county, examining different farms and unimproved tracts. They were introduced to Mr. Purdy, the land agent, by the hotel clerk, and from him they obtained a map of the county. It was then agreed that Mr. Purdy should go out with Cottrell and Marriott on Tuesday, December 5, to look at some pieces of property which the railroad company wished to sell. During Sunday and Monday both of the detectives were trying to learn where Durham lived, but no one seemed to know; neither could any one tell them anything about John Ellis, upon whose farm Durham had said he was living. The idea that Mrs. Farrington was rapidly pushing west, toward Durham's place, made Cottrell very anxious to begin operations as quickly as possible, since, if she should arrive before the detectives were established in the vicinity, there would be great difficulty in working into her confidence, as she would instantly suspect their true character; whereas, if she should find them already there, she would have no possible occasion to distrust them. They therefore thought best to confide the real object of their visit to Mr. Purdy, the land agent, and to ask his advice and assistance. Mr. Purdy had been an officer in the Union army during the war of the rebellion, and had settled in Verona at the close of the war. He was evidently an honorable man, who would always be found on the side of law and order, and as he was very popular in Verona, he would be able to give them a great deal of assistance in capturing the Farrington party. On communicating with me by telegraph on this point, they stated the facts briefly, and I authorized them to confer with Mr. Purdy on the subject, at the same time forwarding full instructions by letter.

On Tuesday, therefore, they told the whole story to Mr. Purdy, and showed him their credentials. He was quite astonished at their revelations, but he was very hearty and sincere in his expressions of good will toward them, and he promised to aid them in every possible way. He knew John Ellis quite well, having sold him the farm on which he was living, and he had heard of Durham, who hired a small portion of the Ellis farm. He said that if force should be necessary to capture the Farrington party, he could raise fifty determined men in ten minutes to help the officers. He said that after the war Verona had been a very bad place for a short time, but that, as Eastern men began to settle there, the respectable people had tried to drive out the hard cases; this had been slow work at first, but they eventually had been completely successful; they not only had driven out the dangerous characters, but they had closed all the liquor saloons also; and now, having once got rid of them, they would take care not to let any of that class of people back again.

Mr. Purdy was called away for a day or two on business, but he promised, on his return, to go with the detectives to Durham's place, and, meantime, he said he would speak of them as gentlemen who intended buying land in that section, and who wished to ride over the country until they found a place which satisfied them. During the next three days, therefore, they learned nothing new, their time being occupied in scouting the road along which they expected Mrs. Farrington to come.

Thus the first week of December passed, and the operation was not progressing very favorably anywhere. Ball and Bledsoe had reported Mrs. Farrington's route up to the thirtieth of November, and she had moved quite rapidly up to that date, but nothing had been learned since, and I expected to hear of her arrival at Verona every day. She had gone from Cairo to Frederickstown, Missouri, and thence to Ironton; then, instead of following a direct road, she had struck up north to Potosi, in Washington County; again taking a westerly route, she had passed through Steelville, Crawford County, and on the thirtieth of November, she had camped at Waynesville, Pulaski County. Beyond this we knew nothing of her movements, although by the eighth of December she had had ample time to reach Verona.

William had spent this week in following up a clue received from Louisville, Kentucky. It will be remembered that about November 9, a pair of dashing women had been reported as having visited the banks in Kansas City, trying to get large bills for about eight thousand dollars in small bills. I had not believed the story at that time, and therefore had taken no steps to follow them. When William learned from Louisville, however, that a woman named Annie Martin, whom Levi Farrington had been in the habit of supporting on the proceeds of his robberies, had been staying there with another woman named Lillie Baker, who had sustained the same relations to Barton, it occurred to him that these might have been the women who were said to have been in Kansas City with so much money. He started at once for Louisville, at the same time telegraphing to me his suspicions in the matter, and I began inquiries again in Kansas City by telegraph. I could learn very little except from the teller of one bank, who described the women as well as he could remember their appearance; but the description was not accurate enough to determine whether these two women had or had not been Annie Martin and Lillie Baker. In Louisville, however, William learned that these women had been there recently, and they had appeared to be well supplied with money. They had not remained very long, but had gone to New Orleans, where they were then living in good style. As Mr. O'Brien, the general superintendent of the express company, was in New Orleans, the information was sent to him, and he agreed to have a sharp watch kept to discover Farrington and Barton, in case they should follow these women.

On the eighth of December, Cottrell, Marriott, and Mr. Purdy started on horseback to visit John Ellis's farm, where the Durhams lived. About a mile before arriving there, they met a farmer named Wisbey, who was a neighbor of Ellis and the Durhams. Without letting him into their confidence, they talked with him a long time, and gradually drew out a number of important facts. The Durham family consisted of two brothers and a young sister living with their mother, old Mrs. Durham, and they rented a small house on a part of the Ellis farm. Nothing positive had ever been discovered against the character of either Jam. or Tilman Durham, but the neighbors had a poor opinion of them, and kept a pretty close watch upon their actions. During the previous fall a young man had visited them for some time, and his description was exactly that of Levi Farrington; but Wisbey could not tell his name, though he promised to learn it, and let Mr. Purdy know. Mr. Wisbey was a downright honest, intelligent man, and Mr. Purdy asked him to learn everything possible about the Durhams and their visitors; in case any wagons should arrive, it was agreed that he should send word to Mr. Purdy instantly. There was no occasion for telling him the whole story, as he was quite willing to undertake the trust on the strength of Mr. Purdy's request, without asking further particulars; and, as he was a thoroughly discreet man, there was little danger that he would betray his mission by idle talking. The detectives and Mr. Purdy then returned to Verona, it being considered undesirable that they should visit the Durhams, lest they might possibly excite suspicion.

The day following their visit to Wisbey, he arrived in Verona and told Cottrell that he had sent his son-in-law, Mr. Stone, to see Jim Durham, and the latter had said that he was expecting the arrival of some relatives very soon. He had learned further that the young man who had visited Durham in the latter part of the previous September had given his name as Levi Farrington, and had passed as the beau of the young Durham girl. In speaking of him, Jim Durham had told Mr. Stone that he did not wish his sister to marry Farrington, as the latter was a dangerous man, and had recently killed a man in a quarrel, while those who stood about were too much afraid of him to arrest him. Mr. Wisbey then returned home, with instructions to alternate with Mr. Stone in secretly watching Durham's place, so that every occurrence might be at once reported.

On the tenth of December I received a dispatch from Mr. O'Brien, saying that the express agent at Springfield, Missouri, had telegraphed to him on the eighth that the wagons of Mrs. Farrington's party had camped five miles from Springfield, and that the three men were known to be sixty miles south of Rolla. Mr. O'Brien therefore requested me to send a good detective to meet Connell in St. Louis, whence they would go together to capture the men at Rolla. I at once sent one of my best men, named Martin Galway, with instructions to join Connell, and, in case the Rolla report should prove to be a false alarm, they were to go on to Verona to assist Cottrell and Marriott. I had hardly completed my instructions to Galway, ere I received a telegram in cipher from Cottrell, as follows:

"Levi Farrington and a man calling himself George Cousins are at Durham's. They came on Thursday evening. Shall I arrest them? I can get all the help I need."

I immediately replied, also by a cipher dispatch, as follows:

"Are you sure it is Levi Farrington? His brother and Barton will probably be at Verona soon. We must get the whole. I think they will come from Douglas County. Probably Connell and Galway will be with you by Monday or Tuesday night; they can identify the men. Mrs. Farrington will be at Durham's by Sunday night or Monday morning. Keep a cool, clear head, and advise with Purdy. Have written by mail tonight. Keep me posted. William will arrive by Tuesday."

At the same time I wrote full instructions to Cottrell, ordering him to keep a close watch upon the men at Durham's, but to take no action until William should arrive, unless they attempted to go away. I did not alter Galway's instructions, but I telegraphed to William to start for Verona at once, to take charge of the operations there. The chase was now becoming hot, and a few days would decide the question of success or failure. I had reason to believe that the outlaws would not be taken without a desperate resistance, and I was anxious to have William present to direct the attack.

On Sunday, the tenth, Cottrell and Marriott rode out to see Wisbey, who met them just outside of Verona and informed them that Levi Farrington had arrived at Jim Durham's late Thursday night, accompanied by a young man named George Cousins. They did not receive my reply to their telegram announcing this fact until late that day, and so they could do nothing toward satisfying themselves as to Levi Farrington's identity until next morning, when they visited Wisbey at his own house. Mr. Stone,

Wisbey's son-in-law, had met a man named Smothers, who worked for Jim Durham, and Smothers had told him all about the two men who had just arrived. According to their own account, they had left Mrs. Farrington at Ash Grove, in Greene County, where she was going to buy a farm, Levi having given her five thousand dollars for that purpose; Levi and Cousins were on their way to Kansas, where they intended to settle down to raise cattle; Levi's brother was said to be at Lester's Landing for the purpose of selling off a stock of groceries which they owned there. Both men were well armed, having three navy revolvers and a shot-gun.

When this news was transmitted to me by telegraph, I decided that this man Cousins must be Barton, and that Hillary Farrington might possibly be at Lester's Landing, as they said. I therefore telegraphed to William, who I knew would be in St. Louis that day, *en route* to Verona, that he had better take Connell and Galway back to Lester's to capture Hillary, while Cottrell and Marriott undertook the arrest of Levi and Barton at Durham's. I also sent a dispatch to Cottrell to take no steps for their arrest until after William should have captured Hillary.

William, having previously thoroughly examined the contents of the store at Lester's, knew that they were not worth over two hundred dollars, and he telegraphed me to that effect, suggesting that it was improbable that Hillary should run so much risk for so small a sum. On learning this fact, I coincided with him, and ordered him to go on to Verona, as I had originally intended. I desired that he should keep the Durham place carefully watched until the arrival of the other Farrington, who, I believed, would soon join the rest of the party; then, in case he arrived, we should get all three together; but, if the other two should show any signs of moving off, they could be taken at any time.

Mr. O'Brien obtained requisitions from the Governor of Tennessee on the Governor of Missouri for the three men, and I felt that success was only delayed a day or two at most.

---

## CHAPTER VIII.

*A determined Party of Horsemen.—The Outlaws surrounded and the Birds caged.—A Parley.—An affecting Scene.—The burning Cabin.—Its Occupants finally surrender.*

WHILE the telegrams were flying back and forth on Tuesday, the twelfth, Cottrell and Marriott were busily engaged. Early that morning Mr. Stone came to Verona, and told them that he had learned that Farrington and cousins intended to leave Durham's for the Indian Territory the next day. The news was doubtless authentic, Stone having heard it from

*Burning out the Outlaws!*

Smothers, who had said that Farrington had told him so himself. It was clearly impossible to wait for William's arrival, as, by that time, the men might be safely hidden in the wild country to the westward. Instant action was absolutely necessary, and Cottrell so informed Mr. Purdy, who soon gathered a force of eight men. Very little would have been needed to obtain even a larger number of recruits, for, had Mr. Purdy and the detectives publicly told the story of the men whom they wished to capture, there would have been plenty of eager volunteers, all anxious to aid in ridding the country of such a band of outlaws. It was not deemed advisable, however, to summon a large posse, lest the news might spread so fast as to reach the ears of the criminals before the detectives could surround them; on this account only a few reliable men were let into the secret, and they left town singly and in pairs to avoid observation, having a rendezvous outside.

Just before starting, Mr. Purdy received a dispatch from the general land agent, ordering him to Pearce City instantly, as several purchasers of land were awaiting him there; although he tried to have his visit postponed one day, he was unsuccessful, his orders being imperatively repeated by telegraph, and so he was unable to accompany the detectives and citizens on their expedition to Durham's. The party of eight met the detectives outside the town, and they were joined on their way by three others, who lived on the road.

They were all substantial business men or farmers, but they were accustomed to a life in the saddle, and they had all borne arms during the war on one side or the other. In spite of their present peaceful occupations they were not a body who could be trifled with, and it was evident that any gang of desperadoes would find their match in these cool, determined, law-abiding men.

A few miles from Verona they met a young lady riding a large brown mule, but none of the men in the party knew her. Cottrell felt sure, however, that she was Durham's sister, and that she was riding Farrington's mule. The descriptions he had received of the girl from Stone and Wisbey coincided exactly with her appearance, while the mule could not be mistaken. He therefore sent a man back to watch her, lest she should have taken alarm at so large a cavalcade of armed men. She rode on to Verona, however, without showing any signs of uneasiness, and the scout soon overtook the party.

On arriving one mile from Wisbey's, Marriott went on to Stone's house with six men, while Cottrell went to Wisbey's with the other five. Stone and Wisbey soon gathered a number of the neighbors, among whom was John Ellis, who owned the house and land where the Durhams were living; he was a very highly respected citizen, and was not at all displeased at the idea of getting rid of his semi-disreputable tenants. The management of the affair was then unanimously voted to Cottrell, and the party rode rapidly toward the Durham house. It was situated at the edge of a clearing, with underbrush and woodland close to it on three sides, so that great caution was necessary, lest the villains should see them approaching, and escape into the woods. At a reasonable distance from the house, therefore, the party divided, a part, under Marriott's direction, dismounting and making their way to the rear of the house on foot. When sufficient time had elapsed to enable the latter party to surround the house, Cottrell, with the remainder, dashed up to the front of the house and spread out, so as to make sure that no one should escape. As they approached, a man, who proved to be Jim Durham, appeared on the porch and asked what they wanted; to which Cottrell replied that he wanted the men in the house.

The words had hardly passed his lips ere Barton sprang into the open doorway with a navy revolver leveled at Cottrell; but, seeing that the latter, as well as several others, had him covered, he shut the door quickly and started for the back of the house. By this time, however, the cordon of guards had drawn close around, and, as he emerged at the rear, he found himself confronted by half a dozen determined men, who ordered him to surrender. He then hastily tried to close the back door also, and pointed his revolver through the crack; but the discharge of several shots, which struck close to him, caused him to withdraw his pistol and tightly close the door. It was evident that the birds were caged at last, and it was now only a question of time when they would be taken; as it was only one o'clock in the afternoon, there were still four hours of daylight to conduct the siege.

Jim Durham, when he saw the rifles and revolvers of so large a force pointed at him, was thoroughly frightened, and he begged piteously that they would not shoot him. Cottrell placed his men behind trees, fences, and other protections, so as to be safe from any attempt to pick them off by the men in the house, and yet to guard every means of exit from the place; he then called Jim Durham out and searched him, finding nothing but a single-barreled pistol. He then sent Jim to the door of the house to summon the men inside to surrender, telling them that he was determined to have them—alive if possible, but if not, dead.

They refused to surrender, saying that they would kill any man who should approach the house. When Durham brought back their answer, Cottrell sent word that he would give them five minutes in which to decide whether they would yield peaceably or be burned out and shot to death. Just then Mrs. Durham, the mother of the Durham boys, begged Cottrell to allow her to go speak to Farrington and Barton, as she believed she could induce them to surrender. Accordingly, she went to the front window and implored them not to have the house burned down, as all her household goods would be destroyed. They replied that they might as well die inside as to come out and be shot down. Cottrell sent back word that they should be treated like all other prisoners if they would pass out their arms and surrender quietly; but if they tried to fight or resist, they would surely be killed.

As they still refused, Jim Durham was sent to barricade the doors with fence rails, so that they should not be able to rush out unexpectedly. He whined and complained that the men inside would shoot him, but he was obliged to go, and though they did threaten him, he was able to crawl up and lay the rails without getting within range. The house was a solid log cabin, with only two doors and very few windows, so that it was possible to approach it in one or two directions without exposure to a fire from within. When the doors had been securely barricaded, Cottrell ordered him to get on the roof, which was a common shingle roof, and set fire to the house. Mrs. Durham was carrying on at a great rate, first begging Farrington to surrender, and then praying to Cottrell not to burn her property. John Ellis, to whom the house belonged, gave full permission to burn it, and a fire was built in the open air to make brands to set it afire.

Mrs. Durham was allowed to make one more appeal to the ruffians inside, but they would not listen to her entreaties. They asked her, however, what kind of a looking man Cottrell was, and what he wanted to arrest them for. Cottrell was standing near enough to hear the question, and after Mrs. Durham had described his appearance, he told them that he wanted them for an express robbery; that he would treat them kindly if they should yield peaceably; but if they should refuse this, his last offer, he should set fire to the house and shoot them down as they ran out. He said he had no wish to kill them, but that he was determined they should not escape; rather than allow them to get away, he would have them shot on sight; but they would be protected and brought to trial if they would surrender.

To this they replied that they intended killing some of their besiegers first, anyhow. Finding further parley useless, therefore, Cottrell gave the order to burn the building, and Durham was forced to carry the embers and brands to burn his own premises. Just at this time, the young girl, whom they had met riding a mule toward Verona, rode up to the house and asked what was the matter. As Cottrell had surmised, this was Miss Durham, and she was very much frightened at what she saw.

The afternoon sun was buried in a deep bank of clouds, so that the twilight was rapidly drawing on, there being just enough light to show the barricaded doors, the deserted porch, and the determined men scattered around, with shot-guns and rifles pointed at the low log cabin, above which a frightened man stood out in bold relief against the sky, tearing off the shingles and piling them upon a glowing flame at his feet. Everything was now hushed in deathly silence, a . it needed no explanation for any one to understand that a bloody tragedy was about to occur if that flame should be allowed to envelop the building. It was now the prison of its two occupants, but only a short time would elapse before it would be their tomb.

On seeing the situation, Miss Durham asked to be allowed to speak to the men, as she said she knew they would listen to her. On Cottrell's refusal to hold any more parley with them, she burst into tears, threw her arms around his neck, and implored him to let her speak to Barton just once, if only for five minutes. Finally, seeing that most of his party wished to give the girl a chance to speak to her sweetheart, Cottrell said that she could have three minutes to obtain their arms; if they surrendered immediately, the fire should be put out; but, if they should still refuse, their last chance of saving the house and their lives would be gone. Miss Durham then went to the window, and talked with the men in the most imploring manner, urging them not to sacrifice themselves, as they would surely do if they remained in the burning house. Her entreaties did not seem to affect them at first; and, as the flames were then beginning to gather strength, Cottrell ordered her to come away from the house, and leave them to their fate. She made one more appeal, and Barton handed her a navy revolver; then Farrington did the same, and she brought them to Cottrell, saying that they would surrender if they could be sure that their lives would be spared. Cottrell told her to go back and get the rest of their arms, and assure them that they should be taken to Tennessee for trial. She soon returned with another revolver and a shot-gun, and said that the men would come out. Cottrell therefore removed the rails, opened the front door, and called them out—Barton coming first, and then Farrington. The latter proved to be Hillary, not Levi, as he had called himself. It was not known why he had used his brother's name, but it was supposed that Hillary had taken his name to enable him to prove an *alibi* in case he should be arrested.

Cottrell's party first secured the prisoners with ropes, and then assisted Jim Durham to extinguish the fire on the roof; the latter was quite rotten, and it had burned so slowly that very little damage had been done. The prisoners were thoroughly searched, but nothing of any consequence was found upon them, the total of their funds being less than three dollars. A prolonged search through the house revealed nothing of importance, except the fact that it was quite an arsenal for arms, there being found six navy revolvers, two double-barreled shot-guns, and a Spencer repeating rifle. The siege had lasted nearly three hours, and, another hour having been spent in searching the house and saddling their animals, it was nearly dark by the time they started for Verona. Farrington and Barton were carefully tied upon the horse and mule respectively, and, after thanking the neighboring farmers for their assistance, Cottrell took the road back, accompanied by the eleven men who belonged in and about Verona. The greatest care was taken that the prisoners should have no opportunity for escape, and they were informed that any attempt to get away would be the signal for riddling them with bullets.

While riding along, Cottrell learned from Barton that the party had been very lucky in finding the two men in the house, since their usual custom had been to spend the days in the woods, coming in only at night to sleep. On this occasion, however, the weather was so cold that they were spending the day indoors.

When asked why they had not surrendered before, they both made the same reply, namely: that they believed the posse of citizens intended either to shoot them immediately, or to hang them after a trial by lynch law.

On arriving in Verona early in the evening, the prisoners were securely tied up with ropes, and Cottrell alternated during the night with Marriott in watching them. A blacksmith was also called up, and shortly after midnight he completed two pair of leg shackles, with which they were fastened together. My men were greatly fatigued, having ridden a large number of miles every day for a week, and the excitement of the affair added, of course, to their prostration, but they resolutely paced the floor in alternate four-hour watches, determined that no possible loophole for escape should again be afforded to such daring villains as these two.

The result of the expedition was, of course, transmitted to me in telegraphic cipher at once; but the arrest was kept secret for the time, in order to prevent a knowledge of it coming to Levi Farrington, who was still at large. According to Barton, Levi was concealed somewhere in Tennessee, but this statement was proof positive that he was not in Tennessee at all, since Barton's object in telling anything about him was evidently intended to mislead us; hence, no faith was put in his story, and other steps were taken to capture Levi.

William arrived in Verona on the morning after the fight, and he prepared to return with the prisoners to St. Louis by the noon train. It was supposed that Levi Farrington was also on his way to the rendezvous at Durham's farm, and that he would probably approach by the direct road through Douglas County. Cottrell and Marriott were left, therefore, to attend to Levi and the old lady, whose whereabouts were still uncertain. William saw most of the citizens engaged in the affair, and heartily thanked them for their aid; being questioned as to whether they should receive the reward of one thousand dollars offered by the express company for the capture of the two Farringtons and Barton, he informed them that he considered them entitled to it, and that he should recommend its payment, but that the matter would be decided by the officers of the company. I may here anticipate events somewhat to state that the company paid the citizens and farmers a liberal amount for their services in capturing the robbers, and a settlement was made which was satisfactory to all parties.

William left Verona about noon of the day he arrived, taking Hillary Farrington and Barton with him, under guard of Galway and Connell. On arriving in St. Louis, he separated the prisoners in order to induce Barton to confess; and, after a long conversation, in which he showed Barton how conclusive was the evidence against all three of the men, he obtained a very full confession, of which the greater part is here given exactly as it was taken down from Barton's lips.

## CHAPTER IX.

*Barton's Confession.—The Express Robberies and the Outlaws' subsequent Experiences fully set forth therein.—A Clue that had been suddenly dropped taken up with so much Profit, that, after a desperate Struggle, another Desperado is Captured.*

"I AM twenty-two years of age," said Barton, "and my native place was Columbus, Mississippi. When quite young, I left home and took to following the army. About five or six years ago I moved to Normandy, Tennessee, and lived with the family of Major Landis, and two or three years later, I went to work on the Nashville and Northwestern Railroad as a brakeman, remaining as such over two years. About three years since I formed the acquaintance of Hillary and Levi Farrington, at Waverly, Tennessee. These are the men otherwise known as J. H. Clark and Edward J. Russell. Afterward I opened a saloon in Nashville, and Levi Harrington visited me there several times. Last April or May he was arrested on suspicion of counterfeiting, but as there was no case against him, he was discharged. After a short time, I went down to visit Levi at Mrs. Farrington's; she lived at the head of Tumbling Run Creek, twelve miles back of Gillem Station. Hillary was in jail at Memphis at that time, charged with murder and horse-stealing. When he got out of jail, Levi, Hillary, and myself all made a trip to Little Rock, Arkansas, gambling by throwing three-card monte, and we won about thirteen hundred dollars; we then returned to Gillem Station, where we remained until the twenty-first of July, this year. During this time, Levi, who frequently rode back and forth on the express trains, spoke of the feasibility of robbing them.

"On the morning of July 21, Levi, Hillary, and myself left Gillem Station for the purpose of robbing the express train at some of the stations either on that road or on the Mobile and Ohio Railroad. At Union City we changed cars, and arrived at Moscow just after dark. The plan was, that we all three should enter the car and overpower the messenger; but Levi and Hillary were the only ones who entered. I remained on the platform of the first passenger coach and kept watch. When the train was passing the water tank, they slacked up the speed, and we all jumped off and struck for the woods. The messenger had nothing whatever to do with this robbery, so far as I was ever informed.

"As I said before, we struck into the woods and reached the river just above Hickman, where we stole a fisherman's skiff, and all three of us started down the river. Finding that we were pursued, we left the skiff on the Tennessee shore, near Island Number Ten. We then took the river road and walked back as far as Lester's Landing, arriving there about dinner-time, July 23. Levi divided the money, giving me one-third of one thousand dollars, which was all, he said, in the safe, although I always believed there was more.

"So far as I know, neither of the Farringtons had ever met Lester before, and I am sure that I had never set eyes on him until we went to his place at this time. On account of the spot being so lonely and isolated, Hillary proposed that we put up a store there, as it would be a good cover for our actual business. We started the store, and applied to the postmaster to establish a post-office, to be known as Lester's Landing; our object in this move was, of course, to give an added color of respectability and *bonâ fide* business to our transactions. From this time until the middle of October, I remained at the store nearly all the time; Hillary was also there most of the time, but Levi very seldom. During one of the latter's western trips, he said he had been out to see his Aunt Durham.

"Along in October, Levi proposed that we again strike the express company when the train stopped for supper at Union City. Hillary had been in the habit of riding back and forth on the engine, and he understood how to run a train. Levi suggested that we take a man named Bill Taylor into the robbery with us; he was then employed chopping wood for Lester, and when Levi approached him on the subject he agreed to go. Levi left Lester's a few days before the robbery. Hillary and I did not leave until the nineteenth, when we went up to Columbus by steamer, taking along a large quantity of fish. Having sold our fish, we took the train for Union City, where we arrived the same evening. On getting off the train, we met Levi and Bill Taylor on the platform, and the only conversation which took place was when Levi asked why we had not arrived sooner, to which we replied that we came as soon as we could. The next morning we met again, having slept in separate places so as not to attract attention, and went down the road some distance toward Hickman. While camped in the woods that evening, about ten o'clock, an old man named Hicks came along with a bottle of whisky and stopped at our camp-fire quite a time. There were present Hillary, Levi, myself, and Bill Taylor. We remained in the woods all that night. The next day we moved further into the woods toward Hickman, and at night, just at dark, we came back to Union City.

"We had been there only a few minutes when the up train came along; she stopped and backed down a little ways, when all the train hands left her and went to supper. Hillary and Taylor then boarded the engine, and Levi and myself jumped aboard the express car. The messenger was eating his supper when we went in, and, seeing Levi point a Derringer at him, he exclaimed: 'Don't shoot me! I will surrender.' Levi compelled him to unlock the safe, and we took all the money. Levi then swung the messenger's lantern, and the train stopped, when we all jumped off and started down the railroad to Hickman. Our intention was to go to the wood-yard near Union City, and steal a ride on a freight train to Hickman. We hid under the platform at the wood-yard, and while there Levi accidentally shot himself in the thigh; but the wound was very slight, and it hardly interfered with his walking. As the freight train did not stop, we were obliged to walk to Hickman, where we arrived Sunday night. We had had some provisions when we first camped out, which Bill Taylor had carried in a valise; but he had left the valise and all its contents on the engine, so that we had very little to eat.

"While in the woods we divided the money, but Levi, who carried it, showed up only twenty-three hundred dollars.

"Sunday night we stole a skiff in Hickman and went down the river to James' Bayou, and while there, on Monday morning, we saw Messenger Cross, whose car had been robbed, making inquiries about us in a grocery-store. We then started off on foot, going down the river on the Missouri shore. About a mile below James' Bayou we found the skiff which we had previously set adrift, and which had evidently been picked up by some one. Taking this skiff again, Hillary, Taylor, and I dropped down to a point about a mile above Lester's, leaving Levi on the Missouri shore, where we started from. We landed on the Tennessee shore, and walked down the river road a short distance, when Taylor left us, remaining in the woods. Hillary and I met Lester on the road soon afterward, and told him that we had come down on a steamboat which was then tied up, on account of the heavy fog. Levi arrived next day, having come across the river with a fisherman.

"The following Sunday, October 29, Hillary left on a steamboat, taking with him a woman named Slaughter, with whom he said he was going to Davidson's wood-yard, nine miles above Cape Girardeau. He expected to return in a few days.

"The next thing of any importance which occurred was on the Tuesday night following, when Messrs. Pinkerton and Connell rode up to Lester's house. At the first glance, I thought they were officers, and Levi told me that he thought the same. I saw him pull his pistol out of his pocket before getting out of his chair."

[The moment Connell opened the door, Levi knew that he was a detective, having seen him acting in that capacity in Memphis, when Hillary was arrested for horse-stealing the previous spring.]

"When I made my escape from Lester's house," continued Barton, "I ran right back through the cornfield; I heard all the shooting, but did not see it. In a short time Levi joined me in the cane-brake back of the cornfield. Levi told me that he had had a shooting match with the two officers, but he did not know whether he had hit either of them or not; they had not hit him, but he had had a very narrow escape.

"After awhile we slipped up to the house, and saw that the officers were gone; so we went in, got our supper, and took our pistols, besides a shawl and blanket. We then got an old skiff, crossed the river, and slept in the woods on the Missouri shore. The next day we remained under cover until nightfall, when we recrossed the river, and went through the woods to Union City, spending Wednesday night and Thursday in the woods on the way. On Thursday night we took the train from Union City to Gillem Station. The conductor of the train was Conductor Roberts, on whose run I had formerly been brakeman; and, being afraid he might recognize me, I laid down in my seat and covered up my face, while Levi paid both fares. We arrived at Gillem Station about three o'clock in the morning, and reached Mrs. Farrington's house about daylight.

"I gave Mrs. Farrington five hundred and fifty dollars in money to keep for me, this amount being the proceeds of both express robberies, and she still has it in her possession. Before leaving Lester's, Hillary had given most of his money to Levi to take to their mother to keep for him, and Levi left with her nearly the whole of his share of the plunder also.

"We had been at Mrs. Farrington's a week when Hillary arrived. Before this, we all thought that the officers had captured him, and we were quite surprised to see him safe. He said that Detective Connell had arrested him at Mrs. Gully's, and that he had made his escape by jumping out of Connell's wagon into a thicket near Allenville; he had then gone right back to the house where he had left Mrs. Slaughter, where he got a pistol and some money, and had his irons removed.

"At the time Hillary arrived at Mrs. Farrington's, the old lady had been gone a day and a night on her way to Texas or Missouri. It was understood that Levi and I were to meet her somewhere on the road, or at Holton's farm, near the line between Lawrence and Dade Counties, Missouri. The day after Hillary arrived, we started for Missouri; I was riding a sorrel horse; Hillary, a chestnut-sorrel horse; and Levi, a large brown mule. We spent two days at the house of Mr. Douglas, near Mrs. Farrington's, and then crossed the Tennessee River at Cuba. We crossed the

Mississippi River by the last ferryboat on Friday evening, November 10, at Hall's Ferry, opposite Point Pleasant, Missouri. We saw no men on guard at the ferries. We struck right out through Nigger-Wool Swamp to Bloomfield, where Levi left us. He said he was going to Farmington, Illinois, as that was a good place to keep under cover. After he left us, nothing important occurred until our arrest. We knew where Mrs. Farrington was every night, and also knew all about the two men who were following her; we did not mind letting them follow her, as they could not have captured us, and we could have shaken them off at any time if we had wanted to do so.

"Levi and Hillary frequently spoke of making other raids upon the express company, and said what a soft thing it was. It was my intention to separate from them as soon as I could get my money from the old lady, as I wished to return to my friends below Columbus, Mississippi.

"The foregoing is all I know of the Farringtons or the express robberies.

(Signed), "WILLIAM BARTON."

It will be observed how completely this confession corroborated our investigations, there being few new points learned. The information that Mrs. Farrington had possession of nearly all the stolen money was valuable, and I sent instructions to Cottrell, at once, to attach all of her property in the name of the Southern Express

Company, if it could be done. But the most important feature brought out was the hiding-place of Levi Farrington, which was given as Farmington, Illinois. It will be remembered that William found, at the store at Lester's Landing, some pieces of paper, upon which was scribbled, "Kate Graham, Farmington, Illinois;" that I sent a detective to that place to see Mrs. Graham; that the latter answered, with every evidence of truthfulness, that she did not know Russell, Clark, or Barton; and that the clue was dropped immediately. From Barton, however, William learned that Mrs. Kate Graham was a cousin of the Farringtons, and that, being a highly respectable and conscientious woman, she knew nothing of their *aliases*, nor of their crimes. It was there that Levi Farrington had gone to hide. Barton's confession was made on the fourteenth, and William instantly sent me a cipher dispatch containing the important features of it. By the evening train of that day, my other son, Robert A. Pinkerton, took passage for Farmington, accompanied by Detective W. T. Brown, of my force. They arrived there about noon the next day, and soon learned that Levi Farrington was staying with his relatives. Having presented letters of introduction to one or two influential men, Robert obtained an introduction to the city marshal, who promised to give all the aid in his power to arrest Farrington.

About two o'clock they saw the latter coming down the street, and, by previous arrangement,

Robert allowed Levi to pass him, both walking toward Brown and the marshal. Levi Farrington was a very powerful man, standing six feet in his stockings, with a frame and muscles in proportion to his size. Remembering the desperate character of the man, Robert did not deem it advisable to give him any chance to draw a weapon or show fight; he therefore followed Farrington closely until he was about ten feet from the marshal, and then, springing at him, he pinioned the desperado's arms by clasping him tightly around the body just at the elbows. Farrington did not stop to question the cause of this proceeding—he knew the reason of his seizure well enough—but, gathering his whole strength, he made one jump away from the two officers who were approaching in front, and landed nearly in the middle of the street, taking Robert along with him. Robert clung to him like a vise, however, and before he could make another such an effort, the other two were upon him. A terrible struggle now ensued in the street, during which both Robert and Brown were badly bruised by being rolled upon and kicked by their powerful prisoner. Robert knew that Farrington was desperate enough to fight to the bitter end, and that he would kill as many as he could before being killed himself; to release his arms, therefore, would enable him to draw a weapon, as he was undoubtedly well armed, hence Robert never relaxed his hold. Having a professional pride in securing his prisoner alive, moreover, he did not wish to resort to extreme measures except to save the lives of other persons, and, as a large crowd had gathered around the moment the struggle began, there would have been evident danger in allowing him an instant's freedom. Over and over they rolled together, therefore, Farrington striving with all his strength to break Robert's clasp upon his arms, while the other two officers were doing their best to pinion his legs. After a ten minutes' struggle, they succeeded at length in holding him down and sitting upon his legs until he could be tied with ropes. By this time, the whole party were pretty thoroughly exhausted, but, after resting a few minutes to recover their breath, the officers got handcuffs on their prisoner's wrists, and took him to the railroad station, where he was searched. Little money was found on his person, but he had a large revolver, two Derringer pistols, and a large dirk concealed about him. He was then placed in the freight office, while Brown and Mr. Graham, Mrs. Kate Graham's husband, went to the latter's house to get Levi's baggage. On their return, the whole party took passage for Chicago, where they did not arrive until next day, owing to the failure to make connections. In Levi's valise were found two revolvers, some jewelry, and a very large sum of money.

They arrived so late on Saturday that there was no train for Cairo before the following evening, and meantime the prisoner required the most careful watching, as none of our handcuffs were large enough to fit his wrists without cutting into the flesh. Robert and Brown were completely prostrated by the strain upon their muscles and the injuries they had received, so that they felt the effects of the struggle for several days.

The moment that Robert arrived in Chicago with his prisoner, the latter was taken to the First Precinct police station, where he was placed in a cell for safe keeping. During the afternoon it was learned that he had sent for a lawyer to obtain a writ of *habeas corpus*. The arrest had been made without any warrant, and no requisition had been obtained for use in Illinois, as I had expected to capture all three of the men in Missouri. Should Farrington succeed in getting the desired writ, I should be forced to give up my hold upon him, and, before the requisition of the Governor of Tennessee upon the Governor of Illinois could be received, he would be probably beyond the reach of pursuit.

I therefore procured a closed vehicle and took the prisoner out for a drive, carefully bound, with two reliable men as guards. The afternoon was thus spent, and, after dark, there being no longer any object in driving around the suburbs of the city, Farrington was taken to my office and kept all night. He behaved very well, and did not seem anxious to get away by force. He tried, however, to induce Robert to let him go, telling him that it would be worth a very large amount of money to him to do so. Finding his offers disregarded, he appeared to take his arrest very coolly, saying that he guessed he had money enough to see him through.

On Sunday evening, Robert and Brown took him to the railroad station, and the party embarked for Cairo.

---

## CHAPTER X.

*A terrible Struggle for Life or Death upon the Transfer-boat "Illinois."—"Overboard!"—One less Desperado.—The Fourth and Last Robber taken.*

AFTER Barton had made his confession to William in St. Louis, the prisoners, Hillary Farrington and Barton, were kept separate, as the latter was afraid that Hillary would find some means of killing him. About midnight of Thursday, December fourteenth, they all took passage by railroad for Cairo, and there they immediately went on board the large transfer-boat to Columbus, Kentucky. All the detectives were thoroughly worn out from excitement and loss of sleep, but they did not for an insant relax their vigilant watch upon their prisoners. William had been talking for some time with Hillary, trying to obtain a confession and to learn what had been done with the money secured at the two robberies. From the questions that William asked, Hillary soon learned, or surmised, that Barton had confessed. He was terribly enraged at this, and without doubt he would have killed Barton if he could have got at him; but being unable to do so, his fury was all turned upon his captors.

My son hoped by threatening to have Mrs. Farrington arrested and imprisoned, to induce Hillary to give up his share of the plunder rather than have his mother punished. This threat seemed to infuriate him beyond anything, and he swore that he would have his revenge on William if he had to wait twenty years for it. After sitting sullenly thinking on the subject for a time, he said he was cold, and wanted to get a drink. William therefore offered to go with him into the bar-room, and they walked toward the forward end of the saloon, leaving Galway and Barton seated together. Connell had gone into the water-closet a few moments before, but, as there was a detective with each of the prisoners, no attempt at escape was anticipated.

The steamer was the powerfully-built transfer-boat "Illinois," and she was running with great speed, her ponderous wheels revolving at an unusually rapid rate. The bar-room was situated just forward of the saloon, after passing through the barber shop, and it could be entered from the saloon or through a door leading upon the guards, just forward of the paddle-box.

As they were about to enter the barber shop from the saloon, Hillary drew back, saying that he did not want to go that way, as there were some men in that room whom he knew. They therefore went out upon the guards to walk along to the outer door of the bar-room. The space was narrow, and the rail quite low, so that it would not have been at all difficult for a man to spring overboard, even though he were in irons. This idea occurred to William, but he did not trouble himself about it, since he knew that the heavy strokes of the paddle-wheel would instantly kill any one who might attempt such a thing. William wore a loose-fitting sack coat with large pockets, in one of which he carried a heavy army revolver, which he had taken from Hillary, his own revolver being in his belt. In walking it was his habit to put his hand on the butt of this army revolver, which protruded somewhat from the pocket. On reaching the door, however, he took his right hand from the pistol to turn the knob. This was a careless action, of which he never would have been guilty, had he been less fatigued, mentally and physically, but, being so used up as to act almost mechanically, his habitual thoughtfulness was momentarily absent, and he was caught off his guard for an instant in a manner which nearly cost him his life. It should be understood that the scene which ensued occurred so rapidly as to occupy less time in its passage than is required to read about it, and that during those few seconds a struggle of life and death was going on.

Hardly had William's hand touched the doorknob ere he felt the pistol drawn out of his coat pocket. He knew there was but one person who could have done it, and that person was a perfect devil thirsting for his blood. Turning like a flash, he seized Farrington by both wrists, just as the latter was trying to cock the pistol; then there was a terrible contest. The pistol was in Farrington's hands, which were held so close together by the irons as to make it impossible to wrench one away from the other; it was pointed directly at William's head, and should Farrington succeed in cocking it, William's death would be instantaneous. All his energies, therefore, were directed toward keeping Farrington's hands far enough apart to prevent him from drawing back the hammer. The space was too narrow to permit of such a struggle without one party or the other being forced back upon the rail, and, in a moment, William had lifted his lighter antagonist from the deck, pressing him against the railing, and at the same time shouting for assistance. In response to his call, Connell came running out in *dishabille*, with his pistol in one hand and his pantaloons in the other. At this moment the cold muzzle of the pistol was pressed against William's temple, and he heard the click of the hammer as his desperate prisoner succeeded in drawing it back. He made a violent plunge forward, ducking his head as he did so, and simultaneously the pistol exploded close to his ear, the ball ploughing a little furrow in the scalp, while the powder scorched his neck and hair. Staggering back stunned and dizzy for a moment, he was caught by Connell, who asked whether he was much hurt. He soon gathered his senses, and, finding his wound to be only trifling, he asked what had become of Farrington. Connell pointed overboard, and no further answer was necessary; no man dropping in front of those wheels could have lived for an instant, and, even had he not been struck, he could not have kept himself up in the rapid current then running filled with fine ice.

By this time the bar-room, barber shop, and saloon had been emptied of their occupants, and the boat had been stopped to see whether the man could be picked up; but, as this was clearly hopeless, the trip was soon resumed. Connell's arrival had been most opportune for William, since he had caught the weapon the moment it was discharged, and succeeded in changing the course of the bullet sufficiently to save William's life. Thinking, however, that William had been killed, Connell had struck Farrington on the head with his pistol almost simultaneously with the explosion, and the blow, aided by the plunge which William made forward in endeavoring to dodge the pistol-shot, had sent Farrington over the rail into the water, where he was undoubtedly killed the next instant by the paddle-wheels.

The fact of the man's death was so absolutely certain that no person could doubt it, if acquainted with the circumstances; yet there were not wanting people who insinuated that he had been allowed to escape by jumping overboard and swimming ashore. The absurdity of such a story is manifest, for, even supposing that his irons had been removed, and that he had escaped injury from the paddle-wheels, he never could have swam ashore at the spot where the affair occurred. The nearest point of the river bank was more than three hundred yards away, and the current at that place was running off the shore; besides, the night was very cold, and the water was covered with a film of ice, so that after five minutes' immersion in it, a man would have become wholly numbed and insensible.

Barton was not at all surprised when he heard of Hillary Farrington's death, for he said that he knew Hillary so well that he had expected nothing else from the time he was taken; he was so desperate that his intention undoubtedly had been to have seized William and dragged him overboard; but, seeing the pistol, another idea had probably occurred to him. Barton said that had Hillary succeeded in killing William, he would have gone up to the pilot-house with the revolver, and forced the pilot to land him immediately; once on shore, his knowledge of the country would have enabled him to escape again. Whatever had been his plans, however, he had failed in his attempt at murder, and had paid the penalty of his rashness with his life.

The rest of the party went on to Columbus, where they took passage for Union City, arriving there Friday morning.

About this time, Mr. Ball, who had been sent to follow the wagon train of Mrs. Farrington, reported, after a silence of several days, that he had traced her into the Indian Territory. In point of fact, she was settled at Ash Grove, near Mount Vernon, in Greene County, Missouri, and had been there ever since Hillary and Barton had left her before their arrest at Durham's. It will thus be seen how fortunate it was that I had not trusted to Ball and Bledsoe to keep track of Mrs. Farrington, since they had utterly lost the trail, and had followed another set of wagons for several days as far as the Indian Territory; when, probably suspecting that he had made a mistake, Ball telegraphed to the express company's officers for instructions. He was then ordered to return at once with Bledsoe, the whole party having been captured by that time.

While speaking of Mrs. Farrington, I may as well give an account of all our dealings with her, irrespective of the chronological order of the story :

Having received Barton's order upon her for all of the wagons and stock, and for five hundred and fifty dollars in money, Cottrell endeavored to attach her property in a civil suit. She insisted that she had none of Barton's money—indeed, that she had no money at all—and she refused to give up anything. At last, finding that he could not legally attach her property, Cottrell took the bold step of arresting her for receiving stolen goods. She was taken to Mount Vernon, where she engaged a lawyer to defend her, and then, of course, Cottrell was also obliged to employ a legal adviser. At length, a compromise was effected, by which Mrs. Farrington was allowed to retain a small portion of the property; Cottrell then took possession of the remainder as agent of the express company, and Mrs. Farrington was discharged from custody. After selling some of the animals, Cottrell shipped all the remaining chattels to St. Louis, where the agent of the express company took charge of them. The two detectives then returned to Chicago, and no further attention was paid to Mrs. Farrington.

On Saturday, after the arrival of William's party, with Barton, in Union City, Detectives Galway and Connell started out to arrest Bill Taylor, the fourth one of the party of robbers.

This man was a long, lank, round-shouldered fellow, with putty face, long, straggling hair and beard, and a vacant expression of countenance, who lived by hunting and chopping wood, below Lester's Landing, in the vicinity of Reel's Foot Lake. William had been satisfied of his complicity in the robbery for some time previous to the arrest of the others, but he had not arrested him for the reason that he was sure of picking him up whenever he wished to do so; and, knowing Taylor to have been merely a weak accomplice, he was anxious to secure the leaders in the crime first. Barton's confession made the suspicion of Taylor's guilt a certainty, and so Galway and Connell were sent to arrest him.

At Mr. Merrick's they obtained a good guide, and four other citizens joined them, so that they had quite a formidable party. After visiting several houses in the cane-brake, they learned where Taylor was staying, and, on going there, they saw him looking at them from a front window. Galway asked Taylor to come down a few minutes to give them some information, and Taylor unsuspectingly complied. He had been allowed to go free so long, and had so often talked with William and others about the robbery, that he did not imagine their object on this occasion. On coming into the yard, therefore, he greeted the men cordially, supposing them to be a party scouting for the other robbers, of whose arrest he had not heard. When he saw a couple of navy revolvers close to his head, and heard an order to throw up his hands, he surrendered without a word. He was evidently badly frightened, but he would not confess having had any part in the robbery, and he refused to tell where his share of the money was concealed. He was placed on Connell's horse and taken to Merrick's, where another horse was obtained, and the party went on to Hickman; thence he was taken by wagon to Union City, arriving there about midnight of Saturday. Both Barton and Taylor were placed in rooms in the hotel, where they were carefully watched night and day by my detectives, the county jail being almost useless as a place for keeping prisoners.

On learning that the whole party had been arrested, Taylor made a very full confession of all the circumstances connected with the robbery, and the movements of the robbers after it had occurred. He confirmed Barton's account in every particular, but revealed nothing new of any importance. His share of the stolen money had been only about one hundred and fifty dollars, as Levi had made him believe that they had obtained only six hundred dollars in all. About fifty dollars were found on Taylor's person; the rest he had spent. He said that Levi Farrington had hidden all the checks, drafts, and unnegotiable paper underneath an old log in the woods, but that he could not tell where the log was, nor find it, since it was not marked in any way, nor had they taken any bearings by which to remember it. He gave an account of the evening when Hicks, the tipsy planter, came to their camp-fire, which agreed exactly with the previous statements of Hicks and Barton; but one slight remark in his confession seemed to account for the fifth man mentioned by Hicks. Taylor said that during most of the time Hicks was at their camp, one or two of the party were lying on the ground with their feet toward the fire, and that there was a log of wood lying beside them. Now, it is probable that Hicks was just drunk enough to be unable to tell the difference between a man and a log, especially as, in his description of the men, he gave the appearance of Hillary Farrington twice as belonging to different persons. Hicks's vision was somewhat uncertain that night, evidently.

## CHAPTER XI.

*The last Scene in the Drama approaching.—A new Character appears.—The Citizens of Union City suddenly seem to have important business on hand.—The Vigilantes and their Work.—Their Bullets and Judge Lynch administer a quietus to Levi Farrington and David Towler.—The End.*

THE last scene in this drama seemed about to end in the complete defeat of the whole gang of villains and the triumph of law and justice, when a new character came upon the stage, and the curtain fell upon a bloody tragedy. That substantial justice was done cannot be denied, though the manner of its execution was beyond and outside all forms of law. It was a striking instance of the manner in which an outraged community, particularly in the West and South, will arrive at a satisfactory settlement of important questions without the intervention of courts, juries, or lawyers. The court of Judge Lynch makes mistakes occasionally, but it rarely admits of an appeal from its decision.

Robert arrived in Union City with Levi Farrington on Monday, December eighteenth, and he took his prisoner to the hotel for safe keeping, with the others. They were kept in separate rooms, and a detective remained with each of them constantly. William spent several hours with Levi Farrington, trying to induce him to tell where he had hidden the stolen papers, and also what he had done with his share of the money, of which he had undoubtedly retained the greater part. Finally he agreed to return all the papers, and about twenty-five hundred dollars besides, on condition that he should receive a sentence of only five years in the penitentiary on entering a plea of guilty. Having agreed to this arrangement, William went to his room, which was a large one, with several beds, occupied by Robert, Brown, and Connell. As the men of my force were all pretty well used up, Taylor and Barton were placed in the same room, with Galway guarding them, while Farrington, being such a desperate fellow, was put in another room, with three of the Union City policemen as guards.

Soon after the arrival of Robert with Levi Farrington, a man, named David Towler, tried to get admission to Farrington's room. On being denied, he was very insolent, and he insisted on seeing Farrington alone. Finding that this would not be permitted, he went away cursing the officers and swearing to be revenged. His actions naturally attracted the attention of the police, and caused him to be regarded with a great deal of suspicion, as a probable member of the Farrington party of robbers. About eleven o'clock that night, a policeman, named Benjamin Kline, discovered this man Towler with a drawn revolver, skulking behind a car standing on the side track near the dépôt. He immediately called for the railroad company's night watchman, and the two approached the thief to arrest him. The man instantly shot Kline through the lungs, and then shot Moran, the watchman. Kline's wound was mortal, and he died in a few minutes, while Moran was supposed to be fatally hurt also. The pistol-shots quickly drew a crowd, and a few determined men gave chase to the murderer. After quite a long pursuit he was captured, and brought back to the station where Kline had just died. A justice of the peace held a preliminary examination at once, and the prisoner, David Towler, was held for murder, without bail. He was known to be a low, desperate fellow, who had been imprisoned for horse-stealing and other kindred crimes, until he was regarded almost as an outlaw. He had long lived near Reel's Foot Lake, and while there he had become acquainted with the Farringtons. That their friendship was more than that of two casual acquaintances was shown by an important circumstance discovered by William. It will be remembered that when Levi Farrington stopped in Cairo to send eight hundred dollars to his mother, he purchased two of the largest-sized Smith & Wesson revolvers. They were exact fac-similes of each other, and were numbered 1,278 and 1,279 respectively. At the time of Levi's arrest, only one of these revolvers was found, and he said that he had given away the other to a friend, retaining number 1,279 himself. When Towler was captured, William happened to notice that his revolver was similar to the one Levi had carried. This would have been nothing to be remarked under ordinary circumstances, since there were, undoubtedly, many of these revolvers in use, all exactly alike except in number; but William connected this man Towler's appearance in Union City with the arrival of the express robbers, and the new revolver caught his eye at once. On closely examining it, his suspicions were fully confirmed: *it was numbered* 1,278, and was, without question, the mate to Levi's, bought by him in Cairo and given to Towler.

When this news became known to the throng of citizens whom the shooting of Kline and Moran had drawn together, the feeling against all the prisoners became intense, and when Towler was committed by the justice to the guard of the men who were watching Levi, the citizens began to depart very suddenly, as if they either had important business elsewhere, or were in a hurry to get home. By midnight the town was quiet, and after a visit to the guards, to caution them to be extra vigilant, William and Robert retired to their room, together with Brown and Connell.

Young Kline, whom Towler had murdered, was very highly esteemed in Union City, and his death at the hands of an outlaw would have aroused deep indignation at any time; but just now there were additional reasons why the affair should excite a desire for summary vengeance upon his assassin. It had been shown that Towler must have formerly been on intimate terms with the

Farringtons, and these latter were well known as desperadoes, whose hand was turned against every man; hence, the crimes of the whole party were considered as a sort of partnership affair, for which each member of the firm was individually liable. But, besides the natural indignation of the law-abiding citizens for the crimes committed by these men, there was a widespread sense of insecurity so long as they were in that vicinity. Towler had remarked, when captured, that he would soon be out again, and all the prisoners bore themselves with an air of bravado, as if they had no fear nor expectation of punishment. It was believed that a number of friends of the gang among the desperadoes living in Nigger-Wool Swamp and near Reel's Foot Lake intended to attempt the rescue of the whole party of express robbers, before they could be consigned to a secure place of confinement. The citizens who had risked their lives to capture Towler and the others, who had turned out in time to see poor Kline die in agony, were determined that nothing should occur to prevent justice from reaching the criminals, and exacting the fullest penalty for their numerous crimes; hence the sudden departure of the throng who had attended Towler's preliminary examination before the justice. They did not go to their homes, but gathered in a secluded place, and formed a Committee of Safety. The question as to what course would best protect the lives and property of the community was then discussed, and a conclusion was soon reached, without a dissenting voice.

Throughout the town all was hushed in the usual stillness of a winter's night; no lights were burning anywhere, save in an occasional sick-chamber, and sleep seemed to have fallen alike upon the just and unjust. In one room of the hotel were Barton and Taylor, guarded by Galway and an employé of the express company, while near by was the room where Levi Farrington and David Towler were watched by three of the city policemen. A dim light burned in each room, and, while the guards paced the floor in their stocking feet, the prisoners lay on their beds in deep slumber. Not a memory of the past, full as it was of scenes of crime and blood, came to break their repose; not a thought of the future, with its possibilities of punishment, caused them to lose one moment of their customary rest. Fear they had never known; remorse was long since forgotten; unconscious or careless of their impending doom, they slept the night away.

About two o'clock there was a stealthy gathering of masked men at the door of the hotel, and, at a given signal from the leader, a certain number slipped up-stairs with little noise, and filled the corridor from which the prisoners' rooms opened. So sudden was their appearance and so quiet their approach that even the wakeful guards scarce heard them until the doors were forced open. Then the policy of silence was dropped, and a rush upon the guards was made. A battery of pistols suddenly confronted them, and, as resistance was clearly impossible, an unconditional surrender was at once made. The bursting in of the doors awakened William and Robert, who hastily sprang up, and, without stopping to put on any clothing, opened their door, pistol in hand. This move, however, had been anticipated by the vigilantes, and a dozen or more pistols were thrust in their faces as they appeared in the doorway.

"Go back, Pinkerton, we don't want to hurt you," said one of the men outside, and they were pushed back into the room, while the door was hastily closed in their faces.

To resist such a body with the few men at his command, William knew, would be suicidal, and he did not especially care to sacrifice himself in the interest of such a villainous band as those whom the vigilantes were seeking. The four detectives, therefore, dressed themselves and remained in their room awaiting further developments.

Having overpowered the guards, the leader of the vigilantes ordered the removal of Towler, and, as the latter was hustled out of the door, Levi Farrington knew that his hour had come. Standing up and facing the remainder of the crowd, who had withdrawn to the further side of the room, he defied them all, and told them to fire away. A volley of pistol-shots was the reply to his words, and a rattling fire continued for two or three minutes; when it ceased, Levi Farrington was no more, his body having been struck by more than thirty balls, almost any one of which would have been instantaneously fatal. His

"The work of the Vigilante's." — Page —

body was left where it fell, and the room was soon deserted as the party hastened after the detachment which had Towler in charge. The whole affair was over in ten minutes, and when the detectives again left their room none of the masked party were to be seen. Levi Farrington's body was found in his room, but no trace of Towler could be discovered. Finding that the excitement was over, the detectives returned to bed, leaving Barton and Taylor still carefully guarded. The former had slept through the con fusion and noise without even a start or restless movement, but Taylor was terribly frightened, and he fully expected to be lynched also.

The next morning at breakfast, William was informed that the body of Towler had been found hanging to a tree near the graveyard, and, on going to the spot, they found him as represented. At the coroner's inquest little testimony could be obtained further than that one man had been shot to death and the other hung by parties unknown, and the verdict was rendered accordingly. There was naturally considerable excitement over the affair for two or three days, but the general verdict was, "Served 'em right." However violent had been their taking off, there were few who did not feel that society demanded their death, not only as a punishment for their past crimes, but as a means of security in the future. Believing that a sentence to the penitentiary was wholly inadequate, and that their escape therefrom was not only possible, but probable, the citizens preferred to take no risks of future robberies and murders by these desperadoes, and they therefore took the most effectual method of preventing their occurrence. Their action was illegal, it is true, but then it was just—which is a more important consideration sometimes.

On the following Friday, Barton and Taylor had their preliminary hearing before a justice, when they waived examination, and were committed for trial in default of bail in the sum of ten thousand dollars each. Upon the representation to the justice that the county jail was an unsafe place to confine the prisoners, permission was obtained to remove them to the jail in Memphis; the proper papers were made out, and the transfer was made under William's management.

The death of Levi Farrington made the recovery of the missing checks, papers, and money an impossibility, since neither Barton nor Taylor were able to conduct the officers to the place where they were hidden. Barton gave the company a bill of sale of the goods in the store at Lester's Landing, however, and an assignment of all debts due the firm, from which about five or six hundred dollars were eventually realized. Robert and Brown attended to this matter and returned to Chicago. William was on duty until the two remaining prisoners were safely lodged in jail in Memphis, and then, having settled up all the business of which he had had charge, he also returned home.

At the next term of court in Obion County.

Tennessee, Barton and Taylor pleaded guilty of grand larceny, and were each sentenced to five years' confinement at hard labor in the penitentiary. Thus, out of a party of four engaged in this robbery, two were finally brought to trial and appropriately punished, while the other two would have been so punished also, had not a higher penalty been demanded by the circumstances of their cases, aggravated by their own brutal and revengeful dispositions. No reminiscence in my experience shows a more striking illustration of the certainty of retribution for crime than does the career and fate of these outlaws of the Southwest.

THE END.

# DON PEDRO AND THE DETECTIVES.

## CHAPTER I.

*A Fraudulent Scheme contemplated.—A Dashing Peruvian Don and Donna.— A Regal Forger.—Mr. Pinkerton engaged by Senator Muirhead to unveil the Mystery of his Life.—The Don and Donna Morito arrive at Gloster.—"Personnel" of Gloster's "First Families."*

THE history of crimes against prosperity is of vital interest to the public. The ingenuity of thieves, burglars, forgers, and confidence men is active and incessant, so that their plans are often successful even against the experience and precautions of men of the most wary and cautious character. This seems to be especially true when the amounts at stake are large, for petty attempts to defraud are so frequent, that when a criminal plays for a large sum, the suspicion of the capitalist is wholly allayed by the improbability that a mere swindler should undertake an operation of such magnitude. Indeed, in many cases the cupidity of the victim is so great that the sharper hardly offers the bait ere it is swallowed by some confiding simpleton. Hence, as a warning for the future, the lessons of past frauds possess no small degree of interest and value to the world;

and as there is no portion of society free from the depredations of these schemers, their various wiles and snares cannot be exposed too often.

More than twenty years ago, the city of Gloster was one of the most thriving cities of the West. Controlling the interior trade to a large extent, its interests were of the most varied character, and its inhabitants were already distinguished as being more cosmopolitan than those of any other city in the Union, except New York. They had imbibed, perhaps, some of the genius of the prairies, and their scorn of petty methods of doing business, their breadth of charity and hearty hospitality, were as boundless as the great plains of which the city was the business center at that time. Among such a people, a plausible adventurer had a fine field of operation, and I was not surprised when I was asked to go to Gloster in the latter part of the winter to investigate the character of some persons who were living there.

The application came from Senator Muirhead, a man whom I had long known, both in his public and private life. His suspicions were of the vaguest possible character, and a hasty examination of the case failed to convince me that they were well founded; yet he was convinced in his own mind that there was a fraudulent scheme in contemplation, and his positive conviction had great weight with me. The Senator's interest in the case had led him to make extensive inquiries into the antecedents of these parties, but he was unable to trace them further back than their arrival in New York, several months before. There they had suddenly appeared in society with a great display of wealth, stating that they had been traveling in Europe for some time, and were gradually making their way back to Peru, where they lived. Don Pedro P. L. de Morito and his wife, having enjoyed life in New York for several months, now proposed to spend at least a year in Gloster, and it was this couple whose character was suspected by the Senator. Indeed, he felt sure that, at least, they were traveling under assumed names, and certain coincidences led him to believe that they were adroit swindlers of the most capable, dangerous type. He had discovered a chain of circumstantial evidence which needed only one link to make a clear connection between certain crimes and these fascinating Peruvians, and it was for the purpose of discovering this link that he had requested my aid. In brief, his suspicions were, that after innumerable frauds in other countries, this plausible pair had settled in Gloster to add to their ill-gotten wealth by some new scheme of villainy. His theoretic history of the man, derived from various sources, mainly newspapers in which crimes had been described bearing the same style of workmanship, was as follows:

José Gomez, a cadet of the ancient Brazilian family of that name, began life with a fine physique, ample mental endowments, and a high social position. He was the heir-expectant of a valuable estate, and no pains were spared upon his education. As he grew to manhood, however, his habits became such as to excite the gravest apprehensions as to his future, and by the time he was thirty years of age he was a reckless libertine, gambler, and spendthrift. Finding that his source of supplies was about to be cut off by his family, he obtained large sums of money by means of forged paper, with which he fled from Rio Janeiro to Lima, Peru. His whereabouts were not discovered for a long time, but when the information was received, the Brazilian Government made an effort to obtain his extradition. He was living in fine style in Lima, under the assumed name of Juan Sanchez, and, in some way, he was warned of his danger. Before any steps had been taken to expose or arrest him, he perpetrated another series of forgeries, by which he obtained a large amount of money, and then wholly disappeared. The aggregate of his forgeries was so great that a considerable notoriety attached to the case, and the facts were published in full in the leading newspapers of this country.

About the time of the great rush to California, after the gold discoveries there, a gentleman known as Don José Michel appeared in San Francisco, where he lived in regal splendor; indeed, his extravagance was so great as to make him conspicuous even among the reckless throng who filled the Golden City. After wasting a fortune with a prodigal hand, however, he suddenly vanished, and, although little was known positively on the subject, it was commonly understood that he had swindled a number of bankers and capitalists by worthless notes, drafts, and checks, many of which were wholly or partly forged. The men thus defrauded kept the matter quiet, both because they were ashamed to acknowledge how easily they had been imposed upon, and because they hoped to facilitate the capture of the criminal by working in secret. The incidents were related to Senator Muirhead in a casual conversation with a friend who had recently returned from the Pacific coast, and the description given of Don José Michel tallied exactly with that of Juan Sanchez and José Gomez.

By an odd coincidence, the month after the departure of Don José Michel from San Francisco, a brilliant gentleman of nearly the same name appeared in Quito, Ecuador, where he pursued a course so exactly similar in character to that of Gomez, Sanchez, and Michel, that it was not difficult to imagine that that ubiquitous person was identical with the elegant Don Pedro Michel who created such a brief excitement in Quito, terminating with forgery and a hasty flight.

About two years previous to the time of which I write, a wealthy Brazilian arrived in London, and became a great favorite in society. His wife was a beautiful Spaniard, and her exquisite taste, courtesy, and knowledge of the world were highly appreciated by the select circle of aristocracy into which she and her husband were soon admitted.

Don José Arias was the name of this gentleman, and he was soon known in nearly every drawing-room in Belgravia. He was introduced by the Brazilian *chargé d'affaires*, in the absence of the Minister Resident, and this semi-official guarantee of his position in Brazil gave him a passport everywhere. It was not strange, therefore, that such a handsome, refined, and agreeable couple should be cordially and hospitably received, especially as their wealth was undoubtedly enormous, while their manners showed that they had been born in the purple of aristocracy. It was a sad shock to society when it was learned that Don José and Donna Maria had absconded suddenly, taking with them about fifty thousand pounds sterling, obtained by forgery. It was then learned that the Brazilian legation had been the victim of forged documents also, though the intimate acquaintance of Don José with the policy and statecraft of Brazil in many important affairs had contributed largely to his success in deceiving the young diplomat who was temporarily in charge of the legation.

It was not until more than a year after this occurrence that Don Pedro P. L. de Morito arrived in New York, with his beautiful wife, Donna Lucia. They did not stop long in New York after their arrival, but spent the latter part of the summer in the White Mountains in a very retired manner, although they lived in the best style that the place afforded. In August, they made a hasty trip to Washington and back to New

York again, where they began a more pretentious mode of life than they had chosen theretofore. Don Pedro kept a yacht elegantly fitted up, and his horses were the best that money could obtain. His bachelor suppers were models of epicurean perfection, and when his wife gave a reception, everything was in the best taste and style. While visiting Washington, Don Pedro had met Senator Muirhead, who had gone there for a few days on public business, and the acquaintance was renewed in New York, where the Senator had some private interests demanding his attention. Something had led the Senator to connect Don Pedro with Gomez, Sanchez, Michel, and Arias, and though the idea was a vague one in his mind, it was sufficiently fixed to cause him to institute inquiries into Señor Morito's antecedents. As previously stated, nothing could be learned of him previous to his arrival in New York, and the only circumstance which could possibly be regarded as suspicious was, that both in Washington and New York he had avoided meeting the Peruvian Minister and other fellow-countrymen.

The peculiarity of the case interested me, and, after a long conversation with the Senator, I agreed to unravel the slight mystery surrounding the parties, and to make a complete review of their past history so far as it might be possible to obtain it. No harm could result from such a course, whether they were honest or the reverse; and so, having decided upon a simple plan, I returned to Chicago to select the persons to represent me in Gloster.

My preliminary survey of the field had brought me into contact with many of the most fashionable people in Gloster; and, as I foresaw that my operatives would be called upon to move in the best society while engaged in this investigation, I obtained as extended information about the members of the *crême de la crême* as possible. Since many of them will figure conspicuously in the incidents of this story, a brief description of the leaders will be necessary.

One of the wealthiest men of Gloster was a bachelor, named Henry O. Mather. He was about fifty years old, but he still retained much of the fire of youth, and he was one of the most popular members of society. At an early day in the history of the Great West he had settled at Gloster, where he had invested largely in unimproved lands; and, by forethought and good judgment in his speculations, he had rapidly increased his property in extent and value, until, at this time, he was one of the few millionaires west of the Alleghanies. About three years previous to the time of which I write, he had invested largely in the new railroad schemes then organized, and his importance as a railway magnate was recognized throughout the whole country. His reputation as a shrewd business man made him a species of authority among his fellow-townspeople, and few persons would have ventured to distrust the safety of any enterprise in which he was actively interested. Indeed, so complete was the confidence of most men in him, that it was not considered necessary in buying real estate to trace the title further back than to Henry O. Mather, a deed from him being considered as secure as a patent from the government. Personally he was a very agreeable man, being gallant without affectation, and brilliant without priggishness. His figure was of medium height, compactly built, and he carried himself with an erect bearing and springy gait, which greatly aided in deceiving strangers as to his age. His hair was brown, turning gradually to gray, and he wore full gray side-whiskers. His features were quite pleasing except the mouth, which was rather large and sensual. On the whole, he was a man with uncommon ability to please when he felt disposed to exert himself, and his great wealth was an additional charm which society was not slow to recognize. He owned a large house, occupying the whole of a square in the most fashionable part of the city, and his sister-in-law was installed as its mistress.

Richard Perkins was an Englishman who had long lived in Gloster, where he owned the largest brewery in the West. He was of middle height, but being quite fleshy, his gait was a kind of waddle—the reverse of elegant or dignified. His smooth, round, jovial face was strongly expressive of an appreciation of the good things of this world, and he rarely denied himself any indulgence that passion craved and that money could procure.

It was while Mather and Perkins were on their annual visit to New York that they met Señor Morito and his beautiful wife, Donna Lucia. The distinguished foreigners soon made a complete conquest of both the western gentlemen, who invited them in the most cordial manner to visit Gloster at their earliest convenience.

The delights of New York society were enjoyed for several months by these wealthy and aristocratic foreigners before they were able to keep the promise made to Mather and Perkins; for they were entertained by the old Knickerbocker families of Manhattan in a princely style. They were the guests of the most exclusive circles of the city, and everywhere they displayed such perfect courtesy, good breeding, and *savoir faire*, that it was evident they were accustomed to wealth and high social position. They had elegant apartments in the leading hotel of the city, and their cash expenditures showed the possession of an unlimited fortune. They finally tore themselves away from New York, arriving in Gloster during the comparatively dull season of Lent. Here their fame had become known in society through the incessant praises of Mather and Perkins, and their reception into the highest circles was coincident with their arrival. The unanimous verdict of those who made their acquaintance was, that Gloster had never entertained two more thoroughly pleasing guests than the Don and Donna Morito.

Don Pedro was about forty years of age, but

he had all the brilliancy and ease of a man of thirty. His figure was very fine, being slightly above the medium height, erect, compact, and muscular. His hands and feet were small and elegantly shaped, but were not effeminate. His rich olive complexion was in admirable harmony with his soft black eyes and deep red lips. His face was a good oval, without being unmanly, and his black, glossy hair was beautifully curly and wavy. He wore side-whiskers and a long moustache, beneath which his smile, the ladies said, was faultless. Like most South Americans, he seemed too lazy to be unamiable, and his general style was that of a man who, having possessed wealth always, would be perfectly lost without it.

Donna Lucia was a fine specimen of Spanish beauty, education, and refinement. It was easy to see that she possessed more force of character than her husband, and that her passionate nature was like a volcano, which might burst forth at any time, driving her to the most dangerous courses if it took possession of her. A detailed description of such a woman is an impossibility. In general, she was a beauty of the Andalusian type, as nearly perfect in form and feature as can be conceived; but her expression was of an infinite variety of characters, each one giving the precise shade of meaning most applicable to the time, place, person, and sentiment. In short, she was so near perfection that nearly all the men she met were in love with her, and nine-tenths of them more than half believed that she regretted her marriage for their sake. Nevertheless, she kept all admirers at a certain distance, which only bewitched them the more.

At the time of which I write, Don Pedro was so much pleased with Gloster, that he had rented a large residence in a very fashionable locality, and was making preparations to spend a year there. The charming manner in which they had entertained their friends at the hotel was ample guarantee that when the Don and Donna were established in their new home, they would surpass anything in the way of festivities ever seen in Gloster; hence, all the best society of the place rejoiced greatly at the arrival of this new constellation in the social firmament.

Among the bachelors most noted in *salons* and parlors of the city were Daniel McCarthy and Charles Sylvanus, the former a lawyer, and the latter a journalist. McCarthy was an Irishman, of brilliant talents and ready wit. Although still comparatively a young man, he was the county prosecuting attorney, and was considered one of the foremost lawyers of the city. He was very good-looking and good-hearted, and his natural drollery made him a most entertaining companion. While speaking in court, and often in society, he had a habit of running his fingers through his long, thick hair, which he would also, at times, throw back with a peculiar jerk of his head. This habit was especially frequent when he became deeply interested in his subject, and the spectators could always tell whether Dan was doing his best, even when they could not hear his words.

Sylvanus was editor and part proprietor of an evening newspaper. As a journalist he was not above mediocrity, but he was well received in society, where even a moderate allowance of brains will suffice for success.

A conspicuous member of society and a pillar of the Swedenborgian church was Mr. John Preston, a banker and capitalist. With a book of Swedenborgian revelations in one hand and a bundle of tax titles in the other, he would frequently orate to a crowd of unbelievers, from a text drawn from his book, in a manner calculated to quite convert them, were it not that they knew he was only working up a fresh head of steam to enable him to grind the faces of the poor upon whose property he held tax titles. In fact, many people were of the opinion that this man was a dangerous character, in spite of his pretense of piety, his ostentatious charity, and his assumption of the *rôle* of a professional philanthropist. They insinuated that a man could afford to give largely to an astronomical society, a college, an academy of sciences, and other objects of education, when he had appropriated many thousands of dollars belonging to the school fund to his own use; that he could easily contribute freely to his church, when he used the church property in his own interests and managed the society to suit himself; and that there was no great amount of philanthropy in giving a few hundred dollars to miscellaneous charities, when he made ten times the amount in shaving notes at usurious interest and acquiring land by means only one remove from actual theft; these things were becoming so notorious that a man of less indomitable brass than John Preston would have long since been sent to Coventry, if not to jail; but he revolved on his own center, sublimely indifferent to the attacks of his enemies, for whom, by the way, he used to pray with most fervent unction. His wife was a pleasant, motherly woman, who gave liberally to charitable objects, and who regarded her husband as one of the saints of the earth.

There were three children—a young man and two girls. The former gave no promise of either ability, probity, or ambition, and there was about him a noticeable air of deficiency in both mental and moral worth. The girls were commonplace nonentities, with no pretensions to beauty or grace.

One of the most prominent citizens of Gloster was a wealthy tanner, named Charles H. Sanders. Having foreseen at an early day the great progress which the city would make in population and importance, he had invested largely in tracts of unimproved land, which he held against all offers to purchase until his real estate was more extended and valuable than that of any other property-owner in the city. Personally he was very thin and angular, with such a sickly look that his death seemed possible any day, though his constitution was of that character which might hold out much longer than that of a more robust type. His wife was a very charming woman, and they had two young daughters, who gave promise of considerable beauty when they should arrive at maturity.

Mr. Thomas Burke and his wife were, perhaps, the most general favorites in Gloster society. Mr. Burke was tall and well built, and his large head and commanding appearance made him conspicuous in any group. He had a broad, high forehead, heavy eyebrows, deep-set black eyes, a Roman nose, and a heavy black moustache, which completely covered his mouth. His straight, black hair, high cheek-bones, and swarthy complexion, gave him slightly the look of having Indian blood in his veins; but the rest of his features were unmistakably Celtic, and the moment he spoke, the Irishman stood confessed. He was a man of such extensive reading and general information that few persons excelled him in conversation. His wife was also cultivated and intelligent, so that either as guest or hostess she was equally agreeable and popular. They had a large family of bright and interesting children.

One of the social curiosities of the city was known as Deacon Humphrey. He was a striking instance of the importance which self-complacent mediocrity can obtain in a newly-settled community, in spite of ponderous stupidity. His large head gave him his only excuse for professing to have brains, and his air of preoccupation made him in appearance the personification of wisdom; indeed, a witty journalist, who had sounded the depths of Humphrey's ignorance, once said that "no man *could* be as wise as Humphrey *looked.*" No better condensation of this character in a few words could be made. He was part proprietor of a morning newspaper, and at times, to the dismay of the other stockholders, he aspired to the editorial tripod. The mighty lucubrations of his intellect were generally assigned to the waste-basket, and in the city it was well known that his influence in the columns of the paper was absolutely nothing, though in the country he was still regarded with awe by the bucolic mind. He was generally known as "Deacon" from his honorary occupancy of that office in a Presbyterian church. Mrs. Humphrey was seldom seen, being in poor health almost constantly, but their only daughter, Jennie, was one of the foremost of the fashionable of the *dilettanti* of the city. Indeed, it was confidently anticipated that, some day, Miss Jennie would burst forth as a full-blown authoress, and overpower an expectant public with the radiance of her intellect and the elegance of her style.

No description of Gloster celebrities would be complete without that of Ethan Allen Benson, Esq., formerly Member of Congress, and late Minister Plenipotentiary at an important European court. The suggestion having once been made to him by some waggish diplomat that he resembled the first Napoleon, he was ever afterward desirous of drawing attention to this fancied resemblance. He was a vain, fussy, consequential politician, whose principal strength was in the ward caucus and the saloon.

Judge Peter B. Taylor was another old settler, and he was frequently seen in social circles in spite of his age. His forehead was very broad indeed, but his face tapered so rapidly to a pointed chin as to make his head wedge-shaped. He had coarse, faded hair, but no whiskers nor beard, and only a scrubby, gray moustache. He had a singular habit of working his eyes independently of each other, and the effect upon a stranger who was not aware of this peculiarity was sometimes startling. His mouth was quite large, one side appearing larger than the other, and his lower lip slightly protruded, giving him a very harsh and forbidding appearance. He had at one time occupied a seat on the judicial bench, but few persons could understand on what grounds he deserved the office, unless it were that people believed the adage about a poor lawyer making a good judge. He was quite wealthy, and his business was that of a money loaner and real estate speculator. He was considered to be very pious and charitable—on Sunday; during the rest of the week no Shylock ever demanded his pound of flesh more relentlessly than he his three per cent. a month.

It was among a society of which the foregoing were shining lights, that I was to operate at the request of Senator Muirhead. On returning to

Chicago from Gloster, I gave a great deal of thought to the case, for there was so little to act upon that none of the ordinary plans could be depended upon. During his stay in this country, Don Pedro had apparently acted in a perfectly honorable manner toward every one, and it would be impossible to proceed against him legally in the United States for crimes committed elsewhere, until the aggrieved parties should take the necessary steps for his extradition; with several of the countries in which he was supposed to have committed his crimes we had no extradition treaty, and nothing could be done here to arrest or punish him; hence, the task of exposing his previous career might be fruitless, even though the Senator's suspicions should be confirmed in every particular. Nothing whatever could be adduced against his character since his arrival in the United States, and I was, therefore, confined to the prevention of future frauds rather than the detection of old ones. The primary object of my efforts was thus made to be the discovery of the Don's intentions, as, without some slight forecast of his plans, I might be unable to circumvent them. Accordingly, I decided that I must furnish him with a friend who would be sufficiently intimate with him to become his trusted companion and adviser. At the same time, it would be essential to learn as much as possible relative to the previous career of both the Don and Donna, for it might be desirable to use a little moral suasion with them by showing that their history was known. This plan would involve no injustice to them, for, if innocent of wrong-doing, they would never know that they had been under surveillance; while, if guilty, they deserved no consideration.

## CHAPTER II.

*Madame Sevier, Widow, of Chicago, and Monsieur Lesparre, of Bordeaux, also arrive at Gloster.— Mr. Pinkerton, as a Laborer, anxious for a Job, inspects the Morito Mansion.—A Tender Scene, resulting in Profit to the fascinating Señora.— Madame Sevier is installed as a Guest at Don Pedro's.*

MY first action in this affair was to detail a man to "shadow" Don Pedro and the Donna until the detectives chosen for the more difficult portions of the work should be in a position to take notice of all their movements. As three detectives would require some little preparation to gain the position I desired them to fill, I hastened to select them and give them their instructions. For this mission I detailed a married couple, who had been several years in my employ. Mr. and Mrs. Rosel were natives of France, and as they had been constantly in my service almost from the time of their arrival in this country, I felt sure they would not be recognized as detectives by any one in the city of

Gloster. They were people of more than average intelligence and education, with a natural refinement which would be especially desirable in the prosecution of this case. In a few days all their preparations were completed, and they went to Gloster by different routes.

Mrs. Rosel was not handsome, but she had a good figure, and she was very attractive, on account of her dashing, spirited ways, and because she could assume a deep interest in every one whom she met. She spoke English with so slight an accent that it was only noticed as an added charm to her winning conversation. I instructed her to represent herself in Gloster as Madame Sevier, the widow of a lace merchant, lately of Chicago, where he had carried on a moderate business. His death had thrown his affairs into some confusion, but the estate would be settled up soon, leaving a comfortable fortune to his widow. Madame Sevier did not like the climate of Chicago, and therefore she had decided to remain in Gloster until her business affairs were settled, when she would probably return to her relatives in France. I intended that she should mix in society as much as would be consistent with her character as a widow, and that she should endeavor to become intimate with Donna Lucia.

Mr. Rosel was to make a slight detour, arriving in Gloster from the east. He would be known as Monsieur Girard Lesparre, and his ostensible character was to be that of a man of moderate capital from Bordeaux, looking for a favorable opportunity to invest some of his means in a profitable business.

I followed the Rosels in a day or two, and found that Monsieur Lesparre was pleasantly located at a fashionable family hotel, while Madame Sevier had taken apartments in a stylish boarding-house only a few doors from the handsome residence which the Moritos were to occupy. This was quite satisfactory, and I turned my attention to the examination of the reports made by my "shadow." The reports were very monotonous in character, except as evidences of the popularity of the Don and Donna. The dull days of Lent had just passed, and the close of the season was now more crowded with parties and balls than the earlier portion had been. The presence of two such distinguished guests as Don Pedro and Donna Lucia contributed largely to the reasons for this rush of gayety, and they were overwhelmed with visitors and invitations. Mr. Mather had set the example by giving a large dinner-party in their honor, followed in the evening by a grand ball; and they had so charmed the other leaders of society that no entertainment was considered complete without the presence of Don Pedro P. L. de Morito and his beautiful wife.

On leaving my hotel to visit the house which Don Pedro was fitting up for his residence, I met Charlie Morton, the United States Commissioner of Gloster. Morton was a capable lawyer and a shrewd politician. He was equally attentive to ladies as to gentlemen, and it was well known that Charlie would never slight any one who could cast or influence a vote. His acquaintance extended through all classes, from the lowest to the highest, and few men were more generally popular. His powers of observation were only equaled by his tact, so that, while he saw all that went on about him, he never talked indiscreetly. He and I were quite intimate, and we chatted for some time about various people before I succeeded in bringing up the names of those in Gloster in whom I was just then most interested.

"I suppose you are quite glad that the gay season is over, Charlie," I said, interrogatively. "As usual, you will not have many social events of any consequence after Lent, I presume?"

"Oh! yes, indeed," he replied; "we shall be more active in society for the next month or two than ever before. You see, we have two wealthy and aristocratic Peruvians visiting Gloster, and they are so fascinating that they have quite taken our people by storm. They have been accustomed to the finest society of Europe and South America, so that we are put upon our mettle to show how well Gloster can compare in wealth, luxury, and refinement with older cities at home and abroad."

"Are they then such remarkable lions?" I asked, "or do people run after them simply because they are rich foreigners?"

"Of course their wealth and foreign birth

would cause many people to pay them attention," said Morton; "but their popularity is something exceptional, and is undoubtedly due to their perfect knowledge of all the courtesies and customs of modern society, to their charming manners, and largely to their personal good looks. Señor Morito has fascinated all the ladies, while nearly every man in society is in love with the Señora."

"Well, take care of yourself, my boy," I said, jokingly. "If the lovely Donna causes Charlie Morton to strike his colors, she must be dangerous indeed."

After leaving Morton, I sauntered along to the house which Don Pedro had rented, and which was now nearly ready for occupancy. It was a large residence, with ample grounds fronting on the principal avenue, and its imposing front of heavy columns gave it a striking appearance as compared with the more commonplace stone fronts around it. While I was glancing curiously about, a truck arrived laden with costly furniture. I was rather roughly dressed, and the driver asked me if I wanted a job of work. I accepted his offer to aid in carrying the furniture into the house, as I was anxious to examine the interior. After finishing the job, the furniture salesman took me over the house to show off the elegance with which it was decorated and furnished. It was certainly a model of good taste, while the paintings, statuary, frescoing, and articles of *bijouterie* were evidences of enormous expenditures. Having obtained a thorough knowledge of the plan of the house, I withdrew, receiving fifty cents for my labor.

The time when Don Pedro was to occupy his residence was to be signalized by a grand reception held therein, and the invitations were already out. Meantime entertainments were given by John Preston, Alexander McIntyre, and Charles H. Sanders. The latter's reception was especially brilliant, and those who knew Mr. Sanders's parsimonious character were much surprised at his profuse expenditure for the occasion. I soon afterwards obtained an explanation of this unusual liberality, by hearing another banker casually remark that Don Pedro had withdrawn a part of his funds from New York, and had deposited them in Mr. Sanders's bank. This gave me a hint, and I immediately acted upon it. Being well acquainted with a number of bankers, I visited several of them, and talked about various business men of Gloster, as if I were desirous of getting information about their commercial standing and credit. In each case I succeeded in learning the extent to which Don Pedro had deposited money in bank. The total amount then due him by the three houses with whom he had made deposits was about $17,000, although his original deposits had amounted to more than double that sum. Heavy drafts to pay his current expenses and to furnish his house had largely reduced his available cash, though he still had an ample sum on hand. Knowing how enormous his expenses were, I felt sure that he would reach the end of his bank account in a short time, unless he should have other funds, of whose existence I was unaware. If this sum of seventeen thousand dollars represented his total capital, however, he would soon show whether he was what he claimed to be, or an adventurer; for, in the former case, he would draw money from his Peruvian estates, and, in the latter, he would accomplish some great swindle. I was, therefore, anxious to put my detectives at work as quickly as possible to enable me to learn something definite of his intentions.

Madame Sevier was making quite rapid progress in her new quarters. Mrs. Courtney, the lady who kept the house, was a widow of some means, who took boarders to enable her to educate her children in the best manner. She was highly regarded by every one, and her visiting-list included all the most fashionable people in the city. She soon became greatly interested in Madame Sevier, and through her assistance the Madame made the acquaintance of a number of the families living in the neighborhood. As the rage for foreigners was at its height just then, Madame Sevier soon became highly popular, and she was invited to several entertainments, where she met Don Pedro and Donna Lucia. The latter, finding that Madame Sevier was to be her near neighbor in her new residence, became very intimate with her, especially as Donna Lucia was desirous of reviving her knowledge and practice of the French language. Consequently, when Don Pedro's arrangements were all completed and the new house occupied, Madame Sevier used to drop in for a few minutes' chat every day. As she was a very capable manager, she was frequently able to give Donna Lucia valuable hints about her household affairs, especially with reference to the approaching reception.

Ever since the arrival of the Moritos, Mr. Henry O. Mather had been a constant attendant upon the Donna. His attentions had not been so publicly marked as to have created scandal; but he had been so assiduous in paying his regards, that he was much more intimate than Mrs. Grundy would have thought strictly proper. He was in the habit of calling very frequently, and he often took the Don and Donna out for a drive. Sometimes the party would consist wholly of ladies, and occasionally the Donna accompanied him alone. In short, he became a sort of intimate friend of the family, welcome at all times, without the necessity of invitation or ceremony.

One day, Madame Sevier went in to see Donna Lucia in the afternoon, and was told by the servant that she would find the Donna in the library. Without permitting the servant to announce her, she passed on toward the room mentioned; but, as she approached the door, hearing voices within, she paused a moment to see who was with Donna Lucia. The room was in a very retired part of the house, and she was able to take a position close to the partly open door without the probability of being noticed by any one. She was thus enabled to overhear a highly interesting conversation between the Donna and Henry O. Mather, who had evidently arrived only a moment or two before her.

"You are not in good spirits to-day, Donna Lucia?" questioned Mather, sympathetically.

"No, Mr. Mather; I have my troubles at times, like other people, but I try not to let others see them."

"Then you do not care for sympathy, Señora," said Mather, with a tender sigh; "I see that you have been in tears, and it grieves me to think that I cannot save you from the painful things which cause you to cry."

"Oh! Mr. Mather, I do appreciate your kindness, I assure you," said the Donna, also sighing deeply; "I am almost tempted to ask your advice, for I feel that you are truly my friend; but I am afraid you will think I have been naughty in having exposed myself to such annoyances."

"No, indeed, my dear Donna," replied the millionaire, quite enraptured at this evident token of her confidence in him; "I know that you are too lovely to be anything but an angel, and I shall be only too happy to give you advice upon any subject that you confide to me."

As the conversation was becoming highly interesting, the tones of the parties being of a really lover-like tenderness, Madame Sevier took a hasty glimpse through the door, and saw that she could watch as well as listen, unperceived. Mather was standing beside the Donna, bending over her and looking into her face, while she had her head half turned away, as if in coy indecision.

"Well, Mr. Mather——"

"Why do you address me always so formally? Can you not call me Henry?" asked Mather, boldly.

"How would it sound if any one should hear me?" said the Donna, casting down her eyes and playing with her watch-chain.

"But when we are alone no one can hear you," replied Mather. "Won't you call me Henry when we have an occasional tête-à-tête?"

"Well, then you must be very discreet, Henry," answered she, looking up, blushing and hesitating as she spoke.

"I will be discretion itself," said the now wholly infatuated Mather, with a look of triumph; and to show that he accepted the conditions of the agreement, he sealed it by raising her hand to his lips.

"Oh! fie! fie!" she exclaimed; "is it thus that you show your discretion? I shall be obliged to retract my promise if you become so rash. Now, sit down beside me, and be more polite in future."

"I will not be so hasty again, my dear Donna; but my pleasure was so great that I was somewhat beside myself. Now tell me what it was that caused your troubles."

"Well, Mr. Math——"

"No, no; not 'Mr. Mather;' recollect your promise," interrupted Mather, as he saw she hesitated to call him by his first name.

"Well, then, Henry, I have been very thoughtless and extravagant, and I do not know what to do. You see, I have always spent money for everything I needed without regard to cost; for my own fortune was ample for everything, and Pedro would give me any amount that I might desire. But last month a draft for six thousand pounds, which was sent me by my trustees, was lost on the way, and so I have used up all my own funds. Having run up several large bills in New York, I asked Pedro to pay them, and he did so; but he said that, having ordered his factors to send him no more money until his arrival in Callao, he should be somewhat embarrassed until he heard from them again. His sudden determination to fit up and occupy a residence here has exhausted all his available funds except a few thousand dollars for current expenses, and he requested me not to make any large purchases until one of us should receive a remittance from our estates. Well, you see, I expected surely to have received a large sum before now, and so I made purchases without regard to consequences; the result is, that I am deeply in debt, my money has not arrived, and I am afraid to tell Pedro, because he will not forgive me for running in debt and disobeying him. Unfortunately, I have done both these things, and I am momentarily in fear that some of the bills will be sent to him

7*

Now, my dear Henry, you see that I have good cause to look sad and cry."

As she finished, the Donna began to whimper and put her handkerchief to her eyes in so touching a manner that Mather was quite overpowered. The artistic expression with which she hastily called him her "dear Henry" was the finishing touch to an already powerful attack, and he surrendered completely.

"My dear Donna," he exclaimed, seizing her hand in both of his, "how glad I am that you confided in me. I will see that you are not troubled by another anxious thought in this matter. Tell me how much you need to settle all your indebtedness."

"Indeed, Henry, I cannot let you do anything of the kind," she protested, feebly. "Why, it is a very large sum in all, and it may be several months before I can repay you."

"Now don't talk about payment, but just tell me how much you need," replied Mather.

"The large bills amount to over four thousand dollars, and there are a number of small ones which I have not figured up," she said, thoughtfully.

"Well, then, I will bring you around five thousand dollars to-morrow, and you can pay the bills without any one knowing where the money comes from," said Mather, again kissing her hand.

"Oh! you dear, good fellow!" exclaimed the Donna; and, overcome by his generous response to her request, she threw her arms about his neck and kissed him several times.

"There, there," she continued, releasing herself and coquettishly tapping his lips with her hand, "I don't know how I came to do such a thing, but you were so kind that I couldn't help it."

"If that is the case," said the overjoyed Mather, "I will add five thousand more to have a similar expression of your gratitude."

"Will you, really? I believe I am half in love with you," she murmured, as she allowed him to embrace her a second time, and press burning kisses on her lips.

The ringing of the door-bell interrupted their happiness, and Madame Sevier hastily retired to the drawing-room, into which other visitors were shown by the servant. Donna Lucia soon entered, perfectly self-possessed, and greeted all her friends with her usual ease and cordiality. Mr. Mather probably passed out by the library entrance, for he did not appear in the parlor. The ladies conversed together for some time, one of the important subjects of their talk being the troubles of household management. Donna Lucia complained bitterly that her servants robbed her, and that they were careless, dirty, and impudent. She knew very little about housekeeping, and every domestic in her employ took advantage of her. She added that, as soon as her housewarming was over, she intended to get, if possible, a lady who would be a member of the family, and who would relieve her of the management of the house.

"Now," said she, in her most winning manner, "here is Madame Sevier, who has nothing to occupy her time, who is a natural manager of other people, and who is so agreeable that she would be a positive charm to any household; and I have been thinking, positively, of asking her to take charge of my whole establishment, and help me entertain my guests. What should you think, Madame Sevier, of such a request?"

The opportunity of becoming domesticated in the Morito mansion was thus afforded to one of my detectives, but she knew better than to accept at once. She therefore professed to treat it as a pleasantry, and said that she had no doubt that she should succeed as a housekeeper, but whether she could add anything of attraction to such a charming home was greatly to be doubted. The other ladies, however, thought the idea an admirable one, and they all urged Madame Sevier to adopt it. Having once broached the subject, Donna Lucia again spoke of it with the greatest interest, showing, by her arguments and determination to coax Madame Sevier to decide favorably, that she had thought about such a plan before, and that she was really in earnest in her request. Finally, Madame Sevier said that she saw no objection to accepting the offer, as she really enjoyed taking care of a large establishment, but she was not prepared to accept it at once, and she would wait a few days to reflect upon it. It was then agreed that she should give her decision at the grand reception to be given as a house-warming.

This part of my plan had worked admirably, and I felt confident of my eventual success in learning all about the affairs of the Morito family. The method by which Donna Lucia had obtained ten thousand dollars from Mr. Mather was a decided confirmation of Senator Muirhead's suspicions; though there was nothing in the transaction which could make her liable to punishment by law, and as there was no danger that her victim would ever appear against her, I paid no further attention to this episode.

I ordered Madame Sevier to accept Donna Lucia's offer on the following terms: she should have full authority over all the female servants in the house; she should have charge of the ordering of all articles for household use; she should be considered in the same light as a guest, so far as social intercourse went; she should go and come as she chose, without regard to the duties of the *ménage;* and she should receive no salary. This last point she was to insist upon, as necessary to preserve her feeling of independence, and enable her to occupy her time as she might see fit.

As the day approached for the Moritos' reception, all Gloster's best society were filled with pleasurable excitement and anticipation, as the preparations were known to be far more magnificent than those for any similar entertainment since Gloster was settled. As Monsieur Lesparre had already made Don Pedro's acquaintance, and had received an invitation, I felt sure that I should be thoroughly informed as to all the occurrences of the evening, and so I awaited developments.

The employment of detectives to penetrate into the social life and domestic surroundings of any family is strongly repugnant to my sense of propriety, and I rarely countenance the practice, if I can possibly attain my object in any other way. I dislike to feel that I am trespassing upon the privacy of any man's home, even though that man may be a criminal. The idea of introducing a spy into a household is opposed to the spirit of our free American institutions, violating, as it does, the unwritten law that "a man's house is his castle;" hence, I never resort to such a measure, except in extreme cases. I saw, however, that there was no other means of protecting the interests of my client, Senator Muirhead; he was acting disinterestedly in the case, to save his constituents from being defrauded, and I could only prevent the threatened swindle by learning in advance the exact plan of operation proposed by the suspected person.

I was careful, however, to employ my most discreet and cautious agents, in order that I should quickly learn whether the Senator's suspicions were based on fact; in case I should find that the suspected parties were innocent, I was determined to withdraw instantly. They would not then suffer any injustice, for my employés would keep their discoveries secret from every one except myself, and no one would ever know that they had been the objects of suspicion.

---

## CHAPTER III.

*Monsieur Lesparre, having a retentive memory, becomes serviceable to Don Pedro.—Diamond Fields and droll Americans.—A pompous Judge in an unfortunate Predicament.—The grand Reception closes with the happy Arrangement that the gay Señor and Señora shall dine with Mr. Pinkerton's Detectives on the next evening.*

THE day of the reception was unusually pleasant, and at nightfall the full moon rose to add her splendor to the attractiveness of the evening. The Morito mansion was ablaze with wax candles, gaslight being considered too common for use on such an occasion. From the street to the door was a passageway of double canvas, with an opening at the sidewalk to prevent interference with passers. This opening was brilliantly lighted, and was hung with flags, pennants, and flowers, artistically arranged so as to give the guests a charming prospect when alighting from their carriages. The rooms of the house needed no decoration beyond that already given by the frescoes and paintings adorning the walls and ceilings. Nevertheless, flowers were abundantly distributed about the spacious apartments. The beautiful conservatory contained a superb fountain, whose jets and sprays gave forth exquisite odor and rippling music. Everywhere throughout the house the most artistic grouping of furniture, pictures, and statuary could be seen, and the variety of taste displayed was only equaled by the unity of arrangements as a whole. At ten o'clock the guests began to arrive, and as the throng of carriages became thicker, it seemed as if the house would be over-crowded. This did not happen to any noticeable degree, however, as the whole of two floors were thrown open to accommodate the guests. The music was furnished by the best musicians of the city, and the supper was a miracle of epicurean excellence, Delmonico having sent one of his chief assistants from New York to superintend its preparation. Never had Gloster seen an affair where such elegance and good taste had been displayed; even the smallest details were perfect, and the Don and Donna received innumerable congratulations and good wishes from their guests.

During his brief stay in Gloster, Monsieur Lesparre had been very active in forming acquaintances, and he was already well known in society. He had a very retentive memory, and, when once introduced to any gentleman, he immediately t ok pains to learn everything possible about him. By careful observation and perseverance, he had learned the general history of a very large number of the leading people in society, and his droll comments and half-sarcastic criticism of them, expressed *sotto voce* to the Don on various occasions, had caught the latter's attention. The Don therefore frequently singled out Lesparre for a companion in society, in order to obtain information about the social and business standing of various people.

"You see, my dear Lesparre," said the Don, "I am such a poor judge of character that I am liable to be imposed upon unless I know something about the previous history of people who seek my friendship. And, as I have a miserable memory for faces, names, places, and everything else, it is a great pleasure to find some one who can keep me posted as to the status of the people I meet. You must let me see as much of you as possible, for, being both foreigners, we ought to have a common bond of sympathy."

"It will give me great pleasure," replied Lesparre. "Of course our friends here are very attentive; but then, you know, they lack the polish one meets in European *salons*, and they are too apt to obtrude their business into their social relations."

"Exactly; I agree with you perfectly, and it is for that reason that I enjoy a conversation with a gentleman of Continental education and tastes. It is wonderful how keen these Americans are in their pursuit of the 'Almighty Dollar.' Why, only a week or two ago, I happened to mention to Mr. Mather and a few others, that some of my estates in the Peruvian Andes contained extensive diamond fields, when they began to upbraid me for not working them and adding to my already ample revenue. They seemed positively shocked when I told them, that I saw no reason for increasing my income, as I had as much money as I could use now. They insisted that I was doing a positive wrong to my fellow mortals in refusing to burden myself with a new enterprise, and I assure you they were quite in earnest in their remonstrances. Ah! how droll they are, Monsieur Lesparre!"

"Yes, indeed, I have found the same spirit even with reference to my humble means," replied Lesparre. "They want me to invest in something right away, and I have very many disinterested offers of advice; but they cannot understand my delay, and they think I am throwing away so many good chances by waiting. Now, I should be content to settle down for a year, before investing, just to examine at length all the openings offered me; but I doubt whether I could afford to do that, unless I could obtain a satisfactory salaried position, and I feel that that is impossible. There are very few such positions as I would be willing to accept, as I do not care to be tied down to regular duties."

The gentlemen had stepped into the supper-room while this conversation was going on, and were about to take a glass of wine together. Lesparre's last remark seemed to give a sudden idea to Don Pedro, and he sipped his wine in silence for a moment or two. Then he said, inquiringly:

"I suppose you would like a position of a responsible character, where your knowledge of commercial and financial affairs would be available, but where your whole time would not be absorbed?"

"Yes, that was my wish," answered Lesparre; "but, of course, I do not expect to realize my hopes."

"Possibly you may, Monsieur Lesparre," said Don Pedro; "but let us leave the subject of business until to-morrow, when I should like to talk with you more fully about this matter. Now, let us return to the drawing-room, and when you see any of my guests approaching, please tell me briefly who and what they are. For instance, tell me about that stiff and military-looking person crossing the room."

"That is Captain Adrian L. Kerr, a retired army officer, who has lived here a long time. He has been unsuccessful in business, and it would be difficult to account for his means of livelihood were it not that his wife, the brilliant brunette near the mantel-piece, is supposed to have an income of her own. Some people are so ill-natured as to suggest that Alexander McIntyre, the wealthy Scotch banker now talking to her, is the source of her revenue, but that may be pure gossip. At any rate, she is always elegantly dressed, and she moves in the best society."

"If people suspect her of improper intimacy

with McIntyre, why do they admit her to their houses?" asked Don Pedro.

"Well, you see, many of the merchants and business men have financial dealings with McIntyre, and they do not dare to offend him. As an illustration of his power, I will relate an incident that occurred recently. The wife of a well-known merchant was about to give a large party, and, in making out her list of invitations, she purposely left out the name of Mrs. Kerr. Her husband, on going to the bank to obtain the renewal of a note, found McIntyre as surly and savage as a bear, and the renewal was refused. As he had never before had any difficulty in obtaining such an accommodation when hard pressed for money, he could not account for the change in McIntyre's conduct; but when his wife informed him of her action the day previous in withholding an invitation from Mrs. Kerr, he understood it all. His affairs were in such a condition that he could not afford to quarrel with McIntyre, and so he insisted that an invitation be sent to Mrs. Kerr, in spite of his wife's assertion that Mrs. Kerr was an improper character. He was willing to admit that fact, but he preferred to submit to her presence rather than to be seriously crippled in business. An invitation was therefore sent in such a way as to make the delay in its delivery appear accidental, and in a few days Mr. McIntyre was willing to renew the merchant's note."

"Well, she certainly does carry things with a high hand," replied Don Pedro, smiling. "I wonder how she would have retaliated upon me if I had struck her name off my list to-night? However, it is not my business to question her character, and if my wife is satisfied to receive her, I shall not interfere."

As the Don finished speaking, the music sounded the preliminary notes of a quadrille, and he hastened to find a partner. Among the guests were Mr. and Mrs. Arlington, whose minds were of such opposite characters as to keep them continually quarreling. He was a wealthy banker of austere manners and Puritanic tastes, while she was a butterfly of fashion, fit only to be petted, kissed, and caressed. She was all gayety and life; he, all piety and gloom. Her pleasures he considered sinful, while his recreations were to her the most painfully melancholy observances that could be devised. While he believed that she was a child of wrath, a creature of the world, the flesh, and the devil, she was equally satisfied that he was on the highway to fanaticism and hypocrisy. Under these circumstances, it was not unnatural that she should seek her friends among those who mingled in fashionable society, nor that her husband should consider it necessary to follow her into the gay world in order to keep a watch upon her. Her most attentive cavalier was a young bachelor named Harry Bertram, who seemed infatuated with her. Indeed, their preference for each other's society was so marked that the tongue of scandal had already begun to wag, although no overt act could be cited against them. The Don, on leaving Lesparre, chanced to meet Mrs. Arlington, and she readily accorded him the pleasure of dancing with her. In the same set were Daniel McCarthy and Donna Lucia, Charles Sylvanus and Madame Sevier, and Mr. Mather and Mrs. Simon. In the adjoining set were Mr. Benson and Miss Jennie Humphrey, Alexander McIntyre and Mrs. Kerr, Harry Bertram and Mrs. Sanders, and Judge Robert Morgan and Mrs. Middleton.

Judge Morgan was a remarkable-looking person at any time, but his appearance was especially noticeable in a dancing-set, the incongruity of his presence in such a scene being irresistibly comical. He was about fifty years of age, but his face was smooth and unwrinkled; though he was of the medium height, his great size gave him the look of a short man, which effect was partly increased by his long arms. He was very broad and fat, his stomach projecting to an absurd degree. At the same time he stood very erect, so that a profile view gave him a general resemblance to a loggerhead turtle set on end. His eyes were small and treacherous, his cheeks were puffy and flabby, his mouth was large and sensual. His hair and whiskers were brown and fine, but they always seemed unkempt. He wore closely-fitting black clothes, and he was fond of displaying an unusual amount of jewelry. He had obtained the office of judge of the criminal court by currying favor with the very classes

*The Fudges' downfall.*

most likely to be brought before him for trial, and his judicial ermine was not considered free from the foulest stains. His private life was, in many respects, a counterpart of his official conduct; though married to an agreeable woman, he was a notorious libertine and profligate. Still, he held his position in society, and was admitted to the acquaintance of the most reputable people in the city; hence, he frequently appeared at balls and dancing-parties, where he always tried to act like a light and graceful youth.

On this occasion he was especially anxious to display his manly form in the same set with the Donna, but being disappointed in this, he chose the set next to hers, and acted like a playful hippopotamus. While backing rapidly, in an attempt to balance to his partner, he came in contact with Mrs. Simon of the next set, and, tripping on her dress, he fell violently upon her. Her partner, Mr. Mather, tried to catch her as she also fell, but the ponderous form of the Judge came upon them both with crushing effect, and all three were brought to the floor at once. Mr. Mather and Mrs. Simon were quickly on their feet again, flushed with mortification but unhurt. But it was no such easy matter for the corpulent Judge to raise himself erect; he lay on his back a moment groaning, and it was thought that he might be seriously injured, as his fall had jarred the whole house. Several gentlemen carefully lifted him upright, and the ladies gathered about to condole with him, when it was suddenly discovered that, if the Judge's person had not suffered, his clothing had. His tight dress coat was split several inches down the back, while a hasty glimpse behind his coat-tails satisfied the spectators that his pants were in an even worse condition than his coat. It may be imagined that the situation caused some merriment, in spite of the efforts of the more well-bred guests to preserve their gravity; but when the Judge, having regained his feet, vociferated in great wrath: "You are a pack of monkeys. I don't see anything to laugh at," there was a universal burst of laughter which could not be repressed. This so enraged him that it was difficult to make him understand his absurd position, but at length Don Pedro and Monsieur Lesparre induced him to go to the dressing-room for repairs. As there was no coat in the house large enough for him, the Don was at his wits' end to make him sufficiently presentable to enable him to return to the drawing-room; but at length the Judge was arrayed in one of the Don's gorgeous dressing-gowns, which was large enough to hide most of the effects of the fall. He soon returned to the lower rooms dressed in the most remarkable costume ever worn at a full-dress party in Gloster.

With the exception of this accident, the evening passed off with the most perfect success, and the unanimous verdict was that there had never been a more thoroughly enjoyable entertainment given in the city. During the evening, Madame Sevier informed Donna Lucia of her willingness to take charge of the Morito establishment, and agreed to begin her reign the next day. Donna Lucia was delighted at this news, and willingly accepted all the conditions, though she insisted for some time on giving Madame Sevier a liberal salary. Finding that Madame Sevier was resolute in her refusal to receive pay, the Donna informed her friends that she had invited Madame Sevier to live with her, and that the Madame had kindly agreed to assist her in entertaining her numerous guests.

It was not until nearly daybreak that the more indefatigable revelers became weary of dancing and flirting, so that the Donna was quite exhausted when the last guest had departed. Madame Sevier remained to the end, as she intended occupying her room in the Morito mansion at once, instead of returning to her boarding-place. Donna Lucia left orders that she was not to be disturbed until five o'clock in the afternoon, but Madame Sevier decided to get up at twelve o'clock, in order to superintend the work of clearing away the decorations and *débris* of the ball. The Don had invited Monsieur Lesparre to dine with him at six o'clock, and so it was arranged that they should all meet at that hour.

## CHAPTER IV.

*Madame Sevier and Her Work.—Unaccountable Coquettishness between Man and Wife.—A Startling Scheme, illustrating the Rashness and Gullibility of American Business Men and the Supreme Assurance of Don Pedro.—Disaster approaching the Gloster Capitalists.—Other Suspicions Aroused.—The Story of Mr. Warne, English Diplomatic Agent.—A New Move.*

MADAME SEVIER began her work of reform in the household as soon as she was dressed that afternoon. Finding that they now had a mistress competent to control them, the servants showed a greater willingness to be useful, though some of them were inclined to be lazy and impudent as before. The Madame made mental notes of everything, took charge of the keys to all storerooms and closets, and clearly demonstrated that she was able to manage the house according to her own ideas. The cook, thinking she was indispensable, and that she could act independent of control, was very impertinent to Madame, and she evinced an insubordinate spirit that created a good deal of trouble. Seeing that prompt and severe measures were necessary, Madame Sevier paid this woman her wages and discharged her without a moment's warning. The effect upon the other servants was most satisfactory, and although the Madame was obliged to make some minor changes afterward, she was never again annoyed by impertinence or presumption. The dinner for that day was prepared by the assistant cook, under Madame Sevier's direction, and when the Don and Donna came down from their chamber, they were delighted to find that the house was in perfect order, showing no signs of having been the scene of revelry and dissipation the night before.

During dinner, at which Monsieur Lesparre was the only guest, Don Pedro, after complimenting Madame Sevier very highly upon her success in bringing order out of chaos, turned to his wife and said:

"Lucia, your selection of a companion and advisor has been so fortunate that I am more than ever disposed to follow your example. What do you think, Monsieur Lesparre, cannot you serve me as confidential secretary and financial agent as satisfactorily as Madame Sevier assists my wife?"

"Indeed, Don Pedro," replied Lesparre, gallantly, "if you impose upon me the task of equalling so accomplished and charming a lady as Madame Sevier, you will probably be disappointed in everything I do."

"Bravo, bravo, Monsieur Lesparre!" cried the Donna; "you will certainly be successful in paying delicate compliments, at least. Yes, Pedro, I think you ought to secure Monsieur Lesparre's services at once; when you have nothing for him to do, he will be an agreeable companion for us. What say you, Madame Sevier?"

"I quite agree with you," replied the Madame, casting down her eyes coquettishly; "but I prophesy that Monsieur Lesparre would find his position an onerous one if he should be under obligations to pay me compliments."

"Ah! the obligation would be unnecessary," said Lesparre; "the difficulty would be to avoid doing so constantly."

The Don and Donna smiled at each other significantly, thinking that they saw the incipient signs of a mutual attachment between these two, and that it was not unreasonable to imagine that a wedding might result therefrom. How little they imagined that these apparently distant acquaintances were, in fact, already man and wife!

After dinner, the Don and Lesparre repaired to the billiard-room to smoke, while the ladies entered the drawing-room to receive visitors.

"Monsieur Lesparre," said the Don, as they lounged back in luxuriant easy-chairs, "what do you think of my suggestion at dinner? I should really like to obtain your services as private secretary, and I will gladly give you such a salary as will make you independent of other labor. While you are attending to my affairs you will naturally become well acquainted with many business men, and will be able to investigate a number of enterprises, so that you will be better able a year hence to invest your capital to advantage."

"Your offer is truly liberal," replied Lesparre, puffing his cigar thoughtfully, "and I feel disposed to accept it. What would be my duties?"

*Madame Sevier discharging the servants.*

"Well, I will explain what I wish fully, and then you can judge how the position would suit you," answered Don Pedro. "In the first place, I wish a financial agent, a man whom I can trust, who will attend to all my affairs. You see, I detest the details of business. I desire to live free from the vexing annoyances consequent upon the providing and disbursing of money. My estates produce as much as I can use, and I do not trouble myself to inquire whether they might not yield more. I am accustomed to buy whatever I wish, but I hate to bother my head to know whether I have enough on hand to pay for my purchases; hence I want my secretary to attend to such matters for me. There is another thing in which you could be of the greatest service to me; for, while it is an affair of great importance, involving large interests, I am positively too fond of my own ease to give it the attention which it deserves. I know I can trust you not to repeat the slightest portion of what I am about to tell you, for it is not desirable that it should be talked about, unless the enterprise is successfully carried out."

"Indeed, you can rest assured that I shall never mention a hint of it to any one," replied Lesparre.

"Well, you recollect I told you last night that Mather, Perkins, and some others were anxious to have me explore and open up the diamond fields which, I have reason to believe, constitute a large part of one of my estates in Peru? Some time after I spoke to you, toward the end of the party, I missed Mather, Perkins, McIntyre, Sanders, and several others from the rooms, and while I was wondering what had become of them, Mather came up and asked me to go up to my dressing-room, which, you recollect, adjoined the room used for the gentlemen's dressing room last night. On arriving there, I found about a dozen of the wealthiest men of Gloster sitting around the room, with Dan McCarthy at the table acting as secretary. Will you believe it? They had actually formed a business meeting in my own house, and had made speeches, passed resolutions, and voted upon two propositions, which they wished to submit to me; they had then sent the chairman, Mr. Mather, to bring me in, and I was expected to stand and deliver my decision at a moment's notice. The idea was perfectly ludicrous to me, yet it did not strike any of them that they were doing anything unusual. I believe that if a party of these Gloster business men were to be landed suddenly in hell, they would organize a stock exchange to deal in brimstone and ashes!"

"They certainly carry their business instincts everywhere," said Lesparre, laughing heartily. "I suppose they had fully arranged everything before you were sent for?"

"Yes, indeed; the very minor details were provided for, and I could not raise an objection which had not already been discussed and removed. Both propositions provided for the formation of a stock company for the mining, cutting, and sale of diamonds. According to the first plan, I was to fix a price upon my diamond fields, which the company would then purchase, paying me three-fourths in cash, and one-fourth in stock. In case, however, that I should be unwilling to part with my controlling interest, the second plan provided that I should receive one-fourth the estimated value of the land in money, giving to the company therefor the privilege of mining for a certain length of time, and receiving also one-half of the value of the diamonds found. The idea of disposing of this property had never before occurred to me, and naturally I was not prepared to give any answer on such short notice; but if I had done so then, I should have positively rejected both propositions. In fact, I said as much to Mather, and he then suggested to the meeting that 'Señor Morito be given a week to decide upon the propositions submitted to him.' The cool impudence of thus graciously giving me a week did not seem to strike them, and the meeting broke up with great satisfaction, every man feeling certain that I *must* accept one proposition or the other. It was further decided to appoint a committee to draw up a charter and by-laws, 'so as to save time,' as one gentleman remarked. After the gentlemen had left the room, Mather urged the matter upon me very strongly. He apologized for having acted with such precipitation, but, he said, the others were so eager, as soon as they heard that

I owned a vast tract of unworked diamond fields, that he could not restrain them. He begged me to make some arrangement with the proposed company, as the men who had become interested in it were wealthy and enterprising, and they would surely push it to a profitable conclusion. In answer to my remark that I was rich enough already, he said that I ought to give others a chance to make some money who needed it, perhaps, more than I. Finally, as he urged it as a personal favor to himself, I agreed to give the most favorable answer that I could, and so the matter stands."

"When are you to give your answer?" asked Lesparre.

"The committee adjourned until a week from last night," replied the Don, "and I shall then again be summoned before them, I presume. Now, although the first proposition would not probably pay me so well in the end as the second, I much prefer it. You see I do not wish to keep a controlling interest because I should have the continual annoyance of supervising the business; and, as I have said before, I wish to be perfectly free from cares and responsibilities. My object is to enjoy life, and I can't be happy if I am obliged to work. Nevertheless, I do not wish to turn over this property to a body of men who will squeeze it like a sponge, leaving it a mere waste. There are a large body of tenants occupying portions of it, whose rights must be respected. They will make willing and honest laborers if properly treated, and I wish to protect them as far as possible from cruelty and extortion. Hence, I desire to learn all I can about the men who will create and manage the company before I agree to put the property into their hands, no matter what price they may be willing to pay for it; it is here, my dear Lesparre, that you can be of great service to me. You are well acquainted among all classes of business men in Gloster, and you can readily learn all about the people who purpose buying stock. This will be considered very natural and proper if you become my private secretary, and your duties will not be severe. What do you say?"

"I think I can do what you wish," said Lesparre, "but I should like a day for reflection. I never like to act hastily in an important matter, even where my mind is already made up."

"You are quite right," said the Don; "but I hope your mind will remain unchanged in regard to this matter. I will give you whatever salary you wish, and shall expect you, of course, to live here on equal terms with myself and wife. Now, let us join the ladies."

On receiving Lesparre's report, I saw the whole scheme at a glance, and I was now convinced that Senator Muirhead's suspicions with regard to Don Pedro were correct. I immediately visited the Senator, and laid the latest developments before him. We could not help admiring the consummate knowledge of human nature which the Don displayed; he had baited his hook so skillfully that the gudgeons were actually fearful lest something should prevent them from swallowing it; but there seemed to be no probability of defeating his schemes unless we could obtain positive proofs of his dishonesty elsewhere, or detect him in some criminal offense in this country. We therefore decided to keep a close watch upon all his movements, and await further developments. It was evident that the sufferers by Don José Michel's forgeries in California would not take any active steps against him unless they were sure of the identity of the man, and so we had no ground of accusation against him which we could rely upon. Both Senator Muirhead and myself were indignant at the audacity displayed in his swindling projects, but we did not dare to attempt his exposure without absolute proof of our charges. The waiting game is never a pleasant one to play, but I could not do otherwise under the circumstances.

About this time I was called back to Chicago on important business, but I immediately sent my superintendent, Mr. Bangs, to Gloster, to take charge of the case there. During my absence little of note occurred, except the meeting to hear the Don's answer to the propositions to purchase the diamond fields. At this meeting the Don was apparently anxious to decline all offers, saying that the property had been in the possession of his family for about two hundred years, and that he considered himself in honor bound to retain an interest in it. Also, he tried to cool the ardor of the would-be purchasers by telling them that he had no positive certainty that there were valuable diamond fields on the property, though such was probably the case. His reluctance to sell the land only made them more determined to buy, for they argued that he was so well satisfied with it as a means of revenue that he wished to retain possession of it all himself. At length he found that they would give him no peace until he yielded, and so he graciously agreed to accept the first proposition. The question of price then remained to be discussed, but, on this point, there was little opportunity for disagreement. Having had so much difficulty in inducing the Don to sell at all, they were not disposed to endanger the sale by haggling about the price; and when the latter was fixed at one million five hundred thousand dollars, they made no demur, although the sum rather staggered their enthusiasm at first. This effect was only momentary, however, for the vivid anticipations of dividends in proportion to this price quickly banished their fears, and they hastened to subscribe the amounts required. These facts were all reported to me immediately after my return to Gloster, which occurred a day or two after the meeting, and I saw that the day of disaster to the trusting capitalists of that city was fast approaching.

Neither Monsieur Lesparre nor Madame Sevier had learned much about the private affairs of the Moritos, for, whenever the latter had anything important to say to each other, they usually spoke Spanish. The Don's remaining funds amounted to only about eight thousand dollars, and at the rate with which he had hitherto spent money, this sum would not last much more than five or six weeks. The time might be extended to two months by running the establishment on credit; but the Don was averse to such a course, and all bills were paid promptly at the end of each month. He showed no uneasiness as his cash began to run low, but merely said that if the first installment on the mine should be paid in soon, it would obviate the necessity of drawing upon his agents in Lima, otherwise he should call upon them for fifty thousand dollars to carry him through the year. There was nothing in his manner or actions to excite suspicion, and certainly, if he intended to defraud the Diamond Company, he had too much nerve to betray himself, even to so close an observer as Monsieur Lesparre.

Having heard the reports, I strolled out in the evening for a walk with Mr. Bangs, and while passing one of the leading hotels, I met a very intimate friend, named Judge Key. The Judge was an old resident of Gloster, and his character was highly esteemed by all who knew him. He was a man of great ability and force; but, possessing little ambition, he was not nearly so well known as many of those who were his inferiors in point of intellect and morals. We had a great deal of business between us at one time, and our relations to each other were of the most cordial character, partaking more of the nature of personal friendship than mere business acquaintance. I had not visited him previously during my stay in Gloster, for the reason that, even to my intimate friends, I never make my presence known when engaged in an operation, if I can avoid doing so. On this occasion, the Judge recognized me instantly, and greeted me with great warmth, at the same time adding that I was just the man above all others whom he wished to see. He then introduced his companion to Mr. Bangs and myself as Mr. Edward Ashley Warne, of London, England.

"Now, Mr. Pinkerton," said the Judge, "let us step into the club close by, and over a social glass of wine, Mr. Warne will tell you about a peculiar case of mistaken identity, or of consummate rascality—it is hard to know which. Possibly you may be able to understand some things which puzzle us, and to frustrate a fraudulent scheme, if our suspicions are correct. You both know each other by reputation, I guess, and I presume, Mr. Warne, that you will not object to tell Mr. Pinkerton what you have told me."

"Oh! yes, I have often heard of Mr. Pinkerton," said Mr. Warne, "and I think, as you say, that he can clear up the mystery, if any one can. I shall be pleased to tell him all that I know with regard to it."

Mr. Edward Ashley Warne was an *attaché* of the British diplomatic service, and, having been entrusted with the settlement of some questions relative to commerce between the United States and Great Britain, he had executed his mission with such fairness, good sense, and courtesy that he was regarded with great kindness and respect by our people as well as by his own government. He was on a rapid tour through the United States, previous to his return to London, and he had spent a week in Gloster with Judge Key at the time when we met in front of the hotel. We were soon comfortably seated in one of the private dining-rooms of the club, and, after a few sips of wine, Mr. Warne began his story.

"I don't know whether I am the victim of imagination, or the gentlemen of Gloster are likely to be the victims of an impostor; but one thing is certain, that a gentleman here known as Don Pedro P. L. de Morito is the exact image of a man who was known in London as Don José Arias."

This information came so unawares that I almost betrayed my interest in the case by uttering a hasty exclamation. I restrained my feelings, however, and asked Mr. Warne to tell me all he knew about this man.

"Well, I first met him in Paris, when I was a member of the French Legation," replied Mr. Warne. "He was then moving in the most aristocratic society, and his wealth was reputed enormous. I saw a great deal of him at times, and, indeed, I was better acquainted with him than I was with many of my countrymen; but I was recalled to London about that time, and I soon forgot all about Don José Arias."

"Pardon me," I interrupted; "was the Don married?"

"Oh! yes; he had a beautiful wife, I have been told, but I never happened to see her. I think she was Spanish, if I recollect rightly. One day, after my return to England, as I was entering the Foreign Office, I met Don José coming out, and he seemed delighted to see me. He said that he had come to spend some months in London, and he hoped to enjoy my society frequently. I was then engaged in studying a very difficult diplomatic question, and I was unable to give any time whatever to society; I therefore expressed my regrets that I should be obliged to decline all invitations, and, after some further conversation, we separated. I often heard of him in connection with social events in the best circles, and, on one or two occasions, I met him in the street; but I did not renew our former degree of intimacy, for the simple reason that I did not have the time to do so. Just before I left London on the mission for which I had been preparing myself, I was astonished to learn that Don José Arias had proved to be a scoundrel of the most dangerous character. He had not hunted small game, it is true, but this was probably a part of his whole scheme. So far as I could learn, he had left no unpaid bills in the hands of tradesmen, but he had taken enough out of bankers and capitalists to pay his tradesmen's bills for half a century. The aggregate fraudulently obtained by him was never known, for many of his victims refused to state their loss; but it was surmised that he obtained as much as forty or fifty thousand pounds sterling in London alone, while several Paris bankers also suffered heavily. I was not specially interested in the affair, and it had wholly passed from my mind, when suddenly, while walking in the streets of this city last week, I came upon Don José Arias again. He wore his hair differently from his old way in London and Paris, having now full side-whiskers, whereas then he wore only moustache and goatee; but I could not be mistaken, and I said to Judge Key: 'There is a man who forged paper to an immense amount in London less than two years ago.' 'Impossible!' replied the Judge; 'he is a very wealthy man, moving in the best society in the city.' The Judge then vouched for him with such earnestness that I began to believe that I was mistaken; but I determined to meet him face to face, to see whether there could be two persons so nearly resembling each other. Unfortunately he had an opportunity to see me before I saw him when I next met him, so that I lost the chance of surprising him into betraying himself. He appeared to glance at me casually, as any stranger would do, and then went on with his conversation without hesitation or embarrassment. I have met him several times since then, and he always acts with the same natural ease of manner, as if we had always been perfect strangers to each other; but, Mr. Pinkerton, the more I see of him, the more fully am I convinced that Don José Arias, of London, and Don Pedro P. L. de Morito, of Gloster, are identical; and, believing this, I consider it my duty to tell you these facts in order that your citizens may be protected against him, if possible."

"Well, Mr. Pinkerton," said Judge Key, "what do you think of this affair? Mr. Warne does not admit that he can be mistaken, and there are some corroboratory evidences that he may be right; yet, it seems incredible. It is a pity that Mr. Warne should have never seen Don José's wife, because he could then compare her with Señora Morito, and if they, too, were exact resemblances, there would be no longer any room for doubt."

"That would certainly be a strong proof," I remarked; "but I think it is unnecessary. The suspicion you have spoken of, Mr. Warne, has already been raised by another gentleman in this city, and I have been requested to discover whether or not it is correct."

"Why, you astonish me!" exclaimed Judge Key, "for Mr. Warne has not mentioned the subject to any one but me, and I have never even hinted anything about it except to you gentlemen."

"Nevertheless, I have suspected for some time that this Don Pedro was an impostor, and have been trying to obtain positive proof of my opinion, in order to save many persons here from being swindled by him. You are acquainted with Senator Muirhead, Judge?"

"Oh! yes, quite well."

"He has taken enough interest in the affairs of his constituents to place in my hands the task of exposing this man, Don Pedro, in his true light."

"That seems very kind and disinterested on the part of our Senator," said Judge Key, with a quizzical smile; "but I will venture to say that his interest has been excited more by the Don's marked attentions to Mrs. Muirhead, than by the fear that some of his constituents would be defrauded."

Of course I took no notice of this remark, although I was quite convinced that such was the fact; but as the Senator was my client, it would have been eminently improper for me to discuss his motives, and so I turned to Mr. Warne.

"As you have already met this man under another name, Mr. Warne," I said, "can you not go with me to meet Senator Muirhead, and tell him what you know about him?"

"I must beg you to excuse me, Mr. Pinkerton," he replied. "You see, I am in this country in an official capacity, and, while I am personally perfectly satisfied of the truth of the statements I have made to you, I cannot prove them; hence, I must be careful not to involve myself in a difficulty which would compromise my position as a diplomatic agent of Great Britain. I shall immediately give to the police, on my arrival in London, a description of this man, and I presume that prompt action will be taken to insure his arrest and extradition, in case his offenses should come under the extradition treaty. But as this is a question upon which the decision of both governments may be required, the delay may enable this man to escape. I will use all my influence with the London authorities; you will readily see, however, that personally I cannot appear here as an accuser against him."

I recognized the force of Mr. Warne's objection, and did not press him further, but Judge Key agreed to visit the Senator as soon as the latter should return to the city. When I left Mr. Warne we had agreed that any British official who might be sent to identify and arrest Don Pedro, should communicate with me the moment he arrived in this country, so that we could work together for the same object, though my whole duty in the case would be to protect the interests of my client, Senator Muirhead. I then returned to my room with Mr. Bangs, and made a new move. I saw that more than two months would elapse before any news could be expected from London, as Mr. Warne would be somewhat delayed in his return home, and meantime, the Don would probably obtain a large advance payment for his fictitious mines. If anything should occur to prevent us from sending him to England, he might succeed in getting away with his plunder before we could find any new grounds upon which to hold him. I therefore instructed Mr. Bangs to write to the proper authorities in Peru, Brazil, and Ecuador, describing Don Pedro and his numerous suspected *aliases* accurately, and asking that some steps be taken by his victims to bring him to justice. It was true that we had no extradition treaties with those countries, but nevertheless he might be arrested and frightened into surrendering himself voluntarily. The letters were dispatched at once, and duplicates were also forwarded by the next steamer. There remained nothing further for me to do except to keep a strict watch upon the Moritos to see that they should not slip off suddenly with a large sum of money. The Diamond Company were in such haste to bind the bargain with Don Pedro, by making him a large payment, that there could be no hope of preventing the partial success of his scheme. Whether I might not be able to force him to disgorge afterward was uncertain, but I determined to use every means in my power to accomplish such a result.

## CHAPTER V.

*The third Detective is made welcome at Don Pedro's.— The Señor is paid the first half-million dollars from the great Diamond Company.—How Don Pedro is "working" his Diamond Mines.—Very suspicious preparations.—The Don describes his proposed Fête Champêtre.*

ONE evening, as the members of the Morito family were about to retire, Monsieur Lesparre noticed a nervousness and abstraction in Don Pedro such as he had never shown before. Thinking that something new might be learned by overhearing the conversation between the Don and Donna when they should be alone, Lesparre, instead of going to his own room, slipped into an unused closet adjoining the Don's dressing-room, and communicating therewith by a door, which was kept locked. There was a transom over this door, and, by climbing to one of the shelves, Lesparre could hear all that was said in either room of the Don's bedroom *suite*. He had hardly taken this position when the two entered their apartments.

"See what a handsome necklace that old fool Mather sent me to-day," said the Donna.

"Yes, it is very elegant and valuable," said Don Pedro, with a yawn; "but what we most need is money. However, I do not imagine we shall have any difficulty, for I expect a large sum in a few days from the stockholders in this Diamond Company. Still, you may as well get all you can out of Mather and the others, for we must keep up our present style of living to the end."

Just at this moment the shelf upon which Lesparre was sitting gave a loud creak, and he had only just time to slip down and regain his own room before the Don came out to see what was the matter. Fortunately, there was a large pet cat in the hall, and she received the credit of having made the noise.

The next day, on hearing Lesparre's report, I decided to place still another detective in the Morito mansion, and so I instructed Lesparre to recommend the employment of a young man to assist the butler and to do general work about the house. As I expected, Don Pedro acquiesced in the suggestion, and told Lesparre to engage such men-servants as he considered necessary. Accordingly, I at once telegraphed to Chicago to have a young fellow named George Salter sent to Gloster at once. He was a very intelligent French Canadian, and I chose him because of his slim build, his ingenuity, and his capacity as an eavesdropper. He could listen to a conversation with such a stolid expression that no one would imagine he had an idea in his head beyond the performance of his regular tasks, and even when caught in a place where he had no right to be, he could invent a plausible reason on the instant, which would divert all suspicion from him. On his arrival in Gloster, he was sent to ask employment of Monsieur Lesparre, and, of course, the latter was so pleased with him as to engage him at once. He made himself very useful in the house, and soon became popular with every inmate.

A few days later a meeting of the stockholders of the Diamond Company was held, and it was agreed to make a payment of five hundred thousand dollars at once, another like sum when the title-deeds should be delivered, and the balance within one year from that time. This arrangement was satisfactory to the Don, and the sum of half a million dollars was paid over that day in the checks of the different original subscribers. The meeting then appointed a committee of two to visit Peru and examine the property. There was some difficulty in selecting two gentlemen who would be willing to go, and yet who would be satisfactory to the others; but Deacon Humphrey and John Preston were finally chosen. Either of these gentlemen was willing to go anywhere at others' expense, and it was believed that John Preston was too well versed in fraudulent practices to let any one else do any cheating; hence, he was sent to investigate the mines, and Deacon Humphrey was sent to see that John Preston should not steal them. They were not to depart on their mission, however, until the title-deeds were received from Peru and delivered to the directors.

Don Pedro passed the checks over to Lesparre, and informed the meeting that he had already sent to Peru for the deeds, and that the directors should be informed the moment they should arrive; thereafter, all business matters relative to his interest in the mines would be attended to by Robert Harrington, Esq., who would be his attorney in fact. The deeds would be directed to Mr. Harrington, and that gentleman would deliver them to the directors, receive the second payment, and give his receipt therefor.

This arrangement was satisfactory to all, and the meeting adjourned in good spirits, every man feeling that the Don had done him a personal favor in accepting his check in part payment for such a valuable property.

The Don, having indorsed the checks, instructed Lesparre to present them at once for payment, each at its own bank, and to bring the money to the house; he was to obtain as much as possible in gold, as the Don professed to have little confidence in the bills of private banks.

"They may be perfectly sound, Lesparre," he said, in an off-hand way, "but then, you know, we foreigners are accustomed to government bills, or gold, and so I prefer to have the latter."

Taking Don Pedro's carriage, Lesparre visited each bank, and by the time he had cashed the last check, he had a considerable weight of gold and a large amount of bills, about two-thirds having been paid in coin. Lesparre and Salter carried all the money up to the Don's dressing-room, where the Don and Donna were sitting.

"There, my dear," said Don Pedro to his wife,

"this is the first installment of the purchase money of the diamond fields, so that now it will not be long before they will be thoroughly worked. The directors have promised me that you shall have the finest diamond set that the mines can produce within a year from this time, as a present from the company, and you need no longer plague me for not having tried to work them before."

"Oh! Pedro, how lovely!" exclaimed the Donna; "you know I have always wanted you to open those mines, and I am so glad that you have consented. Now I shall have a set that I shall be proud of."

"Well, I did not like to give up the old estate to strangers, I confess," replied the Don; "but now that it is done, I do not regret it. If you wish any money, help yourself; you can write to your agents in Rio that they need not send any more for the present, for we shall have as much as we can use for a year or two. George," he continued, addressing Salter, "you will find a stout iron box in the attic, and I think it will serve as a safe for the present. Bring it down here and put it in this room."

The box was soon brought, and the Don checked off the packages of gold and bills as Lesparre packed them away, the gold at the bottom.

"Now, you can check against my bank accounts for our current expenses, Lesparre," said Don Pedro, with a complacent smile; "and when the funds on deposit are exhausted, I will give you cash monthly to pay all bills as heretofore. I intend to give a grand *fête champêtre* soon, as a lesson to these Gloster people how to enjoy life. I propose to engage one of the islands in the river at once, and begin the necessary work of preparing it artistically for the scene of our revelry. I shall choose one of the large wooded islands with ridges and ravines running through it, and it will take about two weeks to clear away the underbrush, to clean up the grass and prepare the landing-places. Then, by the end of another week, the weather will be delightful, and our arrangements will be completed. I will make the place a fairy spectacle, such as the unimaginative inhabitants of Gloster never dreamed of, and then we will prepare for our summer trip to Newport and Saratoga. What do you think of the plan, Monsieur Lesparre?"

"It is an admirable one, and I feel sure that the people of Gloster will enjoy such an entertainment far more than any that has ever been given here."

"Well, I shall rely largely upon your assistance," continued the Don, carefully locking his safe as he spoke, "and we must divide the duties between us, though of course my time will be somewhat taken up by society. Suppose we issue invitations for three weeks from to-day?"

"Better say five weeks, if not six," replied Lesparre, anxious to delay Don Pedro's departure as much as possible in order to obtain an answer to our letters to Peru and Brazil. "You see, the people here are not accustomed to such gayeties, and it will take some time to prepare their minds to appreciate it."

"Yes, that is true," said the Don, reflectively; "but I do not like to defer it so long. However, let us compromise by fixing one month hence as the time, and we will make it a masquerade as well as an outdoor *fête*. The guests will then have ample time to prepare their costumes, and we can give that as a reason for issuing the invitations so long in advance."

The Don was in no special hurry to escape with his plunder, but neither was he desirous of remaining too long in the vicinity of his victims; hence, although he had no suspicion that his schemes had been discovered by any one, he fixed an earlier date than that suggested by Lesparre in order to prevent the probability of any accident occurring to mar his plans.

Lesparre immediately ordered the cards of invitation, and in a few days all Gloster was in a state of pleasurable excitement over the news of the coming event. Never had such a commotion been created in the placid waters of society as was raised by the delicate cards of invitation to Señora Morito's *fête champêtre* and *bal masque*. The number who received invitations was enormous, including every individual having any claims to be regarded as a member of good society. From that time forward, Lesparre was so busy with the preparations for the *fête* that he was able to see very little of the rest of the family except in the evening. The Don and Donna and Madame Sevier continued their usual round of dissipation and gayety, however, and "all went merry as a marriage bell."

Still there were some curious features of their conduct which I regarded with suspicion. Every day the Don gave Lesparre a large sum in bank-bills to be exchanged for gold, and the coin was then locked up in the iron safe. Then the Don and Donna held frequent conversations in Spanish, during which it was easy to see by their manner that they were discussing an affair of great importance. Madame Sevier found a newly-purchased traveler's guide-book in the Donna's bureau, and from various marks and turned pages it was evident that it had been carefully consulted with reference to an ocean voyage. These things led me to the conclusion that the Don was preparing for a journey, and the fact that he made no mention of it, even to Lesparre, showed that he intended to go secretly. To all his acquaintances he spoke freely of his contemplated tour of the watering-places during the summer, but he always promised to spend the following winter in Gloster, without fail; hence it was clear that he was playing a double game, to deceive some one. I could only wait further developments, and heartily wish for advices from Peru or England.

In company with Judge Key I called upon Senator Muirhead, on the return of that gentleman from the session of Congress, and we discussed together the best plan to pursue, to foil the schemes of Don Pedro. The Senator was very anxious to proceed against him immediately, with the intention of showing him up in his true character, and thus saving his victims from any further loss.

"Indeed, Senator Muirhead," I replied, "I am as desirous to arrest his fraudulent operations as yourself, but I want to be sure of success before I do anything, and I do not see my way clear to act just now. At present we can prove nothing whatever against him; in fact, the only charge we could make would be that of obtaining money under false pretenses. Now, what evidence could we bring to substantiate the accusation? There is no judge living that would hold him on my or your individual opinion that he has sold mines which do not exist, and we should have nothing else to offer."

"Yes, but you forget his forgeries in other countries," interrupted the Senator.

"In the first place," I replied, "you could not charge him in this country with crimes committed elsewhere, even though you had the positive proof of those crimes. If you charged him here with obtaining money under false pretenses, you could produce no testimony except such as bore upon the specific act alleged in your complaint; all other testimony would be ruled out. But, even suppose that such testimony were admissible, can you produce any witness to his crimes in other countries? Indeed, admitting again that these crimes were proven, can we establish the identity of Don Pedro P. L. de Morito as the perpetrator of those crimes? No, sir; we have not a single witness; I ask you as a lawyer, Judge Key, am I not right?"

"You are correct in every particular, Mr. Pinkerton," replied the Judge. "I confess that you present the difficulties of the case more forcibly than I could have done myself."

"Yes, you are right, Mr. Pinkerton," said Senator Muirhead; "I do not see that we can do anything; yet it seems shameful to sit idly doing nothing, when we know that this scoundrel is obtaining such immense sums from our people. What do you propose to do in the future, Mr. Pinkerton?"

"I can hardly tell what may be possible as yet," I answered; "but I feel sure that I shall not only prevent him from securing any more plunder, but also wrest from him that which has already fallen into his hands. He feels secure in the possession of this large sum, and he is in no great hurry to get away; he will undoubtedly remain until after his *fête champêtre* at least. Before that time, I hope to hear something definite from either England or Peru, and then I can act with a power in reserve in case our own means should be insufficient to enforce our demands for restitution. Any action against him now would only result in hastening his departure with all the money he has gained, for I am certain that we could not hold him."

"Well, I see that nothing can be done now," said the Senator, despondently; "but do not lose sight of this man for a moment, Mr. Pinkerton, for he seems an adept in all the tricks of crime."

"Never fear, Senator Muirhead," I replied, cheerfully; "I feel sure that we shall eventually not only bring his career here to a hasty close, but also recover the money which he has fraudulently obtained."

When we parted, the Senator was a little more hopeful, though he said that he should not be at all surprised if Don Pedro outwitted us after all. The loss to the Senator's friends would, of course, be very large; but, perhaps, the lesson would not be a bad thing for them; they would know better thereafter than to part with their money so foolishly.

That same evening the Don and Donna, Monsieur Lesparre, and Madame Sevier, were engaged for the evening at a dancing party given by Judge Peter B. Taylor. Knowing of their intentions to attend this party, I saw an excellent opportunity for Salter to examine the private apartments of the Don and Donna. Accordingly, after the family had gone away in the carriage, Salter began to talk to the other servants about the advantages of belonging to a family where the domestics were allowed to do as they pleased, instead of being so carefully watched. The laundress then related how much less pleasure they had, now that Madame Sevier was in charge of the household.

"Why," said she, "before this French woman came, the servants here had as good a time as any one could ask. Many a fine ribbon, or handkerchief, or bit of a collar, they picked up unbeknownst to the Donna; and, as for aitin', why there was niver a lock on any storeroom in the house, so that there was lashins of good livin' in the kitchen as well as in the dinin'-room. But when this Madame Sevyay came, she put everything under lock and key, and she snapped off the old cook's head in no time for sassin' her. Jist so with the men; this Lesparre, the Don's private secretary, is as close with the men as the Madame is with the women. The butler used to often bring a nice bottle of wine into the kitchen for us to be merry over, but he can't do it now."

"Well, I believe I can find something to drink by a little search," said Salter, with a knowing wink at the laundress and chambermaid. "You wait here, and I'll see what I can do to provide a glass of wine all 'round.

"Oh! would you dare?" asked the handsome chambermaid, looking at Salter admiringly. "Ain't you 'fraid you'll be caught?"

"No, indeed; I believe I can get a bottle of port out of one of the rooms upstairs, without any one ever discovering its loss. Anyhow, I'm going to try, so you all stay here while I make search."

Accordingly, Salter went straight to the Don's room, to which he had a key. Having received from Lesparre an impression of the locks of the house several days before, I had had a skeleton key made, which would open almost any door about the place. While apparently engaged in cleaning the door-knobs, it had been a very easy matter for him to take, in wax, a complete impression of the wards of all the door-locks, without attracting suspicion. He now had no difficulty, therefore, in entering the Don's room, where he found that the Don had removed his iron chest from his dressing-room to his chamber, it being placed at the head of the bedstead. On trying to lift the box, he found that it was very heavy indeed, requiring all his strength to stir it. This was due, of course, to the coin which had been put into it, and Salter's testimony, therefore, corroborated Lesparre's. Salter then, in accordance with my instructions, carefully bored holes through the door leading into the closet in which Lesparre had once listened to a short conversation between the Don and Donna. He arranged these holes so that they would not be detected by the eye, and having thus prepared an excellent place for listening to the occupants of the chamber suite, Salter returned to the kitchen. On the way, he opened the dining-room sideboard and captured a bottle of port wine, with which he entertained the other servants in fine style.

Meanwhile, the Don and his party had been received with the utmost cordiality by Judge Taylor and his wife, who felt quite proud to be the first to entertain such distinguished guests after the sale of the diamond mines, and the issue of the invitations to the Don's grand *fête*.

Every one had talked about the affair, but no one felt exactly sure what a *fête champêtre* was, and so United States Commissioner Charlie Morton determined to ask the Don himself what his entertainment would be. Accordingly, as Dor Pedro approached with Mrs. Arlington on his arm, Morton greeted him pleasantly, and said:

"Don Pedro, every one who has received an invitation to your *fête champêtre* is dying of curiosity to know what it means, and so I am going to take the liberty of asking you to explain it. I freely confess my own ignorance, and I know that there are a great many others no better informed than I am, who would be ashamed to admit that fact; but I cheerfully acknowledge that I have never attended one, and I don't know how I shall be expected to dress nor to act. So please tell me all about it, and I will promise to spread the news among my acquaintances."

"My dear sir," replied Don Pedro, politely, "I admire your frankness, and I shall take pleasure in explaining the principal features of our *fête champêtre*. It was the Donna Lucia's desire and mine to devote one day to enjoyment, and we therefore decided upon giving an entertainment in the open air which should combine every species of gayety and social recreation. It is our intention to embark in the forenoon and proceed by steamer to one of the large islands in the river. There everything will be prepared for out-door

*Don Pedro explaining the Fête Champêtre.*

enjoyment; there will be boats and bathing-houses; swings and archery-grounds; billiard-tables and bowling-alleys; in short, opportunities will be provided for the gratification of every one's tastes. About five o'clock a dinner will be served, the *mènu* for which will include every procurable luxury of the table, and after dinner, the evening will be spent in dancing on the open platforms or in enclosed ballrooms, according to the preferences of the guests, while magnesium lights and colored lanterns will give all possible brilliancy to the scene. Dazzling displays of fire-works will be given at intervals during the evening, and when we finally leave the island on our return to the city, a grand illumination of the whole island will take place as we steam off into the darkness."

Quite a group had gathered around while the Don was speaking, and as he closed, there was a general murmur of admiration. The whole affair was planned on a scale of such magnificence as to appear almost too wonderful to be believed, but the Don had shown such fertility of invention previously, that there was no doubt he was quite equal to creating a scene of oriental splendor such as had never before been witnessed in this country.

"Well, I admit frankly," said Charlie Morton, "that we Americans must learn the art of enjoying life from foreigners, and I think there is no doubt that Don Pedro is a most adept master of its mysteries. Is there not something said in the invitations about appearing in masks, Don Pedro?"

"Oh, yes; I forgot to say at first that there will be much amusement in requiring every guest to be dressed in fancy costume and to wear a mask. The masks will not be removed until the dinner is served, and then, at a given signal, the guests will expose themselves in their own characters."

The Don's description of the intended programme for the *fête* was soon repeated through all the fashionable circles of Gloster, and the expectation of the whole city was raised to a high pitch. No other social event had ever created a like excitement, and it was the theme of conversation at all times and in all places.

The day following the Taylor's party Don Pedro seemed to have determined to get rid of as much paper money in exchange for gold as possible, and during the day he sent more than twenty thousand dollars to be exchanged; of this amount Lesparre and Madame Sevier handled the greater portion, but even the young man, Salter, was entrusted with three thousand dollars in paper, for which he obtained gold at a trifling discount. This method of exchanging money was repeated several times, it being evidently the Don's intention to retain nothing but gold in his possession, and as he had already obtained the greater portion of his plunder in coin, it was not long before he had accomplished his object.

Meantime, the preparations for the *fête* went

on apace, and the time of the Don and Lesparre was quite fully occupied in planning and arranging the details. The Senator called to see me daily, and his constant urging somewhat excited me, so that I became nervous and apprehensive myself. Still, no news came from abroad, and I could do nothing.

---

## CHAPTER VI.

*A Mysterious Stranger.—An unexpected Meeting and a startling Recognition.—An old Friend somewhat disturbs the Equanimity of Don Pedro.—The Detectives fix their Attention upon Pietro Bernardi.—Pietro and his unpalatable Reminiscences.—The Donna shows Spirit.*

EARLY one forenoon Salter was called to the front door by a violent pull at the bell, and on arriving there he confronted a rather disreputable-looking character, who eyed him with an extremely distrustful look. The man appeared to be about thirty years old, and he was evidently a foreigner. He was tall, well-formed, and muscular, and his general bearing was quite at variance with his ragged, dirty clothing. He had black hair and moustache, a swarthy complexion, small feet and hands, the latter soft and well-shaped, and his dark eyes were piercing and brilliant.

"Good morning," he said to Salter, with a haughty nod; "is Don Juan at home?"

"No such person lives here," replied Salter, partially closing the door upon the wolfish-appearing stranger.

"I have good reasons for believing that Don Juan *is* here," replied the man, "and is doubtless the guest of the gentleman who resides here. At any rate, I know that he is now in this house, and I want to see him very much. He would be equally glad to see me if he knew I were here;" and so saying, he pushed Salter aside and entered the hall.

This action still further prejudiced Salter against him, and he said:

"Perhaps you mean Monsieur Lesparre, who is a guest of my employer?"

"That may be," replied the man; "please say that I wish to see him immediately."

Salter did not care to leave the stranger alone, and so he told one of the female servants, who was dusting the parlor furniture, to call Monsieur Lesparre. That gentleman was in Don Pedro's room, discussing some plans for the *fête*, and, when informed that a stranger wished to see him, he told the servant to show him to the room where he usually transacted business. As the man passed before Don Pedro's door, however, Lesparre stepped out to learn who it was.

"This man wishes to see you, Monsieur Lesparre," said Salter, who was following the stranger.

"That is not the gentleman I asked for," the latter replied.

At this instant Don Pedro came into the hall, and, as his eyes fell upon the stranger, he gave a sudden start, and became very pale. The recognition was mutual, for the newcomer rushed forward and said:

"Ah! Don Juan, I am delighted to meet you again. I knew I was not mistaken when I saw you yesterday and recognized——"

"There, there!" interrupted the Don, giving the speaker a warning look, "I am glad to meet you again, Pietro; walk into my room, and sit down."

Lesparre was about to follow, but Don Pedro stopped, and whispered to him:

"Excuse me a short time, my dear Lesparre; this is an old acquaintance whom I knew in better circumstances years ago. He seems quite reduced now, and he may be sensitive enough to object to telling the story of his loss of fortune before a stranger;" and, so saying, the Don retired to his room, leaving Lesparre and Salter outside.

The latter immediately hurried into the closet, where he could hear the whole conversation within the room.

"Well, Pietro," began the Don, "where are you from? You have not been fortunate, it is evident; but how did it happen?"

"You are right; I have had bad luck," replied Pietro. "It is the old story; I have had thousands of dollars at times, and have lived like a prince; and again I have been badly treated by

Dame Fortune, and have lived as I could; but I have never before been so very miserable and poor as now. Positively, it is most providential that I have met you, for I have eaten nothing for twenty-four hours."

"Indeed, Pietro, you shock me," replied the Don, sympathetically; "shall I order some breakfast for you?"

"No; I can wait awhile, and I do not care to be seen by your servants until I get better clothing. But tell me where you have been since we parted in Peru. You have certainly been as fortunate as I have been the reverse; do you make much by gambling?"

"No, Pietro; I gamble very little, except in an occasional game of cards with gentlemen of my acquaintance; but I made a good sum—that is," continued the Don, checking himself a moment, "I made a wealthy marriage, and my wife's fortune is ample for us both. By the way, how did you happen to find me?"

"Well, I have been enjoying life in New Orleans for some time, and, having won quite a large amount there, I decided to come North as the mild weather began. So I started a month ago on one of those enormous Mississippi steamboats, and, of course, I gambled whenever I could. My luck was bad from the start, and, on arriving here, I had nothing except my clothing and jewelry; these I pawned gradually, and soon I was reduced to my present condition. Yesterday I met you as you were entering the Globe Hotel with a party of gentlemen, but I did not want to mortify you by speaking to you in company; so I waited until you came to this house, intending then to call upon you late in the evening, when no one would see me; but you went out in your carriage, and remained so late, that I put off my visit until this morning. I thought that, considering our former relations to each other, you would be willing to set me on my feet again."

"I shall be very glad indeed to do so," replied the Don, eagerly, "and you must tell me what you wish to do, and where you wish to go."

"Well, just now I should like to go to breakfast, Don Juan," said Pietro, with a gaunt smile; "but I have no money to pay for my meal."

"Don't call me 'Don Juan,' my dear friend," said the Don. "I have adopted another name for use in this country, and of course no one knows me except as Don Pedro P. L. de Morito."

"Oh, ho! is that all there is of it?" asked Pietro, with a laugh. "Well, I shall remember in future to call you 'Don Pedro'; but what can you do for me in the way of money and clothes?"

"I will give you fifty dollars at once, and you can get a new outfit yourself; then, when you call again to-morrow morning, we will talk over your future plans. I have a very important engagement to keep in about fifteen minutes, so I must ask you to excuse me now."

"But I can't get any respectable suit of clothes and underclothing for fifty dollars," replied Pietro.

"Well, here are fifty dollars," said the Don, handing a roll of bills to Pietro, "and my secretary, Monsieur Lesparre, will give you an equal amount. You will then have enough to satisfy your immediate wants, and we will arrange the rest to-morrow."

So saying, the Don called Monsieur Lesparre and introduced the stranger as Pietro Bernardi, a fellow-countryman in distress. The Don was quite pale and nervous, and though he did not show any marked signs of agitation, a close observer, like Lesparre, could readily see that his new visitor was anything but a welcome one.

"I wish you to give Señor Bernardi fifty dollars, Monsieur Lesparre," said the Don, "and order breakfast for him here, if he wishes it. I am going out immediately, as I see the carriage is waiting for me, but I shall return at lunchtime. *Au revoir*, gentlemen; call about nine o'clock to-morrow, Pietro."

The Don then went to his carriage, and Pietro followed Lesparre to his business-room, where he received an additional fifty dollars. Pietro quickly stowed the money away in his pocket, and walked abruptly out of the house, saying:

"I'll not trouble you to prepare breakfast for me, as I can get it down town just as well."

The moment Pietro was gone, Lesparre called Salter out of the closet, and sent him out on an errand ostensibly; of course, his real duty was to "shadow" Mr. Pietro Bernardi, and report the occurrences of the morning to me. Salter kept his man in view until he was seated at a popular restaurant table, and then, knowing that some time would be required before the Peruvian's appetite would be satisfied, my detective hurried to my office, and made his report. As it would not be safe to detain Salter long away from his duties at the Morito residence, I decided to keep a watch upon Bernardi myself until Mr. Bangs could send me a man from Chicago. Having sent telegram to Mr. Bangs, I went to the restaurant at once, being joined by Judge Key on the way. Together we entered the restaurant, and I quickly discovered Bernardi still lingering over his breakfast. We each ordered a cup of coffee, and I informed the Judge of the new developments in the case as brought out in the conversation between the Don and Bernardi.

"My opinion is," I said, in a tone audible only to the Judge, "that this man, Bernardi, knows some important facts relative to the past life of Don Pedro, and if we can pump this information out of him, we may thereby obtain valuable assistance in our endeavors to outwit the Don. Now it shall be my aim to learn all that this man knows, for it may give us the means of proceeding against Señor Morito immediately; but even if it should not, we may need such information very much. You see, it is not impossible that we may be forced to use threats to make him disgorge; for I shall not let him escape with his plunder without a struggle, even though no news whatever should come from Peru or England. At present, however, we will devote some time to this Pietro Bernardi, and see what he can tell us."

The Judge fully concurred with me, and said that, as I might be too busy to see Senator Muirhead, he would call upon that gentleman and tell him the latest news. We accordingly sipped our coffee slowly until Bernardi was ready to go, and then I followed him at a little distance, while the Judge went to call upon Senator Muirhead.

Bernardi slowly sauntered down the street, smoking a cigar, and soon reached a large retail clothing store. I remained in the street watching the entrance of the store about an hour, when, as I expected, Bernardi came out in a neat business suit complete, but wearing the same old boots and hat. These articles were soon replaced by new ones, and after a bath and shave, Señor Bernardi was a very different-looking person from the rough customer who had visited Don Pedo in the morning. In addition to his underclothing, linen, hat, boots, and suit of clothes, he purchased at a pawnbroker's shop some very decent jewelry, and he now appeared like a gentlemanly gambler, or a member of the Board of Trade. He did not conclude his business arrangements until he had engaged a boarding-place and bought a trunk, which was sent to his lodgings. He then appeared to have relieved his mind of all care, and he spent the afternoon playing pool and billiards in a fashionable saloon. After dining at a restaurant, he went to a minstrel entertainment, after which he returned to his lodgings to retire for the night. When I went to bed at eleven o'clock, after having followed Bernardi most of the day, I realized that the duties of a faithful "shadow" were sometimes excessively wearying.

The next morning, however, I found that a Mr. Newton had arrived from Chicago in response to my telegram, and I was thus relieved from any further anxiety. He was a cool, shrewd fellow, of attractive appearance and pleasing manners, so that he was peculiarly fitted to obtain the confidence of a man like Bernardi, and it was on that account that I had selected him for the work. He had no difficulty in tracking Bernardi to Don Pedro's residence, and having seen him admitted there, Newton hurried back to report to me. I then instructed him to follow Bernardi until he should have an opportunity to make his acquaintance; this could be done without difficulty in a drinking or billiard saloon, and he was then to cultivate an intimacy with him.

On asking to see Señor Morito, Bernardi was at once admitted, and as soon as the Don closed his door, Salter slipped into the closet to listen.

"Ah! you are looking much better this morning," said the Don, as he scratched a match and handed it to Bernardi to light his cigar.

"Yes, I am feeling much better too. This seems quite like old times, doesn't it? As I sit here and puff your fragrant Havanas, I could almost imagine you were again in the real estate business in Peru. Ha! ha! that was a speculation that paid well, eh?"

"Pietro, you must be careful not to drop a hint of those times to any one, or I should be ruined," replied the Don; "I am in good society here, and I hope to make a little money out of a scheme I have on hand; but it is still quite uncertain whether I shall succeed, and my expenses in engineering the affair are fast eating up all my capital. Now, I shall be happy to assist you as far as I can, but it will be on condition that you leave town; for if you should get tipsy and begin to talk about me, I should lose everything. Next month, I may realize my hopes, but I am playing a risky game, and I cannot afford to jeopardize it. What do you want? Tell me how I can serve you, and how much money you need, and if I can help you, I will gladly do so."

"That is fair enough, Don Juan—Pedro, I mean—I only want a start, and I shall get along without any difficulty; but to tell the truth, I don't know where to go. I could not return to Peru—neither could you, for that matter—and I know of only one place where I could succeed and be satisfied to stay. I have been thinking of going to Buenos Ayres, if I could have a fair sum to start me in good style on arriving there; but it is a long journey, and I am in no haste to start. By the way, where is your present señorita? or are you really married as you said? Is she as handsome as the other was?"

"Yes, she is very handsome," replied the Don, curtly; "but she knows nothing about my history previous to our meeting, and I do not wish that she should; so let us leave her out of our discussion. I have some money left, though it is decreasing rapidly, and I will assist you as far as possible, if you will leave Gloster at once; for I am afraid that you will begin drinking to excess again, and you know that when you are half drunk there is nothing in the world you will not tell. How much do you want?"

"Oh! Don Pedro, you need not fear that I shall betray you; but I can't start off on a long journey so soon after the fatigue and hardship I have undergone during the last month. Just let me have three or four hundred dollars to enable me to live in good style for a week or two, and to get some better jewelry than this cheap stuff, and I will be ready to start for Buenos Ayres as soon as you wish."

"Well, I will give you three hundred dollars now, and as soon as you have spent that, you must be ready to leave Gloster on your way out of the United States."

So saying, the Don stepped to his dressing-case, opened and then closed a drawer, and said:

"There are three rouleaux of gold pieces, each containing one hundred dollars. When that is gone, I will buy your ticket to Buenos Ayres or Montevideo, as you prefer, and will give you as much money as I can possibly spare; you must be prepared to go then."

"All right, my dear Pedro," replied Bernardi, rising to go; "I shall be ready at that time. You can trust my discretion, however, as long as I stay here, and no one shall ever hear a word from me to your discredit. I may call to see you occasionally?"

"Oh! certainly; come in the forenoon. By the way, Pietro, let me caution you against gambling while you are here, for I have found that we are no match for these Northern gamblers. They will take every dollar from you if you venture to stake against them. You will surely lose, and then you will want me to supply you again; but I tell you frankly I will not do it. I have hardly money enough to carry through my scheme, and if you choose to betray me, you can do so, but it won't do you any good whatever; whereas, if you are faithful to me, I can spare you a reasonable sum to start you afresh in Buenos Ayres."

"Never fear, Don Pedro, I shall be mute as an oyster," and so saying, Bernardi took his leave.

The foregoing conversation had taken place in the Don's dressing-room, so that Salter had no difficulty in hearing every word, even when the speakers dropped their voices to mere whispers; but there was another listener in the Don's bed-chamber who was equally successful in overhearing all that had been said. The Donna, having heard of the arrival of this mysterious Pietro Bernardi the day before, was anxious to know who he was and what he came for. Accordingly, she placed herself at the keyhole of their chamber door leading into the Don's dressing-room, and when Pietro had gone, she entered the Don's presence.

"Who was that person, Don Pedro?" she asked, with a sharp tone to her voice, foreboding no good to her already nervous and irritated spouse.

"Oh! his name is Pietro Bernardi, and I formerly knew him in Peru. He was quite a fine young fellow then, but he has taken to gambling, drinking, and general dissipation, so that it is very unpleasant to have him turn up here as an acquaintance."

"Is that the only reason why you dislike to see him, Señor Morito?" asked the Donna, her manner becoming more clearly inquisitive and hostile. "You are too anxious to get rid of him for that to be the sole cause of your annoyance at his presence."

"Well, my dear Lucia, the fact is, that he knows enough about me in the past to be a very dangerous person to have around just now, for he might expose me to the people here, and ruin our schemes upon the Diamond Company."

"Why did you not tell me about this? There must be no secrets which I do not share, for I do not intend to be deserted by you as you have deserted others before. No, no, Don Pedro," she continued, passionately, "I heard every word of your conversation with this man, and you must understand that you cannot treat me like a doll, to be thrown away when you are tired of me. I am able and anxious to help you in all your plans, but I must have your full confidence. You know that I love you, and you say that you return my love, but sometimes I distrust you. You deserted a señorita in Lima, and some day you may try to desert me; but I warn you that I would follow you to the ends of the earth, and I could easily find it in my heart to kill you if you played me false."

As the Donna uttered these words, her determined tones clearly showed that she would have no hesitation in executing her threat. The Don had no reply to offer, and finally the Donna closed the conversation by saying:

"This is our first approach to a quarrel, and I hope it will be the last. You know that I am fearfully excited by any suggestion of the possibility of losing you, and this man's words and sneers have made me almost beside myself. But recollect, I am not without friends, for there are plenty of rich men here who would be delighted to obey my lightest whims if I would permit them, and if you should ever desert me, I would tell all I know of you, and invoke their aid to bring you to punishment. Now let us go along together, without any secrets apart from each other in the future, and we shall have no occasion to quarrel again."

The Donna then left the room, and went out to drive with Madame Sevier, leaving the Don alone. Salter quickly slipped downstairs, but was summoned back by the ringing of the Don's bell. On entering the dressing-room, Salter found his employer seated in a large easy-chair, looking quite pale and agitated.

"I wish you would bring me a decanter of brandy and a glass, George," said the Don; "I don't feel very well, and I think a sip of cognac will do me good."

Salter obeyed orders, and then went to Lesparre's room to report the conversations which he had overheard while concealed in the closet. Lesparre soon went into the Don's room to talk over the plans for the *fête*, but Don Pedro was in low spirits, and did not care to converse. He ordered his horse to be brought to the door, and was soon galloping down the avenue as a relief to his depressed nerves. Lesparre immediately came to my office, reported what Salter had told him, and then went about his duty of preparing the island to receive the guests on the day of the *fête*.

## CHAPTER VII.

*Pietro Bernardi and the Detective become Warm Friends. — A "Tête-à-Tête" worth One Thousand Dollars.*

WHEN Pietro Bernardi left the Morito residence, he sauntered down town in a leisurely manner, with Newton carefully following at a safe distance. Bernardi was evidently vain of his personal appearance, for he was dissatisfied with his ready-made outfit, and, entering a fashionable tailoring establishment, he was measured for a complete suit of clothes. The rest of the forenoon was spent in buying shirts, underclothing, trinkets, and toilet articles of quite an expensive character. After a hasty lunch at a restaurant, Bernardi walked to the post-office, where he met a man whose appearance indicated unmistakably the professional gambler. They seemed to be old acquaintances, and, after taking a drink together, they conversed for some time in low tones. Finally they separated, and Bernardi went to his lodgings. About six o'clock he reappeared, and Newton followed him to the post-office again, where the gambler, who was waiting in the morning, was met apparently by appointment. The two men walked a short distance together, and then disappeared up a stairway, which, Newton was certain, led to gambling rooms. He waited outside nearly an hour undecided what to do, but at length he went upstairs among a crowd of young sports, who seemed to know the ways of the place, and he was allowed to pass in with them unquestioned. He found Bernardi just rising from the dinner-table, which the proprietors of the gambling house were in the habit of setting for their regular patrons. The faro-table was in full blast, and Bernardi was soon seated at it with the air of an old *habitué*. He was thenceforward so deeply interested in the game as to pay no attention to anything else, and, as he was unusually lucky, his pile of gold pieces rapidly increased. Newton took a position at his elbow and watched the game in silence for some minutes. At length, seeing Bernardi win a large stake, he said in a familiar tone :

"You are unusually lucky to-night, and I see you play for all the game is worth."

Keeping his eyes intently fastened upon the dealer's box, Bernardi replied carelessly:

"Yes, this is a game where a man must put down his money freely if he wants to win."

The next turn of the cards was doubly lucky for Bernardi, and, as he raked in his winnings, he glanced up at Newton, scanned his face a moment, and said:

"I think I have met you in New Orleans, have I not?"

"Very likely, for I have often been there; but I do not recall your name, though your face is quite familiar to me."

"Why, certainly," continued Bernardi, apparently quite pleased at the idea of meeting an old New Orleans acquaintance; "my name is Pietro Bernardi, and I have often seen you in the rooms of French Joe on Magazine street."

"Oh! yes, I used to go there a good deal, and we must have met frequently. Let us take something for old acquaintance' sake."

This was taking a short cut to Bernardi's friendship, and as the two stood before the sideboard clicking glasses together, a stranger would have supposed them to be old cronies, as indeed Bernardi actually believed to be the case. Newton instantly saw that Bernardi's frequent drinks during the day and his later potations in the evening had rendered him somewhat intoxicated; he was not drunk, for he had a perfect comprehension of his actions, but he had drunk enough to be very happy, and he probably saw in Newton's face a hazy resemblance to some one he had known in New Orleans. He soon returned to the faro-table, and, taking his seat, asked Newton whether he intended to do any betting.

"No, not to-night," Newton replied, yawning. "I am very tired and restless, and I make it a rule never to bet when my nerves are shaky."

"Well, that is a mighty good rule," said Bernardi, as he put out a pile of gold pieces. "If you will only stick to that plan, you will be sure to win. I can always feel when luck is with me, and if I could only make up my mind to stop when I know that I cannot win, I should be as successful as could be wished; but sometimes I get obstinate when the cards begin to run against me, and then I buck against fate until I lose all."

Having an absorbing interest in the game, Bernardi talked very little after this, but about eleven o'clock he counted his winnings, and, finding that they amounted to more than two hundred dollars, he decided to withdraw. In company with Newton, therefore, he left the room, and entered a bar-room below. They drank and chatted together a short time, and then separated, Bernardi going to a well-known house of ill-repute, while Newton carefully dogged his footsteps unseen.

Knowing that Bernardi intended to spend the night where he was, Newton returned to his own lodgings. They had agreed to meet at the post-office about eleven o'clock next day, and Newton knew that his services would not be required before that hour.

About eleven o'clock in the forenoon, Newton and Bernardi met at the post-office, as agreed, and, after a morning dram together, they went to a restaurant for breakfast.

"How did you enjoy yourself yesterday evening?" asked Newton, as they were finishing their meal.

"Oh! very well indeed. I met a young lady whom I used to know in New Orleans, and she was very lovely; but I shall never meet one like my señorita. She was the most beautiful woman living;" and, as he spoke, Bernardi sighed deeply, and became moody, silent, and abstracted.

"Yes; I recollect having seen her with you once in New Orleans," replied Newton, on a venture; "is she dead?"

"No, —— —— her! I wish she was," replied Bernardi, savagely. "She started to come North with me, and I gave her everything she could ask; but when I had won a large sum of money at Natchez, she stole several thousand dollars from me, and disappeared with a Mississippi gambler, whom she had never seen but twice. I didn't care for the money, but I loved her passionately, and I cannot think of her without becoming enraged.

Come, let us go get some brandy; I always have to drink when I think of her."

While they were drinking together, Newton asked Bernardi if he was always fortunate in gaming.

"Oh! no, indeed; why, less than a week ago I had not a cent to buy my breakfast, and I did not know whether to enlist in the army or commit suicide."

"Then your present success is marvelous, for you must have won, in all, four or five hundred dollars," said Newton, inquiringly.

"No, I did not win it all; in fact, I could not have done so, for I did not have a dime to start with; but I met an old friend here who gave me a few hundreds, and who will give me more when I want it."

"That's the kind of a friend to have," said Newton, warmly; "come, let us drink again to his health. I wish I had met you before, for I would have been glad to divide with you. We ought always to stand by each other, especially we Southerners, among these Yankee gamblers."

"Yes, that is true," replied Bernardi, taking an immense drink of brandy; "they are not so generous to each other as we are down South. Now, my friend, whom I spoke of, is one of the right sort. He gave me enough for a new outfit, and has promised to give me a good sum when I am ready to go South again."

"Is he a Southerner too?" asked Newton.

"Oh! yes," Bernardi replied, "he is from Peru,

where I first met him, and we have had many a gay time together. I used to keep a fine suite of gambling rooms, which he frequented, and he used to play with the utmost indifference to the results; he always seemed equally unmoved whether he won or lost."

"I suppose you must have been very warm friends," said Newton, "or he would not now be so ready to assist you?"

"Well, Don Juan is a very liberal fellow, I admit," answered Bernardi; "but he might not be so generous were it not to his interest to be so," he continued, with a knowing wink.

"Oh! ho! I see," replied Newton, nodding his head expressively. "Your friend would not care to have you talk about his past history, I suppose?"

"Exactly; he knows that I could tell some things about him which might spoil his pleasure here, and so he is anxious to keep on good terms with me. However, he needn't fear me as long as he treats me decently, for I do not wish to injure him, and when I am ready to go I shall get a good sum from him to start me in business elsewhere."

"Suppose he should refuse to give you anything more, or have you arrested for blackmailing him," suggested Newton.

"I'd like to see him try it," Bernardi exclaimed, with a volley of oaths. "I guess two could play at the game of swearing out warrants, and when the account was balanced, his imprisonment would be twenty times as long as mine. No, no; I have no fear that he will attempt such a thing."

"I merely spoke of it as a possibility," said Newton, "in order that you should be on your guard. A man with wealth and position might succeed in crushing a friendless poor man in spite of the latter's protestations. However, if any such thing should happen, you can depend upon it that I will work for you until you are released."

"That's right, my friend," replied Bernardi, as he called for another drink of brandy. "If I should suddenly disappear without warning to you, don't fail to search for me everywhere, and I will see that you are handsomely rewarded. If Don Juan should attempt any treachery, I should have him at my mercy as soon as I should get free, and, together, we could squeeze a large sum out of him."

Newton spent the day with Bernardi, and they became quite inseparable. After driving about the city for an hour or two, they attended a matinée performance at one of the theatres, and then had a long and sumptuous dinner at a fashionable restaurant. In the evening they went to the gambling-rooms where they had met the night before, and Bernardi was soon absorbed in the game of faro. His luck still clung to him, and, on leaving the place at midnight, he had won three hundred dollars more. As before, Bernardi went to enjoy the society of his New Orleans charmer, and Newton went to his own lodgings.

After Newton had made his report to me, early the next morning, I told him to continue his intimacy with Bernardi, and to pump him as thoroughly as possible relative to Don Pedro's past history. Soon after his departure to meet Bernardi, Senator Muirhead and Judge Key entered, and we discussed the possibility of doing anything with this new witness, Pietro Bernardi.

"Would it not be possible to frighten him into telling all he knows of Don Pedro?" asked the Senator.

"I hardly think we could," I replied. "In the first place, you have no charge whatever against Bernardi, nor any reason to suppose that he has ever been a criminal anywhere; hence, how could we frighten him? Moreover, he is a man of considerable nerve, and he would see that, as against third parties, his interests would be best served by supporting, instead of attacking, Don Pedro. No, I don't see anything to be gained as yet by showing our hands. Our object is to recover possession of the money paid to the Don for those bogus diamond fields, and to do that, we must wait until we have a sure case against him for his crimes committed elsewhere."

"I agree with you wholly," added Judge Key. "Besides, this fellow, Bernardi, knows nothing of the Don's forgeries and frauds except those committed in Peru, and as we have before shown, we could make no use of those accusations until we hear from Peru. Indeed, it is questionable how far we can proceed even then, for we have no extradition treaty with that country."

"Well, I do not mind that very much," I replied, "for my chief dependence is upon the moral effect upon Don Pedro. I think that we can so work upon him as to obtain his consent to go to Peru voluntarily, rather than to be detained here until a requisition arrives from England. He knows that if he be sent to England, he will be transported for a long term of years; whereas, in Peru, he may avoid conviction altogether, or purchase his escape after conviction."

"But can we make him give up his plunder?" asked the Senator, anxiously.

"I think we can," said I. "You see that he is liable to be held here for obtaining money under false pretenses, and during the trial the money could be taken by attachment. Then, even though he should not be convicted, the delay would enable us to make sure of sending him back to London, where a heavy sentence would undoubtedly be given him. Now, by representing these things to him, we shall induce him to hand over the money voluntarily, and after that we shall not care whether he is taken to Great Britain or Peru."

"If that be the case, why not arrest him now and get the advices from London afterward?" asked the Senator, who was very anxious to hasten matters.

"Because we could not present a sufficient case

to hold him under the preliminary examination," replied Judge Key. " When we get official news of the fellow's character from Peru, we shall have a sure thing against him, and then I shall feel ready to act; but I agree with Mr. Pinkerton that there would be danger in overhaste. You see, we have him carefully watched, and there is no probability that he intends to make off until after this *fête champêtre;* therefore, let us wait for our foreign advices as long as we can, and in case he prepares to go before they arrive, it will be time enough to arrest him then."

" How about the Donna ? " asked Muirhead. " Do you propose to take any steps against her ? "

"I don't see how we can," I replied. " With the exception of the sums she has received from Mather, she has obtained nothing fraudulently; and, as you may well suppose, we could never get Mather to testify against her ; so I guess we need not trouble ourselves to interfere with the lovely Donna at all."

Our conference then broke up with the understanding that we should assemble again the moment any new facts in the case should be developed. Just after the gentlemen had left, Madame Sevier came in and reported a scene between Mather and the Donna which had taken place the previous evening.

The Don had remained at home entertaining various guests until nine o'clock. He had then gone out with Lesparre and several other gentlemen, to attend a banquet and ball given by a semi-political club at one of the hotels. The affair was attended by many highly respectable ladies, particularly by those whose husbands had any political aspirations, but it was not sufficiently exclusive to satisfy the Donna, and she remained at home. The visitors gradually dropped out until only Mr. Mather remained, and then Madame Sevier excused herself, on the plea of fatigue, in order to retire. Instead of going to her room, however, she hastened to the library and hid herself behind a statue standing in a deep bay window, which was heavily shrouded with drapery and curtains. Thus placed, she was completely hidden from the sight of any one in the library, though she had a perfect view herself, and she could hear every word spoken in the room.

As she expected, the Donna soon entered, followed by Mr. Mather. The latter seemed to consider that the Donna could refuse him nothing, for he put his arms around her, and was about to kiss her, when he found her fan quickly interposed between their faces.

"You are too free with your caresses, Señor Mather," she said, coldly, slipping out of his embrace, and pointing out a chair to him at some distance from the sofa, upon which she seated herself.

Poor Mather was quite astonished, for, having kissed her several times before, he supposed that he could continue doing so whenever he wished; but the Donna was an expert fisher of men, and she recognized the force of that old proverb, "Familiarity breeds contempt;" besides, she wanted some more money, and she knew that her elderly lover would gladly purchase her kisses at a round price. The folly of giving them away gratis could not be indulged in, therefore, and she kept her sighing swain at a distance for a little time. She was too politic to give even the slightest hint of her object in the conversation which ensued, but she used every possible allurement to fascinate her victim, while she would allow him no liberties nor caresses. Mather could not fail to recollect the affectionate manner in which she had received his previous gifts, and he therefore decided to try the same policy again.

"I saw a beautiful camel's hair shawl to-day," he said, "and I was going to get it for you, my dear Lucia, but I did not know whether it would suit you, and so I determined to let you select your own gift. The shawl was worth one thousand dollars, and I made up my mind to give you the amount that I should have paid for it, and you could then exercise your own taste."

"Oh! my dear Henry," she exclaimed, "how thoughtful you are! How can I sufficiently thank you?" and she made room for him on the sofa, as he advanced holding out a roll of bills.

"You know how you can please me best," he answered, tenderly, bending over her.

"Oh! really, Henry, you mustn't," she protested, feebly, as he showered kisses on her cheeks and lips; "suppose any one should come in!"

As she spoke, a carriage stopped in front of the house, and their affectionate *tête-à-tête* was interrupted by the unexpected return of Lesparre, who, having left his watch at home, had returned to get it. He did not enter the parlor nor the library, but the Donna seemed very much agitated at the mere possibility of being detected in a compromising situation, and so Mather took his departure. The coolness with which she counted the money, after he had gone, was in striking contrast with her simulated embarrassment while he was present, and it was plain that, having obtained the gift, she was quite glad to get rid of the giver. She went immediately to her room, and Madame Sevier then retired also.

---

## CHAPTER VIII.

*Don Pedro anxious for Pietro Bernardi's Absence.—"Coppering the Jack and Playing the Ace and Queen open."—A Gambler that could not be Bought.—Splendid Winnings.—Diamond cutting Diamond.—Bernardi quieted, and he subsequently departs richer by five thousand dollars.*

AT eleven o'clock, Newton and Bernardi again met at the post-office, and the latter remarked that he intended making a short call upon his wealthy friend.

"Come along with me," he said, "and you will

see what a fine place he has. I shall not remain very long, and if you will wait for me outside, we can pass the day together. I hate to go around alone in a strange city."

Accordingly they strolled along until they reached Don Pedro's house, and Newton agreed to remain near at hand until Bernardi should finish his call. Salter was on the lookout, and when Bernardi was admitted, he led the way to Don Pedro's room. The moment the door closed on Bernardi, Salter took his place at the auger-holes in the adjoining closet, and overheard the entire conversation, as before.

"Well, Pietro, have you decided how soon you will be ready to leave town?" asked the Don. "From your clothes, jewelry, and other purchases you have made, you must have used up most of the money I gave you, and, if so, your departure must take place soon; for I warn you again, I shall give you nothing more until you depart for some distant city!"

"Well, to tell the truth," replied Bernardi, in an independent, indifferent manner, "I am in no hurry to go away just yet. You see, I have been very lucky since I've been here, and if I keep on, I guess I can repay you the amount you kindly loaned me."

"Do you mean that you have been gambling again?" asked the Don, in a vexed tone.

"Yes, and I have won constantly, so that I don't like to change my luck by making a move right away. You know gamblers are superstitious, and I have a strong feeling that it will be for my interest to remain here for some time yet."

"But you promised to go as soon as you felt able to travel," said the Don.

"Well, there is no hurry. I haven't done you any harm yet, and I don't mean to. Why are you so anxious to get rid of me?"

Of course, Don Pedro's principal fear was that Bernardi would learn how large a sum the former had received for his bogus mines, and that he would not be satisfied to go unless he got a large slice of the plunder. It would not do, however, to excite his suspicions by appearing too desirous of sending him away, so the Don changed his tone, and said:

"Oh! I'm sure I don't want to get rid of you as long as you keep sober and don't talk about me; but you know how it is, Pietro; if you should get drunk and talk about me, you would tell everything you know, and the result would be that I should have to flee the town without accomplishing my object. In that case, I should lose not only all that I hoped to make, but also all the immense outlay I have made in preparing my scheme. If you want to go to New Orleans again, I will start you in a faro-bank there, and will come down there next winter to play with you; but I confess I should feel easier if you were out of Gloster for the present."

"Well, I will be ready to go in a few days, if you insist upon it; but I don't see the necessity of such haste. However, I will come in again and talk about it before the end of the week. I want to win a little more before I go."

"How have you been betting?" asked Morito, in a conciliatory manner.

"I have been 'coppering' the jack and playing the ace and queen 'open,'* and I have won constantly. I left them a few times and played other cards, but I always lost when I did so. Now I am going to stick to that scheme right along."

"Where are you playing?" asked the Don, carelessly.

"I generally go to Dave Carter's, in Mahogany Block, for I think he deals a 'square' game."

"Yes, I suppose so," said Morito; "as much so as any of them; but they are all sharpers here, and they may have been letting you win on purpose, thinking that you had a large sum in reserve which they hope to catch hereafter. If you will take my advice, you will stop while you are ahead. You know, from your own experience as a banker, that the 'bank' always wins in the end."

"Well, I shall try a few more games, and then I shall be ready to talk with you about going South. I want to run my luck while it is good," and so saying, Bernardi rose to go.

---

*These are technical terms in playing faro. The player meant that he was in the habit of making one bet that the jack would be a losing card all the time, and another that the ace and queen would be winning cards.

"All right, Pietro," said Don Pedro, "be careful not to get swindled, and to keep silent about me."

The moment Bernardi was gone, the Don rang his bell violently, and sent for Monsieur Lesparre. When the latter entered the Don's room, he found his employer in a more disturbed and excited condition than he had ever before indulged in, and evidently he meant mischief to some one.

"Lesparre, that fellow Bernardi, of whom I spoke to you the other day, has been here again," burst out the Don. "I gave him a considerable sum of money to set him on his feet again, for old acquaintance' sake, expecting that he would return to his friends in the South, or, at least, behave like a decent gentleman; but he has returned to his old habits of gambling and drinking, so that, at any moment, he may come here and mortify me before a party of my guests, or, worse still, claim me as his friend when arraigned in a police court for drunkenness, *etcetera*. He promised to leave town as soon as the money I gave him was gone, and I was to give him then a respectable sum to start him in business elsewhere; but he has won considerably at the faro-table, and he is now independent of me, and therefore declines to keep his promise until he is ready."

"Would he go, do you think, if he should lose all he has?" asked Lesparre.

"Oh! yes, indeed; he would be forced to yield

to my terms then, and I should give him nothing until he started."

"How would it do to suggest to the proprietor of the gambling rooms that it would be doubly for his interest to fleece this man? I think it could easily be done, if the 'bank' were so disposed."

"I have no doubt of it, especially as I know the way he intends to bet all the time," replied the Don, eagerly; "he 'coppers' the jack and plays the ace and queen 'open.' It must be a pretty poor dealer who cannot 'stack' those cards, with such a stake in view. Suppose you drop a hint to Dave Carter, or to the dealer to-night, before Bernardi goes there."

"I will go down at once," replied Lesparre, "and I will promise him three hundred dollars additional if he wins all that Bernardi has; that is not too much, is it?"

"No, indeed!" exclaimed the Don; "I would gladly give five hundred, if necessary."

Lesparre arrived at the gambling rooms about noon, and at that early hour no one was present except the proprietor and one of the dealers. Lesparre obtained an interview with the proprietor alone, and then asked him if he would like to make a thousand dollars.

"Oh! yes," he replied, in an indifferent way, "I should have no objection, although it would not be such a novelty that I need take a great deal of trouble about it. The 'bank' often wins more than that in a single evening."

"Well, there is a South American who has been playing here recently, against whom I have a bitter grudge. He has about six hundred dollars now, most of which he has won here. He has one regular system of playing—'coppering' the jack and playing the ace and queen to win—and you can easily fix those cards so as to clean him out in one evening. The moment you have done that, I will give you five hundred dollars more."

The gambler fixed a keen look upon Lesparre for a moment, and then replied that he was no gudgeon to bite such a stale bait as that. He added that they played a "square" game, and if a man won, he was welcome to his winnings; but that no trickery would be resorted to against any patron of the house. Lesparre was obliged to withdraw, feeling that he had made a mistake in proposing the plan so openly.

That evening, after a day spent in playing billiards and driving about, Bernardi and Newton again entered the gambling saloon. Bernardi did not make any bets for some time, but stood watching the game in silence, apparently guessing as to the winning and losing cards to determine whether he was in luck. Finally he bet fifty dollars on the ace and lost; this was followed by one hundred dollars on the same card, which again lost. He waited a few deals and then placed two hundred dollars on the queen to win, and one hundred dollars on the jack to lose. The cards fell as he had hoped, and gathering in his stakes

*This was taking a short cut to Bernardi's friendship.*

and winnings, he began betting in earnest. His luck was wonderful, and as all his bets were for fifty dollars or more, he soon had quite a large sum. Presently he stopped betting, and went to the bar with Newton. They talked and drank together for some minutes, but Bernardi was not ready to leave just then. His winnings were already quite sufficient to cause the proprietor to regard him with a considerable degree of interest, and when he returned to the faro-table, a seat was given him at once. He made no bets for some minutes, but at length he asked:

"What is your limit to-night?"

"Five hundred dollars," was the reply.

Bernardi then placed four hundred dollars on the nine spot, and, a moment later, he was again a winner. He now seemed satisfied, for he presented his "chips" for payment, and received cash therefor. The proprietor then invited Bernardi and Newton to drink with him, and, while standing at the sideboard, the proprietor asked Bernardi whether he had many acquaintances in the city.

"No," replied Bernardi, "I have very few; why do you ask?"

"Because one of them is your enemy, or else he was trying to play a trick on the 'bank' this morning," continued the proprietor, watching Bernardi narrowly. "He came in about noon, and wanted the cards put up so that you should be cleaned out of all your money."

"The devil you say!" ejaculated Bernardi; "why did he want to clean me out?"

"That I can't say; but he told me that he had a bitter grudge against you, and that he would give a great deal to injure you."

"I do not know any one here who could say that of me," replied Bernardi, thoughtfully. "There is only one man in the city who knows me intimately, and I do not see why he should wish me to lose, even if he did hate me. Was he a South American, like myself?"

"No; he might have been a foreigner, but he was not dark-complexioned."

"Well, I cannot imagine who it could have been," mused Bernardi; "and I guess I need not be afraid of him, if he goes to work in that roundabout way. However, I am obliged to you for the information, and I will take care that he does not drop on me unexpectedly. So-long."

As Bernardi walked down the street with Newton, he was evidently deeply abstracted, for he muttered to himself in Spanish, and swore at intervals in quite an excited manner. Finally, he said aloud:

"I don't know what to think about this story. It may be that this gambler made it up to shake my nerves, or to cover some plot against me; but I have a sort of feeling that Don Juan is at the bottom of it. I don't fear him one bit, but I want to solve the mystery, and if he has been plotting against me, I will have my revenge upon him. But, no; I can't see what he could gain by it, and

I think, perhaps, this gang despair of breaking my luck, and are planning to rob me by force."

"That seems reasonable," replied Newton, "for then you would attribute the act to this unknown enemy, and they would escape suspicion. Still," he continued, anxious to lead the conversation back to Don Pedro as a subject, "your first supposition may be the correct one, and your pretended friend may be scheming to ruin you."

"But why should he want me to lose money?" persisted Bernardi. "He knows that I should come to him for more, and that he would be obliged to give it to me."

"Perhaps he would like to get rid of your presence," cautiously suggested Newton; "and if you were penniless, he could insist upon your departure as a condition upon which alone he would give you money."

"Caramba! I believe you are right, my friend," Bernardi exclaimed, furiously; "and if I find that it is so, I will make Don Juan, or Don Pedro, as he calls himself now, regret the day he played me false."

"Don't be over-hasty," counseled Newton, "for the whole story may be a gambler's lie after all."

"Oh! I will investigate it carefully," answered Bernardi, "and, when I am satisfied about the truth of the matter, I will consult with you as to the best course to pursue. It is a good thing to have a friend to advise with, especially among such a gang of thieves as seem to hang 'round these rooms. Meet me to-morrow, as usual, and I will go see my friend again."

The men then separated, and went to their respective lodgings for the night.

In the morning they met, took breakfast together, and afterwards sauntered down to visit Don Pedro. As before, Bernardi was conducted straight to the Don's room, and Salter again stationed himself in the closet to listen.

"So you are still successful?" was the first remark he heard.

"Yes, moderately so," replied Bernardi; "but it is strange how cards run sometimes."

"Well, you ought not to be astonished at anything after your long experience in gambling."

"Oh! I'm never astonished," said Bernardi, who had drunk a good deal of brandy before and after breakfast; "but I was thinking how lucky it was that I changed my mind last night about playing those three cards—the jack, ace, and queen."

"How so?" asked Morito.

"Well, if I had played the jack 'coppered,' and the ace and queen 'open,' last night, all the evening, I should have been entirely cleaned out; what do you think of that?"

"I think you were very lucky in having played elsewhere," replied the Don; "but what's the matter with you? What makes you look at me so strangely?"

"I want to find out whether it was you who sent a man to tell Dave Carter, the gambler, how

I was playing, and to ask him to fix the cards so that I should lose all I had."

Bernardi's voice was husky with liquor and anger, and he had evidently worked himself up into a great rage; but, in spite of his partial intoxication, he was very determined, and his tones foreboded no good-will to the Don. In a contest of words, however, he was no match for his opponent, and Don Pedro instantly took the most effectual method for quieting his visitor's suspicions.

"My dear Pietro," he began, contemptuously, "I gave you credit for more common-sense than you seem disposed to claim for yourself. Why should I want you to lose? On the contrary, I would like to see you win enough to start in business for yourself, and repay me what I have loaned you, for I assure you that I much prefer to have you spend your money than mine. I have none too much for my own wants, and if you could repay me, I should be delighted. What is the reason for your question?"

Bernardi did not reply for two or three minutes; he was evidently keenly scrutinizing Don Pedro's face; but at length he said:

"Well, it's all right now, and I suppose I was wrong to suspect you; but the proprietor of the place where I gamble told me that some one had been trying to get him to play a trick on me, and I determined to find out who it was."

"Well, Pietro, I don't think you would have thought of suspecting me if your head had not been fuddled with liquor. Why can't you stop drinking for a month or two?"

"What do you care about my drinking?" asked Bernardi, in a half-cowed manner.

"Because Pietro drunk is a very different fellow from Pietro sober; and some day you will let out some damaging reports about me, and then all hope of making anything here will be destroyed. If I could feel sure that you would remain sober, I would gladly start you in a good 'bank' here."

Of course, Don Pedro had no intention of doing anything of the kind, but he saw that Bernardi was in a dangerous mood, and that he must handle him very skillfully if he wished to get him to leave the city. The Don knew that to urge him to leave would be the surest way to make him stay, but that, if left to follow his own inclinations, he would be anxious to go South, where the climate and people were more congenial to him. Hence, Don Pedro boldly took the ground that he was quite willing for Bernardi to stay if he would only keep sober, and Bernardi quickly fell into the trap.

"I don't want to start a 'bank' in this place," he said, "and I can't get along in this climate without drinking. I have been moderately successful here, and I am in no hurry to leave, but I should like to go back to New Orleans, if I could fit up a good place there, and deal a first-class game."

"How much would you need for that purpose?" asked the Don. "If I can let you have it, I will do so, and you can stay here or go back to New Orleans, as you may prefer; only I shall make one condition: that you promise faithfully to drink nothing but wine while you are in this city, until I get ready to leave. Will three thousand dollars be enough?"

"Hardly; I have won some money here, to be sure, but it will cost a good deal to spread a handsome layout in New Orleans—as for this place, there are not enough gentlemen gamesters here; the gamblers are all trying to live on each other. If you will make it five thousand, I will start for New Orleans day after to-morrow."

"That is more than I ought to pay out in my present circumstances," said the Don, thoughtfully; "but I guess I can run the establishment on credit for about a month, and that will help me out; so if you will go to-morrow, I will give you five thousand when you start."

"Done!" replied Bernardi, much gratified at having obtained so large a sum. "I have nothing to do except to get a young lady friend to go with me, and she won't need a great while to make her preparations. So you can have the money ready to-morrow?"

"It shall be awaiting you any time that you call for it," answered Morito, and Bernardi then took his departure.

On joining Newton, Bernardi was in high spirits, and he talked very freely of his intended plans.

"My friend convinced me that he had nothing to do with the trick which the gambler said some one tried to play upon me, and as a proof of his regard, he is going to give me a start in New Orleans. I shall leave here to-morrow, and if you would like to go in with me, we can make a pile of money there."

"I can't very well leave here for some time yet," said Newton, "for I have a large sum staked in bets on the races next month, and I shall have no money until they take place. I have a sure thing on a new horse, and I have got such large odds that I have put up every dollar I could reach. I shall clear about ten thousand dollars sure, and then if you are so disposed, I will join you in New Orleans."

"All right, we'll do it; but then, you may lose everything instead of winning. I don't care to bet on races, myself; there are too many chances to deal from the bottom."

"There is no danger in this case, so you must let me know where I can find you, and within a month I will join you in the Crescent City."

Bernardi then went to see his fair and frail charmer, to obtain her company on his Southern trip, and Newton came to my room to report. I instructed him to stay with Bernardi as much as possible while the latter remained in the city, and to be sure to obtain his address in New Orleans. I then called upon Senator Muirhead and informed him of the proposed departure of Bernardi. The Senator was very anxious to detain him in some way, in order to get his testimony, in case we should fail to hear from England or Peru in time; but I was unable to suggest any plan for holding this man without exposing our whole connection with the case. Bernardi was evidently ready to act in good faith with Don Pedro, and any endeavor to retard his departure would be regarded by him as coming from the gang of gamblers from whom he had won money. There was no doubt but that he would keep up a correspondence with Newton, and we should thus know where to find him in case his presence should be needed. We decided, therefore, to let him go as he intended.

Early in the evening, Bernardi and Newton went as usual to the gaming-rooms. There they met a stranger, who seemed to be a Spaniard or Cuban. Bernardi addressed him in Spanish, and after some conversation, they sat down to play. By some freak of luck, Bernardi continually won his small bets, but whenever he put out a large amount, he lost. The Cuban stranger had the same experience, and at length Bernardi rose in disgust and left the rooms with Newton, having lost about two hundred dollars.

"Those fellows have got some kind of a 'skin-game' at work," he said, "and they tried to beat me and that Cuban out of all our cash. I gave him a hint in Spanish before I came away, and I hope he will stop before they fleece him. Now let us go to the theatre."

They attended one of the theatres, and then

had a glorious supper at Bernardi's expense after the performance was over. About midnight, they parted with mutual good wishes, and Bernardi promised to write to Newton as soon as he should reach New Orleans.

The next morning Bernardi called upon Don Pedro and received the promised amount of five thousand dollars, assuring him that he should leave the city that afternoon. As soon as he left the house, the Don asked Lesparre to keep a watch upon Bernardi to make sure of his leaving according to promise. When Lesparre returned about three o'clock, and reported that Bernardi was then actually on his way to Cairo, accompanied by a young lady, the Don was overjoyed, and he expressed himself greatly relieved thereby.

"Now we can take more interest in our *fête champêtre*, and we will make it the most delightful affair ever known in this country," he said, exultantly. "When it is over, my dear Lesparre, we will make a tour of the fashionable watering-places, and enjoy life to the full."

## CHAPTER IX.

*Important Information from the Peruvian Government.—Arrival in Gloster of the Peruvian Minister and Consul.—In Consultation.—"Robbing Peter to pay Paul."—Mr. Pinkerton's card is presented.— Juan Sanchez, I arrest you, and you are my Prisoner.—Mr. Pinkerton not "For Sale."—A Dramatic Scene.—The Bubble burst.*

SEVERAL days now sped by with no fresh developments, and Don Pedro was almost constantly engaged in his preparations for the *fête champêtre*. As the day approached, society was stirred to its very center, and nothing was spoken of save this grand event of the season.

But four days remained before the *fête*, when I was delighted by receiving a letter from the Secretary of State for Peru, giving full particulars of the forgeries and frauds committed by Don Juan Sanchez in that country, and enclosing a fine portrait of the man. One glance at the picture was sufficient to assure me of the identity of Don Pedro P. L. de Morito with Don Juan Sanchez, and I now felt ready to act. The letter informed me that a Peruvian official would be dispatched to Gloster at once, to obtain the arrest of Don Pedro, though there were a great many difficulties in the way, owing to the lack of an extradition treaty. Every effort would be made, however, to bring him to justice, and the Peru-

11*

vian Minister at Washington would be instructed to confer with me.

I informed Senator Muirhead and Judge Key of this news, and they were both much encouraged at the prospect, especially as we learned that a Peruvian man-of-war had arrived in New York from Aspinwall, it being doubtless intended that this vessel should take the prisoner to Peru, in case he could be frightened into surrendering himself.

The *fête* was to take place on Wednesday, if the weather should be favorable, or on the first pleasant day thereafter, and everything was already in complete order for the grand occasion. A large and elegant steamer had been chartered to convey the guests to the island, and she was to make several trips during the day for the convenience of business men who could not go early. There remained nothing further to be done, except to pray for fine weather on the important day.

On Monday morning I was told that two gentlemen were waiting to see me, on very important business, at one of the leading hotels. I accompanied the messenger, and was at once shown to the room of the Peruvian Minister, who was accompanied by the Peruvian Consul at New York. Before proceeding to business, I informed the Minister that I was acting under the instructions of Senator Muirhead, and that I should like to send for that gentleman, and for my legal adviser, Judge Key. The Peruvian officials made no objection, and both Judge Key and the Senator were soon with us, ready for consultation. As the new arrivals were tired and dusty after their long journey, we merely exchanged information relative to Don Pedro, and agreed to meet at ten o'clock next morning, to make plans for his arrest.

At the appointed hour, we were all prompt in arriving at the parlor of the Minister. The latter and the Consul, in accordance with a suggestion I had made the day previous, had not mentioned their official rank to any one, and had remained as secluded as possible, in order to prevent Morito from knowing of their arrival in the city.

The Minister stated that the forgeries of Don Juan Sanchez in Peru had been so enormous, amounting to more than seven hundred thousand dollars, that the government had taken up the pursuit of the criminal with unusual zeal, and no effort nor expense would be spared to bring him to justice. Unfortunately, however, in the absence of any extradition treaty between Peru and the United States, the chances of securing Don Juan, even now that he had been discovered, were not bright; indeed, the Minister acknowledged that he saw no way of accomplishing it.

"By an appeal to law," said Judge Key, "nothing *can* be gained; but it is possible that my friend, Mr. Pinkerton, may have a plan which will induce Don Pedro, as he now calls himself, to surrender voluntarily rather than stand trial here or in Great Britain. Let us hear your opinion, then, Mr. Pinkerton."

"Well, gentlemen," I replied, "this is a case where the greatest care must be exercised, for the criminal is a bold, skillful man, of good education and address, with, probably, a fair knowledge of his legal rights. We cannot afford to make any mistakes, for he would surely take advantage of them. We must, therefore, present the case to him in such a way that he will believe it to be to his interest to give himself up. The presence of the Peruvian man-of-war in New York is very fortunate, for, once under her flag, he cannot escape; but he must be induced to go on board voluntarily, or else we shall be liable to the charge of kidnapping."

I then explained the method by which he had had swindled the citizens of Gloster, and showed how difficult it would be to convict him of anything, owing to the probability that his victims would refuse to testify against him; besides, for obtaining money under false pretenses, a short imprisonment only could be inflicted, and then he would be free to go where he pleased.

"However," I continued, "I think I can present to him his position in such a light that he will regard a surrender to the Peruvian authorities as preferable to a long trial and detention here, with the possibility of being sent to California or Great Britain for trial on a more serious charge. When he knows that we are fully acquainted with his past career, he may be willing to accept our terms rather than to defy us."

"Suppose, however," said the Minister, "that he should refuse all terms, and determine to fight it out?"

"In that case," I replied, "we should be obliged to arrest him here for obtaining money under false pretenses, and be prepared to arrest him again the moment he should be set free, repeating the operation as often as we could get different victims to enter complaint against him. The number of stockholders in this bogus company is quite large, so that we could easily hold him until a requisition could be obtained from California or England."

"How large a sum has he in his possession now?" asked the Consul.

"About half a million dollars," replied the Senator.

"Well," said the Consul, "that sum will go far toward reimbursing the people whom he swindled in Peru, so I think that Mr. Pinkerton's plan is the best that can be adopted. We might induce him to go aboard our vessel by promising to use our influence to lighten his sentence, in case he makes restitution to his victims in Peru."

The Consul made these remarks with a wise expression, as if he thought he had hit upon a very easy way of solving the problem. The Senator, Judge Key, and I exchanged looks of astonishment and amusement at this cool proposal to take our citizens' money to reimburse the Peruvians; it was a case of "robbing Peter to pay Paul" which we could not appreciate. Finally, I said :

"I presume that there can be no question as to the way to dispose of this money which Don Pedro has in his possession. Not one penny of it came from Peru, and we cannot permit any of it to be taken there. On arriving here Don Pedro had only a few thousand dollars, which he obtained in England by forgery. This sum he has already used up, and the only money in his possession has been obtained by the sale of his fictitious diamond fields in Peru. It would be manifestly unjust to allow this money to be taken away, and it is our intention to obtain it at all hazards, whatever may become of the Don."

"Oh ! I shall make no such claim, Mr. Pinkerton," said the Minister ; "that was only a suggestion of the Consul, who did not understand exactly how the money referred to came into this man's hands. All that I care for is to get Don Pedro on board our vessel, and I shall be pleased to pay for your services in the matter. We must be careful, however, that there shall be no opportunity to charge us with kidnapping, for we wish to avoid any possibility of complications with the United States ; the fellow has made us trouble enough already."

"I will arrange that matter satisfactorily," I replied ; "as for the question of payment, I am acting wholly in the interest of Senator Muirhead, and under his instructions, so that I can accept nothing except from him."

We spent an hour or two more in preparing papers and arranging the details of our plans, the conclusion being that we should make the arrest that evening, about seven o'clock, when there would be few or no visitors at Don Pedro's house. As I had supposed, there was no charge whatever against the Donna, and my only intentions with regard to her were to see that she did not carry off any of the money belonging to the Diamond Company stockholders, nor assist the Don to escape. It was decided to send Don Pedro to New York immediately, in case he yielded to our terms, and the Donna would be at liberty to go or stay, as she might see fit.

On returning to my office, I found Bangs and Lesparre awaiting me, and the latter said that he believed the Don and Donna intended to take flight immediately after the *fête*. They probably desired to finish their career in Gloster in a blaze of glory, and, as they would not be expected to receive visitors for two or three days after the *fête*, they would have a good start before their departure would become known. I told Lesparre to see that Madame Sevier and Salter kept a close watch for the remainder of the day, and in case any attempt should be made to remove the box containing Don Pedro's coin, he must send Salter to me instantly with the news. I also suggested that the servants be kept out of the way that evening, so that no one should know of our visit.

Lesparre departed to attend to his duties, and I remained to complete the details of my plans with Mr. Bangs, who had arrived from Chicago with two detectives, in obedience to my summons.

About six o'clock, Senator Muirhead and Judge Key arrived, and a more nervous man than the former I never saw. In a few minutes the Peruvian Minister and Consul arrived, and we proceeded in carriages to Don Pedro's house, the Senator remaining at the hotel, however. We left the carriages a short distance away, so as not to attract attention, and, while Mr. Bangs's two men stationed themselves to watch the house, the rest of my party ascended the steps and were admitted by Salter.

"The family are still at dinner," said Salter, "but they are finishing the dessert, and I presume Don Pedro will go to the billiard-room after dinner to smoke, as usual."

"Give him my card as he leaves the dining-room," I said, "and tell him that I am waiting to see him in the drawing-room."

In a few minutes, Don Pedro and Lesparre rose from the table, and Salter gave my card to the former.

"Pinkerton! Pinkerton! I don't know any one of that name; do I, Lesparre?"

"Possibly it may be some gentleman having business with you in connection with the *fête*," suggested Lesparre.

"Ah! very true; where is he, George? I will see him at once," said the Don, unsuspectingly.

Salter led the way to the drawing-room, where I alone was waiting, the rest of the party having waited in the vestibule. As he entered, followed by Lesparre, I rose and said:

"Juan Sanchez, I arrest you, and you are now my prisoner!" and, so saying, I put my hand on his shoulder.

He turned very pale, and sat down in the nearest chair, while Lesparre quickly brought him a glass of water. I then continued:

"Juan Sanchez, or José Gomez more properly, we will retire to the library if you wish, as we may be interrupted here by the arrival of some of your friends, and I do not wish to expose you at present."

"What do you mean by addressing me in this manner?" he replied, trying to regain his composure. "My name is neither Sanchez nor Gomez."

"It is a long time since you have been so called," I answered, " but your victims in Brazil and Peru still retain the names in their memories without difficulty. I will now present to you the Minister of Peru and the Peruvian Consul at New York, both of whom have taken a lively interest in your past life and actions."

Just as I spoke, the Donna and Madame Sevier entered, and the former, seeing the abject appearance of her husband, asked what was the matter.

"Your husband is a prisoner, madam," I replied; "and as our interview would be painful to you, I must ask you to withdraw for the present at least."

She immediately gave an hysterical scream, and sank upon a divan sobbing frantically. Madame Sevier succeeded in quieting her somewhat, and she remained on the scene with her face buried in the Madame's lap. I felt confident that much of her emotion was feigned, and that she was an attentive listener to all that took place about her; however, I made no objection, but requested Mr. Bangs, who was watching in the hall, to admit the Minister and the rest of the party. As Mr. Bangs withdrew, the Don stepped up to me and said:

"Mr. Pinkerton, I will give you five thousand dollars if you will leave me alone for half an hour."

I smiled, and looking at my watch, said:

"It is now seven o'clock; at ten o'clock you will be on your way to New York."

"You can have ten thousand, if you will let me go; I will pay you the cash in coin immediately."

"Your offers are useless," I replied; "I will let no guilty man escape if it can be avoided."

As I spoke, the Peruvian Minister, the Consul, and Judge Key entered, and we proceeded in a body to the library, leaving the Donna in the care of Madame Sevier. On the way thither, the Don made one more effort to appear in the *rôle* of an injured innocent

"I don't understand this proceeding at all," he said, "and I claim my liberty. What authority have you for arresting me in my own house?"

"I *have* the authority, and that is sufficient," I replied, coolly. "If you desire to be taken at once to jail, I have no objection to granting your request; but I thought, perhaps, you might first prefer to hear what these gentlemen have to say."

I have arrested and have watched a great many criminals, but I have never seen one who, having carried out such an extensive scheme of villainy, was so utterly broken down as this man was. I had feared that his nerve might be firm enough to answer my threats with defiance, and force me to bring him to trial in Gloster; but I saw that there was no danger of such a misfortune; and so I stood aside while the Peruvian Minister addressed him.

"Juan Sanchez," said the Minister, "I have come here to obtain your removal to Peru, that you may be tried there for your numberless forgeries in that country. A Peruvian war-ship is now in New York harbor, and you will be placed on board of her for transportation to Peru. Mr. Pinkerton's superintendent will proceed with you to-night."

The Don was speechless for a moment, and then, glancing up, he said, in a sullen voice:

"I want to know what I am charged with, and by what right you send me to Peru. I am entitled to a hearing, and a lawyer to defend me."

"My friend, Judge Key, who is present, is a most able lawyer," I replied, "and you can consult with him if you wish advice; but first let me show you your true position. Your real name, Don José Gomez, was given you in Brazil, where it is remembered only to be cursed; Don Juan Sanchez was your name in Peru, and your crimes there are also well known; as Don José Michel, there are serious charges against you in San Francisco; Don Pedro Michel is badly wanted in Quito, where he would probably be shot, as they treat criminals there rather unceremoniously; and Don José Arias would undoubtedly be transported for life if the London detectives should discover his present hiding place, to say nothing of a lively interest which the French *gens d'armes* take in the same person. All of these people are now informed that the person whom they wish to find is living in Gloster as Don Pedro P. L. de Morito, and they are at this moment hastening agents here to arrest him. By chance, the Peruvian authorities are the first to arrive, and they have, therefore, the happy privilege of making the arrest. Now, as you are probably aware, the Minister will have some difficulty in obtaining an order from Washington authorizing me to send you to Peru, for want of an extradition treaty; but while you are under arrest here, we can easily get warrants from either California, England, or France, and then you can take your choice between being shot by vigilantes in California, transported to Van

Dieman's Land by England, or sent to work in the galleys by France. This is your present situation, and I am perfectly indifferent which course you prefer. If you decide to go with the Peruvian Minister, you must agree to do so voluntarily, until you are placed on board the Peruvian vessel, and you must make an assignment of all your money and property here to reimburse the people whom you have swindled by the sale of fictitious diamond-fields. If you are willing to comply with these conditions, you will sign all the necessary papers at once, and you will leave for New York to-night, before the English extradition writ arrives; if you refuse these conditions, 1 shall hold you until that writ, or one from California, arrives."

The Don was evidently in no mood for defiance; the knowledge of his past history which I displayed had wholly cowed him, and my allusions to the vigilantes of California, and the galleys of France, made him tremble like a leaf. He knew perfectly well the extent of his crimes in those places, and, also, that my hints of his probable punishment were not fancy sketches. Finally, he asked to see me alone, but I refused to grant his request, knowing his object. Then he wished to see the Minister alone, and I again objected, but I accompanied the two to another room, where they conversed in Spanish for some time. The Minister told me that the Don offered the whole of his money and property to allow him to escape; but, finding his offers useless, he agreed tc go to Peru for trial. No pledges were made to him to influence his decision, though he begged so hard that the Minister would intercede for him with the authorities in Peru, that his Excellency finally promised, in view of the Don's consent to go willingly, to recommend that his punishment be the lightest that the law could allow. The Don having fully yielded to the arguments of the Minister and myself, nothing remained to be done except to obtain his signature to the papers which had been already prepared, and to pack his trunk for his journey. Lesparre and Salter performed the latter task while the Don was signing the papers, and writing out his voluntary agreement to deliver himself up to the Peruvian authorities. The most important document was a deed assigning his furniture, horses, carriages, paintings, statuary, books, and, in short, all his personal property, to Judge Key, to be disposed of at the latter's discretion, and the proceeds, with the large amount of cash on hand, to be applied to repay the subscribers to the Diamond Company stock. In case there should not be sufficient to pay them in full, the payments should be made *pro rata;* but should there be an excess, such excess should be applied to the payment of the Don's private debts, contracted prior to that date. This provision was, of course, necessary to shut out the bills for supplies and services at the *fête* on the following day. Evidently it was too late to interfere with that interesting entertainment without throwing a heavy loss on many persons who could not afford to be the sufferers, and I saw only one way to prevent this, namely: to let the *fête* go on, and make those who danced pay the piper.

When the documents had all been signed, I said:

"José Gomez, you fully understand the meaning of this paper?" holding up his surrender to the Peruvian authorities; "it gives me power to convey you to New York and place you on board of a Peruvian vessel, using force, if necessary."

The Don bowed his head submissively, and said that he so understood it. The acknowledgment of the deeds was then made by Judge Key, who was a notary public, and our success was complete. The Donna was then informed that her husband would be taken East that night, and she professed to be much affected. I told her that there was no charge against her, and that she could go with her husband, or stay in Gloster, according to her own wishes. She said that she would go with him if Madame Sevier could accompany them. I had no objection to this, and the two ladies retired to pack their trunks. There was some uncertainty in my mind whether some of the Don's cash might not be in the Donna's possession; but I felt rather confident that she kept her money entirely separate from his, and that I could trust to Madame Sevier's acuteness to discover how much the Donna had on hand. I was not disappointed, for, while packing, the Donna told the Madame that she had about nine thousand dollars, the remains of her gifts from Mather, but that she could secure an immense sum out of the iron box if she could get it open. I had already made the Don confess where he had hidden his money, and one of my detectives was placed to guard the box; hence, the Donna was disappointed in her attempts to make a raid on the treasury. While the packing was going on, I sent to the railroad dépôt and bought eight railroad tickets for the party, which was to consist of the Minister, the Consul, the Don and Donna, Mr. Bangs, Madame Sevier, and two of my men. At half-past nine o'clock the party was ready and the trunks were sent off. I had kept a close watch upon the Don until now, and I saw that he hoped to escape while traveling. When the carriages were announced, I stepped up to him and told him that my invariable custom in such cases would require me to put him in irons to prevent any attempt at escape.

"Shall you permit me to be treated in this manner?" he said to the Peruvian Minister.

"You are not yet in the custody of the Peruvian authorities," I replied, "and I am responsible for your safe delivery in New York; hence I must take such precautions as I consider necessary. When you are on board the Peruvian vessel, the Minister can give such orders concerning you as he may think proper; but, until then, I alone have the right to determine what shall be done with you."

In a moment, I had placed a light set of

shackles on his feet, and handcuffs on his wrists; he was quite submissive now, and only seemed anxious to avoid observation.

As we passed out to the carriages, the Donna handed me a note, addressed to Henry O. Mather, and asked me to have it delivered immediately. I agreed to send it at once, though I sent it in such a manner that he should not receive it until the morning after the *fête*. The party arrived at the dépôt in time to secure seats together, and at ten o'clock the train bore them from the city.

―――♦―――

## CHAPTER X.

*The Fête Champêtre.—A Grand Carnival.—The Disappointed Married Lover.—A Vain Request.—Unmasked!—A Shrewd Caterer and his Humiliating Demands.—An Indignant Deacon.—Don Pedro taken to Peru in a Man-of-War, where he is Convicted and Sentenced to Fifteen Years' Imprisonment.—But the Donna manages to Satisfy her Affections in a quiet way in New York.*

TO the great delight of hundreds of people in Gloster, Wednesday morning revealed all the indications of a pleasant day, and by noon the weather was so lovely that nothing could have been more auspicious for the grand occasion. As the hour approached for the departure of the steamer, carriage after carriage drew up at the dock to discharge its load of brilliantly-dressed and masked ladies and gentlemen. The only person who was not completely protected from recognition was Monsieur Lesparre, who stood at the gangway to receive the guests, and wore a plain evening dress, with no mask.

In order to prevent the attendance of persons who had not been invited, each guest was required to present his or her invitation, and, as there were, as usual, many who had forgotten to bring their cards, Lesparre remained at hand to pass them on board, on leaving their names. When the hour of departure arrived, the boat swung out into the stream, amid the laughter and merry shouts of the gay revelers that crowded her decks, as the band flooded the air with music.

At first there was some embarrassment and reserve in the intercourse between the masqueraders, owing to the novelty of their situation, and the fact that the ladies at first clung closely to their own little parties, with whom they had come and to whom they were known; but soon this feeling wore off. They began to enter into the merry spirit of revelry which characterizes such entertainments in the cities of the Old World. The idea of personal identity began to be lost in the gayety of the moment, and in its place was substituted an identification of each person with the character which that person represented. The balmy airs of a perfect spring day wafted to them the sounds of country life along the shores of the river, and gave sensations both novel and pleas-

*The Fête Champêtre.—Page—*

ing to the gay denizens of the city, who rarely experienced any change from their routine of fashionable entertainments. During the trip by steamer there was much speculation as to the disguises worn by the Don and Donna, and though several persons were suspected of being the host and hostess, there was no sufficient way of identifying them.

At length the island was reached, and the party disembarked. The scene, as they took possession of the tents, booths, and pleasure-grounds, was brilliant and attractive beyond anything which the guests had ever witnessed. The island was covered with large trees, whose branches and foliage afforded a delightful shade. The close underbrush had been removed everywhere, except in certain ravines and other picturesque spots, so that the island presented a fine example of the beauties of landscape gardening. The foreground, at the place of landing, was a level expanse of green turf, which had been laid there weeks before. This was partly arranged for archery grounds, while rustic seats and swings were to be found under every tree. A large platform, for open-air dancing, was placed at the foot of the first ridge from the landing, while near by was an enclosed dancing-hall, to be used in the evening. Two bands were in attendance to play dance music constantly, one resting while the other played. It was understood that dinner would be served, at four o'clock exactly, in a long dining-room near the dancing-hall, and at that time every one was to unmask.

As the party spread over the grounds and began to enjoy all the opportunities for pleasure afforded them, they presented a most novel appearance. There were representatives, both male and female, of nearly every known nationality, and all the leading characters of historical and fictional literature were admirably delineated. Of course, among such members there were many accidental repetitions of the same character, but there were also instances of *fac similes*, which were intentional. This was a frequent cause of mistakes and embarrassing adventures, and often, when a gay cavalier was talking in tender tones to some lovely señorita whom he believed he knew, he would be astonished to see a second señorita, exactly like the first, passing unconcernedly by.

The afternoon was spent in rowing, sailing, shooting, dancing, and flirting, and all agreed that they had never known a more truly delightful day. An elegant lunch was kept ready at all times in a large *buffet*, adjoining the dining-room, and all kinds of wines and liquors were served freely. The hour for dinner was fast approaching, and, of course, by that time, many recognitions had been made, though large numbers still carefully and successfully preserved their own secrets; some, however, had already abandoned their masks, still retaining the fancy costumes. Among these was Mr. Mather, who wandered over the island half distraught. He had vainly searched for the Donna all day, and had been unable to enjoy anything because he could not distinguish her. Often he had believed he had found her, but again and again he had discovered that he was mistaken; so he continued his search without his mask, hoping that she would make herself known to him. At last he approached Lesparre, just before four o'clock.

"My dear Lesparre," he asked, in imploring tones, "I beg that you will tell me how to recognize Donna Lucia. I have talked with every person who could possibly be taken for her, and I acknowledge that she is so perfectly disguised that I cannot discover her. Won't you please tell me how she is dressed?"

"That I do not know myself," replied Lesparre. "She was very careful to keep the knowledge from me, for fear I might be teased into telling some one."

"Well, how is the Don dressed, then?" asked Mather. "Perhaps he will tell me about the Donna."

"I do not know how he is dressed, either," answered Lesparre. "He was as secret in his preparations as his wife."

"What! haven't you seen him to speak to since the *fête* commenced?" inquired Mather, in astonishment.

"No, I have not seen him since last night," said Lesparre. "You see, the Don and I made all arrangements yesterday afternoon, and I came down to the island to superintend the placing of the fireworks in the evening. I spent the night down here, and have not gone back to the house since I left it after dinner yesterday evening. The Don has not spoken to me to-day, and, for all that I know about him, he may not have come to his own *fête*."

Lesparre said this in a jocular manner, as though he had made quite an impossible supposition; but Mather seemed to catch an idea from it.

"By Jove! I begin to think so myself," he exclaimed, as if confirming a thought which had already occurred to him.

Just then Judge Morgan, dressed to represent the Fat Boy of the Pickwick Papers, rang a large bell, which could be heard all over the island, and the guests began flocking into the dancing-hall, preparatory to unmasking and having a grand march into the dining-room. When all were present, the bustle and talk quieted down, and all looked expectantly for the Don to give the signal for unmasking. Several of the intimate friends of the host had assembled on the *dais* at the head of the hall; and each of these looked at the others to see which among them was the Don. At last, Mather stepped forward and addressed the whole company:

"Ladies and gentlemen, somewhere among us are the host and hostess of this, the most elegant entertainment ever given in Gloster; they have been successful not only in producing hero a fairy spectacle of unequaled beauty, but also in effectually hiding themselves from discovery in their assumed characters. So far as I know, not any person present can state positively the disguise of either Don Pedro or Donna Lucia. Am I right? If any one has discovered either of them, I ask him to let us all know it before the signal for unmasking is given."

Mr. Mather waited a moment amid profound stillness, but no one replied to his request.

"Well, now," he continued, "I respectfully call upon the Don and Donna to come forward to the *dais*, assume their rightful positions as host and hostess, and give the order to unmask."

Alas! he was calling upon a pair of unfortunate travelers, who were then far on their way to New York, one in irons, and the other in tears. There was no answer nor movement among the gay masqueraders, and whispers of wonder began to run through the throng.

"Oh! come, Don Pedro," said Judge Morgan, whose appetite called loudly to be satisfied, "you have shown that your disguise defies discovery; now come forward and take your place. You can laugh at our dullness all you please, but don't keep us in suspense any longer."

Still there was no reply, and the astonishment of all the guests began to assume a form of vague suspicion. At length, Mather again spoke up, in a husky voice:

"As our host is so retiring, I will take the liberty of asking those present to unmask, and we shall then discover his disguise. Tap the bell, Morgan."

Judge Morgan immediately pulled the bell-rope three times, and, as this was the concerted signal, a gun was fired on board the steamer, and the band struck up a spirited march. The confusion of unmasking was quickly over, and the guests formed a long procession around two sides of the hall, preparatory to marching to dinner; but on the *dais* the confusion only increased, as face after face was revealed, and neither host nor hostess was to be found. Robert Harrington, Charlie Morton, Captain and Mrs. Kerr, Alexander McIntyre, Judge Taylor, Mr. and Mrs. Benson, Mr. and Mrs. Simon, Charles H. Sanders, wife and daughter, Deacon Humphrey and daughter, John Preston and family, and several others, were there, but not a trace could be seen of Don Pedro P. L. de Morito and Donna Lucia.

"Where in the devil is the Don?" was the forcible manner in which Charlie Morton expressed the sentiments of all present.

The absence of the host and hostess could not fail to cause great confusion at any time, but, in this instance, there seemed to be a host of suspicions flying about in a few minutes. Madame Sevier's absence was also noted, and a sort of panic seized every one. No movement toward the dining-room was made, but all stood irresolute, anxiously waiting for some one to determine what to do, and set them an example. Lesparre was sought for and questioned closely as to the reason for his employer's absence, but he could give no satisfactory answer. He told all inquirers that he had not seen the Don since the evening previous, and that he was as ignorant of the cause of his absence as any one. Then several questions relative to the Don's pecuniary affairs were asked, and Lesparre told all that he knew. The fact that the Don had exhausted his bank account, and had kept all his money in his own possession, set a good many people to thinking about the circumstances of his arrival there. Then the stockholders in the Diamond Company began to grow suspicious, and it took but a few minutes to put them in such a state of vague uneasiness, that they hardly knew what to believe of the man whom they so lately admired and honored. At length, a consultation was held among some of the more intimate friends of the Morito family, and it was decided to go in to dinner as if nothing had happened. If there had been any accidental detention of the Don and Donna, they would, of course, be desirous that the *fête* should proceed without them the same as if they had been present; while if there was any trickery connected with their absence, there would be no use of waiting for them to come. Accordingly, the procession was again formed, the band struck up another march, and the party proceeded toward the dining-room, headed by Henry O. Mather with Mrs. Simon, and Richard Perkins with Miss Benson.

But now occurred the most humiliating part of

the changed programme: Mr. George P. Westerfield, the caterer, refused to admit the guests to the dining-room unless the payment of his bill was guaranteed. Mr. Westerfield was a man of uncommon shrewdness. He had been accustomed to furnishing the suppers at the grand entertainments of the city for several years, and he was well acquainted with the circumstances of every person in the social world; hence, he had seen a great deal of the Don and Donna during their stay in the city. He had no more reason to suspect them of having taken flight than the others, but his native keenness and good judgment led him to protect himself, and he resolutely declined to open the dining-room doors unless his bill was guaranteed. An animated discussion immediately arose between Mr. Westerfield and the hungry guests; but nothing would induce him to change his resolve. He said that he was already out of pocket largely by the lunch he had served during the afternoon, and he could not afford to lose his dinner too.

"But Don Pedro will pay for everything," said Mr. Mather. "He is immensely wealthy, and he always pays cash promptly for all he buys."

"Yes, that may have been true heretofore, but how do I know where Don Pedro is?" queried the caterer.

"Why, he is probably accidentally detained in Gloster," replied Mather. "I have every confidence in him, and when he explains his unfortunate absence to-day, those who have suspected him will regret their hasty remarks derogatory to his character."

" Well, then, Mr. Mather," said the shrewd caterer, " if you have every confidence in Don Pedro, you can give me your guarantee that I shall be paid in full, and then I shall be happy to serve the guests the same as if the Don were here."

Mr. Mather hesitated a moment, and then refused to do anything of the kind. He was, undoubtedly, so disturbed in mind that he hardly knew what he was doing. If he had kept his wits about him, he would not have hesitated an instant to take the whole expense of the *fête* on his own shoulders rather than have such a scene occur as seemed imminent, for the sum would have been a mere bagatelle to him ; but he knew not what to think, and his suspicions ran far ahead of those of any other person present. He had on his shoulders the whole responsibility of this man, Don Pedro, for he had invited him to Gloster, and had largely vouched for his character; hence, if Don Pedro should prove to be a swindler, a great deal of blame would fall upon Mather. This feeling contributed largely to confuse and annoy him, while his passion for the Donna was another cause of embarrassment. He therefore acted in a most nervous, uncertain way, and seemed quite unable to decide what to do. Mr. Westerfield's proposition was reasonable enough, and he was willing to accept the guarantee of any other gentleman of known responsibility ; but singularly, there was not one among all who had been intimate with the Don who would make himself liable for the cost of the dinner; consequently the caterer refused to admit the throng into the dining-room. By this time every one was worked up into a state of righteous indignation. The apprehensions of the owners of Diamond Company stock were the first causes of the feeling against the Don, and the disappointing termination of the long-anticipated *fête* was another fruitful source of bitterness. As people's appetites began to call loudly for dinner, it became evident that the caterer's demands must be satisfied in some way, and finally it was agreed that the dinner should be paid for by those who partook of it at the rate of ten dollars a plate. This amount was to include the lunch and wine already furnished, and also all the provisions for dinner with the remainder of the wine provided under the contract with Don Pedro. Under this agreement, the dinner was served in the best possible style to the long array of famished and irritated masqueraders. It was not a very cheerful meal, for too many of the participants were preoccupied with thoughts of their possibly lost investments in the stock of the Diamond Company; but, under the influence of excellent viands and good wine, there was a slight reaction in the feelings of the younger members of the party, and when the last course had been served, they proposed to go on with the entertainment the same as though nothing had happened.

On entering the dancing-hall, therefore, the

greater portion of the young people prepared to enjoy the evening in dancing; but here again an obstacle presented itself: the bandsmen had taken alarm from the action of the caterer, and they refused to play unless their account was settled. Not a note would they sound until their demands were satisfied, and so the gentlemen contributed, jointly, enough to pay them in full also. The troubles and annoyances of the later portion of the *fête* were soon forgotten by the greater number of the butterflies who formed the assembly, and as they floated off to the strains of a beautiful waltz, they unanimously decided to spend the evening in a delightful dance.

Meantime, however, many of the more staid and elderly guests, having decided to go home immediately after dinner, had gone down to the steamboat landing to embark. To their astonishment they saw the steamer tied up on the opposite shore, her lights being just visible across the water. After various attempts to hail her, a reply was heard from a small boat, which contained the captain. He pulled in near the shore, and Judge Morgan, in an important tone, ordered him to bring his steamer across the river and convey a party back to Gloster.

"But who is going to pay me for the use of my steamer all day?" asked the captain, resting on his oars, within easy talking distance of the shore. Alas! he, also, had determined to follow the example of the caterer, and demand payment for his services before admitting the excursionists on board his steamer.

"Pay you!" exclaimed the horrified Ethan Allen Benson, who had paid so much for his dinner that his miserly soul was already repenting having come; "why, Don Pedro will pay you, of course."

"Well, I'd like to see him, then," said the captain.

An exciting conversation then ensued between the indignant would-be passengers and the captain of the steamer. The latter, however, had all the advantage, for he knew the masqueraders must eventually come to his terms.

"What do you mean by refusing to take us on board?" demanded Deacon Humphrey, furiously. "Don't you know that we can't stay here all night?"

"I presume not," said the captain, "and I don't suppose you will do so; but I must have payment for the use of my steamer. You can pay me in one sum by a check, or you can pay me at the rate of three dollars a head: I don't care which you choose, only I must be paid."

The altercation continued at some length, and eventually the captain said that he could not afford to waste coal in keeping steam up, and if they did not agree to his terms, he would haul fires and let his steamer stay where she was all night. This threat brought the party to his terms, and he was ordered to bring his steamer over. He refused to make more than one trip, however, and so the dancers were called away from the ballroom at the end of the first waltz, thus spoil-

"What do you mean by refusing to take us on board?" demanded Deacon Humphrey furiously.—Page—

ing their gayety almost ere it had begun. As the motley groups gathered on shore awaiting the steamer's approach, a more deeply disgusted and indignant assemblage was never known in the annals of good society, and curses, both openly and inwardly expressed against the Don, were numerous and bitter. As they passed over the gangway, the captain and clerk were at hand to collect fares, and no one was allowed to pass without paying cash or giving a check for the amount, indorsed by some well-known man of wealth and position. Finally, the whole sorrowful party was embarked, and the steamer turned her head toward Gloster. The excitement and continuous dancing, which most of those on board had indulged in during the day, had left them in a state of nervous and physical fatigue little calculated to improve their spirits, while the financial losses of many were matters of an intensely depressing influence upon them. A more ill-tempered, disappointed, and irritable cargo cannot be imagined. Their troubles were not ended even on their arrival at the wharf in Gloster, for, being so much earlier in returning than they had expected, no carriages were in attendance, and the ladies were obliged to wait on board while their escorts went to the livery stables to order carriages to take them home.

Thus ended the *fête champêtre* which had been anticipated so fondly as a new departure in the social world of Gloster. In this, however, it was a success; for, certainly, its like had never been seen before, and the guests were profoundly hopeful that they never should see its like again.

The following morning the whole city was talking of the flight of the Peruvian adventurers. Their late residence was besieged by the holders of Diamond Company stock, and the fact of their absence was then clearly established. The servants had been paid off by Madame Sevier a day or two before, and no one remained in the house except Lesparre. To all inquirers he gave the same answer as he had given at the *fête:* he was entirely ignorant of the whereabouts of the Don, and was as anxious as any one else to find him, in order to obtain his last quarter's salary, which was unpaid. The affair was a nine-days' wonder, and the mystery was still further increased in the minds of the stockholders on receiving a note from Judge Key requesting their attendance at a meeting to settle their accounts with Don Pedro. The meeting was strictly confidential, only the actual purchasers of stock being admitted. Judge Key explained to them that Don Pedro P. L. de Morito had been arrested and carried away for forgery and other crimes, but that, before going, he had assigned all his property to Judge Key to satisfy the claims of the Diamond Company stockholders.

"But how did you induce him to surrender this money and property?" was the question which was asked in various forms nearly a score of times.

"I cannot give you any particulars," replied

the Judge; "you must be satisfied to know that he made this assignment in due legal form, and that the amount which I shall realize will pay your claims nearly in full. The slight loss which you will sustain will be serviceable as a warning against throwing away your money so recklessly hereafter."

The letter of Donna Lucia to Mr. Henry O. Mather was delivered to that gentleman early the day after the *fête*. Immediately on reading it he packed his trunk and took the next train for New York. Meantime the party under the charge of Mr. Bangs arrived in New York without accident Thursday afternoon. In accordance with telegrams sent by the Peruvian Minister, the captain of the Peruvian man-of-war had taken his vessel down into the lower harbor, and was ready to sail at a moment's notice. A steam-tug was in readiness at Pier 1 to take the party out to the vessel, and Don Pedro was transferred by carriage directly from the Hudson River Railroad dépôt to the steam-tug. The party accompanied him on board the man-of-war, and the tug towed the war-ship through the Narrows.

The Don and Donna had an affectionate and sorrowful parting in the cabin, and as the ship made sail outside the bar, the tug dropped alongside; the Minister, Consul, Donna Lucia, Madame Sevier, and the detectives, leaving the Don in charge of the captain, then returned to New York in the tug.

Two days later, Mr. Mather also arrived in that city, and quickly found his way to the Donna's presence. What they said to each other may never be known, but it is probable that the interview was satisfactory to both parties. Thenceforward the Donna lived in New York in the best style, though for some reason she failed to enter the same social circle that she had known before. As long, however, as she and Mr. Mather were contented, they considered that no one else need be troubled about their arrangements. How long Mr. Mather's infatuation lasted, I have no means of knowing, as I soon recalled Madame Sevier, and lost all interest in the affair.

José Gomez was tried immediately on his arrival in Peru, and was sentenced to fifteen years' imprisonment, but he made his escape within two years from the time of his trial. His future career I never learned, but it is altogether probable that he pursued, during the remainder of his life, the same style of money-making (though perhaps on a smaller scale) as that which rendered notorious the name of Don Pedro P. L. de Morito.

THE END.

# THE POISONER AND DETECTIVES.

## CHAPTER I.

*Mr. Pinkerton, at a Water-Cure, becomes interested in a Couple, one of whom subsequently causes the Detective Operation from which this Story is written.— A wealthy Ship-Owner and his Son.—The Son "found dead."—A Woman that knows too much and too little by turns.—Mr. Pinkerton secured to solve the Mystery.—Chicago after the Great Fire.*

DURING the summer of 1870, I was spending a few weeks at a water-cure for the benefit of my health. The place was one not widely advertised nor generally known, and the number of frequenters was not large; hence, I became somewhat acquainted with most of the visitors, and, as a matter of habit, noticed their traits and peculiarities with more attentiveness than a casual meeting would naturally warrant. Of course I had no idea that I ever should make any use of my observations, but I simply kept up a customary oversight upon everything about me. Among those whom I thus noticed was a lady, about forty-five years of age, and her son, who was about twenty-six years old. The mother, Mrs. R. S. Trafton, was a pleasant woman, well preserved, and comparatively youthful in appearance. She was afflicted by a rheumatic affection, which caused her to visit these springs for relief; and her son accompanied her partly to look after her comfort, and partly to obtain a vacation from work. He was a tall, robust young man, with fine physique and strong constitution, but he showed the effects of overwork. I always make a point of observing the character and habits of those around me, and long experience has given me considerable accuracy of judgment with regard to my acquaintances, even where I am not an intimate associate with them. The more I saw of Stanley D. Trafton, the more I was interested in him. His mother was devoted to him, and he to her, so that they were rarely seen apart.

Springville was a very quiet, dull place, and, aside from the invalid visitors, there was nothing about the society to relieve the usual monotony of an uninteresting country town; hence, I was thrown largely upon my own resources for amusement, and I had little else to do except to observe the different strangers and speculate about them. Among them all there were none who afforded me a more interesting study than young Trafton, and, although I never formed his acquaintance, I began to feel that I understood his character quite thoroughly.

He was about five feet ten inches in height, of compact, muscular build, full chest, stout limbs, and erect carriage. His complexion was clear and healthy, his features regular, his expression intelligent and open, and his manners were very frank and attractive to most people. His general appearance was that of an intelligent, handsome man, of more than ordinary ability and steady character.

I learned that his father, Mr. Richard S. Trafton, of Cleveland, was a wealthy ship-owner and merchant, and that his son attended largely to the purchase of grain in the West for shipment in his father's vessels. I judged that young Trafton was a good business man, with an eye to details as well as general results, and while he had no appearance of being small-minded, he did not despise economy in his business affairs. He did not seem like a person who would spend money for mere display or effect; yet, neither would he deny himself the comforts and luxuries belonging to a man of his wealth and position in society. There was nothing of the profligate about him, and his devotion to his mother showed that he must have a genuine and hearty respect for the whole sex.

In the course of a few weeks I left Springville, much improved in health, and I soon forgot all about Mrs. Trafton and her son, until the latter was brought under my notice again amid very tragical and sorrowful circumstances.

Early in the winter of the following year, I was deeply engrossed in business, having an accumulation of cases on hand which taxed my ingenuity and energies to the utmost. I therefore placed almost all of the less important operations in the hands of my superintendent, Mr. Francis Warner, though I kept a general supervisory control over every case on the books of the Agency. One morning, as I was conversing with Mr. Warner, two gentlemen were admitted to my office by my confidential clerk, who informed me that they had suspicions of foul play as the cause of the death of one of their friends, and they wished the circumstances fully investigated by the Agency. The gentlemen were Mr. John Updike, of Cleveland, and Captain Edward R. Dalton, a ship captain, of Buffalo. They introduced themselves, produced credentials and references, and then told me the following story:

In November previous, Mr. Stanley D. Trafton, of Cleveland, left that city to go to Chicago. He was the son of Mr. Richard S. Trafton, a wealthy shipper of Cleveland, and the father was anxious to keep his vessels employed. Captain Dalton commanded one of Mr. Trafton's schooners, and he expected to arrive in Chicago harbor about November 20. Accordingly, young Trafton was to meet the vessel there, and, in case she did not obtain a charter at a paying rate, he was to purchase a cargo of oats on his own account. He brought, therefore, a considerable amount of money and negotiable paper. He had about eight hundred dollars in currency, two thousand five hundred dollars in United States five-twenty bonds, and a letter from his father authorizing him to draw upon him for a large amount. The bonds were the usual coupon bonds of the denomination of five hundred dollars each, and fortunately Mr. Trafton, senior, had the numbers of these securities.

Stanley Trafton arrived in Chicago November 22, and found the schooner awaiting him. He tried to obtain a room in one of the hotels, but he soon gave this up as a hopeless task, for the reason that there was no hotel in the city which was not already crowded almost to an unsafe degree. He then took up his quarters on board the schooner, getting his meals at a restaurant. This was not at all pleasant, and he finally discovered a place where furnished rooms were to let near one of the hotels. He therefore announced to Captain Dalton that he had taken a room at 92 West Madison street. They met each other every day, however, and at last, seeing no profit to be made by purchasing grain in the then condition of the market, Mr. Trafton informed the captain that he might sail for Cleveland on Friday, December 1. On Thursday he visited the captain and promised to return on board again that evening; he failed to do so, however, and the schooner sailed next morning.

Five days afterward, Captain Dalton received a dispatch, sent by a firm of commission merchants in Chicago, announcing that Stanley D. Trafton had been found dead in his bed. Mr. Updike, who was a warm friend of the family, and Captain Dalton, then visited Chicago, arriving December 8. They found the body of Mr. Trafton at the Morgue awaiting claimants, together with a quantity of valuables which had been in his possession when he died. There were two five-twenty bonds, one being torn in two pieces, a set of diamond studs, a small amount of loose change, and three one-hundred-dollar bills. A coroner's inquest had been held, and a verdict of death by congestion of the lungs had been rendered.

The circumstances of young Trafton's death, as related by the officials in charge of the body, created considerable suspicion in the minds of Messrs. Updike and Dalton, who, therefore, proceeded to investigate the affair. In the first place, they were well aware that fifteen hundred dollars in bonds, and nearly five hundred dollars in currency, were missing; secondly, they learned that Trafton had been found dead in bed Friday morning, December 1, only about eighteen hours after he had left Captain Dalton in perfect health.

Accordingly, Mr. Updike and Captain Dalton visited his late lodging-place, which was kept by a woman named May Sanford.

The building was a two-story frame residence, which, like thousands of others after the Great Fire, had been rearranged for business purposes. The lower floor was occupied as a furniture store, while the second floor was also partly occupied by business offices. A covered stairway on the side led to the upper story, and, while the front hall bedroom, the front parlor and the next room back, were used as offices, the rear portion

"He was lying in bed with froth about his mouth and a ghastly look on his face."—Page—

was occupied by Mrs. Sanford, who rented most of her rooms as sleeping apartments.

On stating their object in calling, the two gentlemen were admitted to Mrs. Sanford's sitting-room, and she then gave her account of the circumstances connected with young Trafton's death. She stated that she met him first on the street and recognized him as an old acquaintance who had been intimate with her husband and herself when they lived in Buffalo; that he stopped and talked with her for a time, and, learning that she had furnished rooms to let, he said he would rent one. He stayed there five days, and, on the sixth, which was Thursday, November 30, he came to his room in the evening and complained of feeling unwell. He had been drinking very hard all the week, and she said that this evening he was quite drunk. He complained that he could not keep anything on his stomach, and asked Mrs. Sanford to cook something nice for him. Accordingly she boiled a chicken, but he could not eat it, and he then went to bed. During the evening, she heard him snoring very loudly as she passed his door, but she thought nothing of it, and went to bed at eleven o'clock. About seven o'clock next morning, she knocked at his door, but he made no answer, and she pushed the door open, the bolt being a very slight one. She then found Mr. Trafton lying diagonally across the bed, with his head hanging down and froth on his lips. Becoming alarmed at his appearance, she called in a gentleman named

Taylor G. Pratt, who occupied her back parlor as a real estate office and sleeping-room. Mr. Pratt examined the body of Mr. Trafton and told her that he was dead, advising her to inform the police authorities of the fact. She immediately closed the room and went to the nearest police station, where she reported the circumstances relative to the death of Mr. Trafton so far as she knew them, and asked what she should do with the body. The police sergeant promised to send the coroner as soon as possible to make an investigation, and she was instructed to leave the body and room untouched until the coroner should arrive. That evening an inquest was held by the County Physician, and a verdict of death by congestion of the lungs was rendered. Mrs. Sanford gave an account of the finding of the money and bonds, which exactly agreed with that given by the County Physician, whom she assisted in making search for Trafton's valuables. In one boot, lying under his head, they found a five-twenty bond for five hundred dollars and half of another one, the remainder of this torn bond being found in the right-hand pocket of his pantaloons. In his vest pocket were found three United States notes for one hundred dollars each, and a small quantity of loose change. A set of diamond studs still remained in his shirt, and, as the story was related by her, there was nothing suspicious about the affair except the suddenness of his death.

Having heard all that Mrs. Sanford and the

County Physician had to say on the subject, Mr. Updike and Captain Dalton took charge of the body, and shipped it to Cleveland, where they placed it in the hands of four experienced surgeons, with instructions to make a thorough and careful examination as to the cause of death. The first thing noticed by them was an evidence of considerable external violence on the right side, over the liver, there being a large bruise, about the size of a saucer, apparently caused by a blow. The coagulation of blood beneath the skin showed that this injury must have been caused during Trafton's lifetime, but very shortly before his death. A similar, though smaller bruise, was found on his thigh, while several bruises on the base of the neck and throat showed that the windpipe must have been severely compressed just previous to death. None of these marks had been noticed by the County Physician in making the post-mortem examination, and it seemed probable that he had first guessed at the cause of death, and then made only a sufficient examination to find some corroboration of his theory. The Cleveland surgeons had great difficulty in accounting for Trafton's death, but they were unanimous in scouting the theory of death by congestion of the lungs. They found the body to be healthy in every part, except the external bruises; and, while these were not of a sufficiently serious character to account for the death of so robust a man, they could find no other cause whatever.

These facts, together with the disappearance of fifteen hundred dollars in bonds, and about five hundred dollars in currency, which Trafton was known to have had in his possession, caused his relatives and friends to believe that he had been murdered for his money, and that the murderer had been shrewd enough to leave a large portion of the plunder to allay suspicion. The trick had proven to be a most excellent one, for, as the County Physician afterward acknowledged, the idea of foul play never occurred to him, owing to the apparent lack of incentive thereto; had there been no money, or only a small amount, found on the body, he would have made a much more rigid examination; but no suspicion even crossed his mind, and he acted with the haste which characterized almost all operations in Chicago at that time.

In order, therefore, to discover all the facts in the case, and to recover, if possible, the missing money and bonds, Mr. Trafton, senior, had decided to put the affair in my hands for a thorough investigation, and Mr. Opdike and Captain Dalton had called upon me for that purpose.

Having heard their statement, I asked a number of questions, which elicited the following additional information:

On returning to Chicago the second time, they had again visited Mrs. Sanford, and found that she had taken every particle of furniture out of the room where Trafton had died. At the time of their call, they saw a policeman whom she called Charlie, with whom she seemed to be very intimate. She said that Charlie was the first person to see Trafton after she found he was dead that morning, he having been sent over by the sergeant as soon as she reported the fact. This story contradicted her former statement, that she first called Mr. Pratt into the room; moreover, the sergeant of police had told them that the policeman did not go to the room at all, but merely took the number of the house and went away.

At this interview, Mrs. Sanford gave them the blank power to draw upon Mr. Trafton, senior, saying that she had found it at the foot of the bed since their former visit. She also showed them a gold coin which she said young Trafton had given her as a keepsake. Both gentlemen recognized this coin as one which Trafton prized very highly for some reason, he having refused to part with it even to his mother; it seemed hardly possible that he should have given it to a chance acquaintance like Mrs. Sanford.

During this conversation she claimed to have lent Mr. Trafton three hundred and twenty-five dollars, though she did not seem greatly disappointed when they refused to repay her that amount. Mr. Updike gave her twenty-five dollars, however, to pay for Mr. Trafton's board and lodging, and to recompense her for her trouble. The story that Trafton had borrowed money of her was absurd on its face, and she acted as if she hardly expected to be believed.

Before coming to Chicago this time, Mr. Updike had written to Mr. T. B. Vernon, of Buffalo, asking for information relative to the antecedents of this Mrs. Sanford. Mr. Vernon had replied that she had a very bad reputation in Buffalo, having been divorced from her husband for adultery, and having been arrested in March previous for being drunk and disorderly. She had a paramour at that time, named James McSandy, a police-station keeper, and it was supposed that he had gone West with her.

Another circumstance had been noticed by Captain Dalton, which led him to believe that Trafton had been murdered with his clothes on, and afterward undressed and put to bed: the sole of one of his boots was covered with whitewash, as if it had been violently pressed and scraped along a wall. Now, the room where he was found had been newly whitewashed when they arrived there, so that any marks on the wall made by him in his struggles would be wholly obliterated.

Having learned all the facts bearing upon the case known by my visitors, I informed them of my terms for conducting an investigation of this character, and sketched a hasty outline of my plan of operation. As they had already hinted their suspicions to a member of the city detective force, who was inclined to make light of them, I suggested that they inform him that they had changed their minds in the matter, having learned from the Cleveland physicians that death was surely caused by congestion of the lungs. They then took their departure, saying that they would lay my plan before Mr. Richard S. Trafton, and he would telegraph to me whether I should proceed with the operation. On Christmas day, I received a telegram from Mr. Trafton, briefly instructing me to proceed, and my plan was put in operation at once.

Before proceeding further with the history of my connection with this case, it will be necessary to remind the reader of the anomalous condition of social and business affairs in Chicago at the time of which I write; for, without any explanation, he might have difficulty in understanding many things in connection with the story.

It will be remembered that the Great Fire of Chicago occurred October 8 and 9, 1871, and this case was placed in my hands only about nine weeks afterward. At the time of Mr. Trafton's death, a pall of smoke hung over the city, and, at night, the still-smouldering heaps of coal throughout the "burned district" glowed like volcanic fissures, casting a weird fantastic light about the ruins, and illumining the clouds of smoke overhead with a ruddy glow which was visible for miles away. The streets were filled with dust and ashes, while the fumes of carbonic acid gas were sometimes almost stifling. To venture, at any time, into the waste of ruins, which stretched more than three miles in one direction, through the formerly richest portion of the city, was not a pleasant undertaking; but to make such an excursion at night was attended with more hazard than most peaceably-disposed men would care to run. There were no gaslights, no sidewalks, no street indicators; in many places, piles of stone and brick were heaped in almost impassable barricades from one side of the street to the other; all landmarks were gone, and the old resident was as liable to lose his way as the stranger.

The city, moreover, was crowded with what is sometimes called "a floating population," a species of driftwood, or scum, gathered from every quarter of the globe; indeed, a large per centage seemed to have come straight from the infernal regions, with all the passions and habits incidental to a prolonged residence there. Hence, the labors of the police force were increased to an extent which taxed their abilities to the utmost, and made the task of protecting the respectable portion of the community about all that could be required of them; that they should be apt to suspect foul play, in a case where the coroner had no suspicions, was hardly to be expected. Besides this, there was nothing settled on any permanent foundation; business men flitted hither and thither wherever they could best obtain accommodations for the time being, and whence people came or whither they went was a matter which no one had time to inquire into, much less to investigate.

The destruction of thousands of business blocks and dwellings left the city without adequate accommodations for offices and residences, even for its own regular population; but when the rush of strangers swelled the aggregate nearly twenty per cent., there seemed hardly sleeping-rooms for them all. Dwelling-houses by thousands were converted into stores, manufactories, and offices, until fabulous prices were offered for the merest closets in the vicinity of the new temporary business centers. Every hotel was thronged from the basement to the Mansard roof, and late arrivals were oftentimes happy if they could get a straw mattress on a billiard-table, or an army cot in a hall.

I call especial attention to these things to account for certain apparent anomalies in the action of different persons connected with this tragedy. For instance: a young gentleman of Mr. Trafton's wealth and respectability would never have rented a mean little room in a petty lodging-house, if he could have found any other place equally convenient to business; the County Physician would not have taken things so much for granted, if he had not been so hard at work and so pressed for time, owing to the immense army of gratuitous patients who thronged the offices of the County Agent and the Relief and Aid Society; the police would not have been so remiss in failing to examine into the death of Mr. Trafton, if they had not had their hands full of other business to an unprecedented extent; and, lastly, when I came to work up the case, I should not have had so much difficulty in finding witnesses, if it had not been that people came and went through Chicago like the waves of the sea in mid-ocean, leaving no trace by which they could be followed or identified.

These circumstances, combined with certain facts which will appear in the course of this narrative, made the task assigned me one of unusual difficulty. Mr. Warner was intrusted with the general management of the case, though he frequently consulted me in relation to it; and, though we were continually working in the dark, we never despaired of our eventual success.

## CHAPTER II.

*The Detectives at Work.—Mrs. Sanford Described.— Charlie, the Policeman.—Mrs. Sanford develops Interest in Government Bonds.—Chicago Relief and Aid Benefits.—Mrs. Sanford's Story of Trafton's Death.—A nice little Arrangement.—Mrs. Sanford explains to the Detective her method of "Quieting People."—Ingham "Makes a Raise."— Mrs. Sanford fears being Haunted, but is not easily Frightened.*

THE day after Christmas a tall, well-built man called at No. 92 Madison street, and asked for the lady of the house. Mrs. Sanford soon entered the sitting-room, and the stranger said that, having seen the sign, "Furnished Rooms to Rent," he had called to engage lodgings. He introduced himself as John Ingham, and said that he was a book-keeper, temporarily out of employment. Mrs. Sanford received him with great cordiality, and seemed much pleased to have him as a lodger. She said that she had no suitable room just then, but that a married couple were about to leave, and then Mr. Ingham could have their room. She then showed him through the house. The two front rooms were occupied by an insurance company, and the back parlor was used as a real estate office and sleeping-room by two brothers, named Pratt. At the head of the stairs was a small bedroom, through which it was necessary to pass to obtain admission to the rear part of the house. The passageway from this bedroom to the sitting-room was made by partitioning off a small entry from the back parlor. There were four doors in this sitting-room: one opened from the entry; at the opposite side was one which opened into another entry; the third was adjoining this second door, and it opened into the large bedroom occupied by the married couple; the fourth door led into Mrs. Sanford's own room. At the end of the back entry was an unfurnished room and a kitchen. The front bedroom was occupied by two young women who worked in a bindery, and their accommodations could hardly have been very agreeable, as every one was obliged to pass through their room on the way to the other rooms in the rear.

Mrs. Sanford was a good-looking woman, about thirty-two years old. Her features were quite pretty, and her expression was pleasing. She was very plump, and her skin was smooth and soft. She had brown hair, a nose slightly *retroussé*, and a pleasant smile. Her eyes, however, were a bluish gray, cold and watchful as those of a hawk. She might have been called handsome but for the effects of dissipation, which were plainly visible in her face. She had a pleasant voice, and she was naturally easy in her manners. If she was in a good humor, she could be quite fascinating; and almost any stranger, after talking with her for a few minutes, would feel satisfied that she had once occupied a social station far above that in which she was now placed. She had a good education, and very frequently she would give evidences of having had a wide range of really good reading. At times, her recitations and declamations, wholly from memory, were exceptionally fine, and, but for her two ruling passions, she might have been an actress of a high rank.

She had two controlling vices, one natural, the other acquired: her greed for money was inborn, and it seemed to absorb at times every other faculty; while the habit of using morphine had become so fastened upon her, that she could not shake it off. She was a most contradictory medley of compounds, however, and while her thirst for money seemed to overpower all other considerations with her as a general rule, on some occasions she would be as wasteful and careless of expense as the most prodigal woman in the world. But when she had set her mind on the acquisition of any particular money or piece of personal property, there was no length to which she would not go to attain her object. The mere sight of money seemed to act upon her with an effect almost of insanity, and she would then have no regard for consequences until after she had secured the coveted prize.

It will be readily understood, of course, that Mr. John Ingham, usually known as Jack, was one of my detectives, sent to obtain lodging with Mrs. Sanford, to win her confidence and learn all that he could.

Ingham agreed to take the large room in the rear, but he wanted to come immediately. Mrs. Sanford agreed, therefore, to make up a bed for him on the sofa in the sitting-room until the departure of Mr. and Mrs. Graves, who were then occupying the back room. Having agreed upon the terms, Ingham went away, promising to return that night. Accordingly, he came in again about nine o'clock in the evening, and found that Mrs. Sanford was entertaining a policeman. He was a rather good-looking fellow, and was in full uniform, except his star. He remained until nearly twelve o'clock, and when he went out, Mrs. Sanford followed him to the door, with many affectionate caresses and tender remarks. After he had gone, she began to converse very confidentially with Ingham, telling him that she was engaged to be married to Charlie, the policeman.

"Don't you think a policeman is good enough to marry?" she asked.

"Oh, yes!" replied Ingham, "and your Charlie seems to be a fine fellow."

"Well, he is awfully fond of me," she continued, "and he spends all his time off duty with me; but I don't know whether I care to marry him. What do you think about it, Mr. Ingham?"

"You ought not to be in any hurry about it," he replied, "for you might see some one whom you would like better."

"Oh! I have had a number of offers lately," she said, laughing. "I have had to work hard for a living, and have saved up quite a good sum; and, besides that, my father sent me two thousand dollars a short time ago, so that I have a snug little fortune. But Charlie doesn't know anything about it, and I shan't tell him until after we are married."

After some further conversation, she said that she was hungry, and wished she had some one to go to the nearest restaurant with. Ingham volunteered to act as her escort, and they went out together. While eating supper, she suddenly asked whether government bonds were good property to invest in. Ingham replied that they were very good indeed, since the interest was payable in gold, and there were no taxes to pay upon them.

"Well, suppose you should lose them," she queried; "could any one who found them make use of them without being discovered?"

"Yes, I think so," said Ingham. "There is no means of learning how they came into the bearer's possession."

"Did you ever own any?" she inquired.

"No, but I used to cash the coupons for my employer in Louisville, and I know a good deal about them."

"What business were you in there?" she asked, with a considerable show of interest.

"I was bookkeeper for a wholesale liquor firm, and the senior partner used to put all his money into government bonds."

"Why did you leave Louisville?" she continued, seemingly desirous of learning as much as possible of his history.

"Oh! well, I got hard up," he replied, evasively, "and there was some mistake in my accounts which I couldn't explain satisfactorily, so I thought best to go out of town for awhile. You know we are all liable to mistakes when we are hard up."

"Yes, indeed, I understand," she replied, in a satisfied tone of voice. "What are you going to do here?"

"Well, I can't tell yet. I have a small job of closing up a set of books for the year, and when that is done I shall look around for something else. I'm not particular what I do, if it pays well."

"Perhaps you could get employment from the Relief and Aid Society," she said, "and then you could get lots of nice things for me. This man,

Graves, whose room you are to have, is employed there, and he steals enough to keep the woman who is with him in good style."

"Why, aren't they married?" asked Ingham.

"No, I don't believe they are married," she replied, "and I've given them notice to leave. Mr. Graves gets hardly any pay, but he brings her all kinds of presents, and she sells them to the pawnbrokers."

On their return to the house, Mrs. Sanford made up a bed on the sofa for Ingham, and then went to her room.

The day following, Ingham went down to his work on the South Side, and did not return until eight o'clock in the evening. He said that he knew of a chance to buy a cigar stand in one of the leading hotels, and that he would like to do it if he could raise the money. Mrs. Sanford seemed to have taken a great fancy to her new lodger, for she told him that she would assist him, if it did not cost too much.

"By the way, I was sorry you were not here this afternoon," she said. "There was a very pretty young lady friend of mine here, and I would like to have you meet her."

"What was her name?'

"Ida Musgrove."

"Have you known her long?"

"Oh! no; I have only lived in Chicago a few months. I used to live in Cleveland before I separated from my husband, and we had a fine stone-front house there."

"How did you happen to leave your husband?" asked Ingham.

" Well, he began running after other women, and, though I forgave him several times, when he brought his mistress to live in the same house with me, I left him."

"He must have been a very hard case to do such a thing as that," said Ingham, sympathizingly.

" Yes; and then he sold the house, promising to give me half if I would sign the deed; but he never gave me a cent, so that I have had to work hard to support myself and my little girl, who is boarding at Riverside. However, I am all right now, for my father sent me three thousand dollars the other day, and I shall have plenty of money hereafter."

"Hadn't you any friends here who would have helped you?" asked Ingham.

" No, I hardly knew any one; but I met an old friend from Cleveland about a month ago, and he died here in my house. Haven't I told you about that?"

" No, indeed; how was it?"

" Well, you see, this Mr. Trafton was a former lover of mine in Cleveland, and he was very rich and handsome. He came here last month and took the back room in my house. He was very kind to me, and wanted to marry me; but he drank hard for a week and began to show the effects of his dissipation. Finally, he came home one evening quite drunk, and he complained of feeling sick. I boiled a chicken for him, but he could not eat it, and he went to bed. Next morning he did not call me as usual, and I went to his door and knocked; there was no answer, and so I pushed open his door. He was lying in bed with froth about his mouth and a ghastly look on his face which frightened me terribly. Then I called in Mr. Pratt, who roomed in the back parlor, and he said that Mr. Trafton was dead. When the coroner came, we found twenty-five thousand dollars in Mr. Trafton's pockets, besides his diamond studs and other property. Oh! it was a dreadful thing for me to think that such a handsome fellow as my Stanley should die in my house."

"What was the matter with him?" asked Ingham.

"The coroner held an inquest, and a post-mortem examination showed that he died of congestion of the lungs."

"Did you know that he had all that money with him?" asked Ingham, significantly lowering his voice.

"No, I did not know it until afterward," she replied; "why do you ask?"

"Oh! for no special reason; but," he added, in a determined way, "you might have helped yourself to some of that money and no one would have been the wiser. I tell you, I wouldn't have let such a chance as that slip."

"Well, I know I might have taken some of it," she answered, thoughtfully, "but I couldn't steal from him. Oh! I have mighty good credit among people here now, for every one knows about that money, and that I could have taken it all if I had wished. A reporter came here, and afterward stated in the paper that there was only a small amount, about fifteen hundred dollars, found; but I had it corrected."

She prattled on for some time about her intimacy with Mr. Trafton, until she was interrupted by a noise in the hall bedroom. On going to see what was the matter, she found the two bindery girls in great excitement, as they had been awakened by a strange man in their room. Ingham also went to the door, when Mrs. Sanford told him to get his revolver, as she wanted to shoot any man who should try to break into her rooms. No one was found, but the lower hall door was open, and Ingham went down to lock it. On his return, Mrs. Sanford said that she had a revolver, and that she knew how to use it too. It was about midnight before they retired, but Mrs. Sanford seemed to consider it quite an early hour.

The next day Ingham was again absent until evening, and Mrs. Sanford scolded him a little for not staying more time with her. He replied that he had been out looking for a chance to make a raise.

"What kind of a raise?" she asked.

"Oh! any kind," he replied; "I'm not particular, provided I can get enough to pay for the trouble. If I knew of any good hiding place, I could get a lot of valuable goods some night without much work, and with no danger."

"You can bring them here, and I will hide them so that they will never be found," she replied, in a whisper.

"That will be a pretty hard thing to do, for these policemen and detectives can find almost anything if they want to. I shouldn't like to bring any plunder here and then have it found in your house, for you would then be punished for receiving stolen goods.

"Never you fear about me; I know some sharp tricks if I *am* a woman. I can hide anything you bring, and if they get after you, I can hide you too."

Ingham then told her about various criminal devices for obtaining money, which he had practiced in New York several years before, and called her attention to the ease with which they might rob strangers by the "panel" game. She was very much interested, and said that she could easily get hold of some fellow with plenty of money, make him drunk, and then rob him.

"How I wish you had been here when Mr. Trafton died, for you could have got away with ten or fifteen thousand dollars without any difficulty whatever."

"Yes, it would have been a good chance," he replied; "but I guess we can do nearly as well, if you will be true to me and help me."

"You can depend upon me for anything," she answered, with great determination, but adding suddenly, in a cautious tone, "that is, anything except murder, you know. I shouldn't like to do that. But I would protect you even if you should kill a man—not willfully—not willfully, you understand; but if you should be obliged to do it to save yourself, I should not blame you very much."

"I am determined to 'make a raise,' soon," said Ingham; "but I don't know whether I can trust you."

"How so?" she asked, as if greatly surprised.

"I am afraid you will 'give me away' to that policeman whom you think so much of."

"You need not fear anything of the kind," she said, leaning forward, and speaking slowly and emphatically. "I can help you a great deal, and I would never betray you to any one. I don't think so much of Charlie as I pretend to."

Soon afterward she had to go into the unfurnished room to get something, and she asked Ingham to hold the light for her.

"Why can't you hold it yourself?" he asked.

"Well, to tell the truth, I don't like to go into that room alone," she replied, trying to laugh in an unconcerned way.

"Why not? You aren't afraid of anything, are you?"

"No, not afraid; but I have never felt like going in there since Mr. Trafton died there. I cannot help recollecting the way he looked when I first saw him hanging over the bedside, with the froth on his lips. I took out all the furniture on that account, but I am going to furnish it again next week, as I can get a good rent for it."

Ingham went with her as she requested, and he noticed that all the time she was in the room overhauling a trunk containing the things she wanted, she was very restless and nervous. Several times when she heard a sudden noise she would start and turn pale, as if much frightened.

Presently the two girls occupying the front room came in and said that they should leave next day, as they were afraid of a man coming into their room as one had done the night before. Mrs. Sanford was evidently not sorry to have them go, and they soon went to bed.

Ingham and Mrs. Sanford then talked together about their plans for getting money for some time. Her whole mind seemed bent upon one object,—to obtain money; and she seemed to have no scruples whatever as to the means employed.

"Don't you know of any wealthy fellow who carries considerable money about with him?" asked Ingham.

"Oh! yes; I know two or three who come here to do business, and I expect one from Canada next week. He always has plenty of money with him, so that I have no doubt we could get a big sum out of him."

"Does he ever drink?" he asked; "I don't want to tackle a sober man, if I can help it."

"That needn't trouble you," she replied, in a whisper; "I can give him something to keep him quiet."

"How can you do that?" he inquired, with apparent astonishment.

She then showed him a bottle of morphine, and said that she always kept it for her own use, and that she knew how to give just enough to produce a deep sleep. They finally agreed to lay their plans together, and to make a big haul at the first opportunity.

Ingham went out again on his prospecting tour next day, but when he returned, in the evening, he had not discovered any good place for a robbery. He told Mrs. Sanford, however, that he thought he could get a quantity of counterfeit money at a very low price, and that they could pass a great deal of it, if they were skillful. She liked the idea, and said that she could pass it on a great many people who would never recollect where they received it. She also said that she had a good place to hide it, and that some time she would show him where she had hidden some property, when the police were looking for it.

"Oh! how I wish you had been here when that man died with eighteen thousand dollars in bonds in his pockets!" she exclaimed. "You could have helped yourself to all you wanted."

"Yes, indeed," he replied, "I should have made myself rich for life."

"But could you have disposed of the bonds without being suspected?" she asked. "Wouldn't his friends catch you if they had the numbers of the bonds?"

"Oh! that wouldn't make any difference.

There are millions of dollars afloat of these bonds, and they cannot be traced any more than money."

"His bonds were all for five hundred dollars each, and they had little tickets on the end, which could be cut off for the interest," she said. "I saw them when the coroner was examining them."

"Yes, they were undoubtedly five-twenty bonds, and were worth their face in gold."

"Well, another time, if we get such a chance," she said, "we will take enough to make ourselves comfortable, and leave the rest to remove suspicion."

On the following day, Ingham returned to his room at Mrs. Sanford's about three o'clock in the afternoon, and she told him that the two girls and Mr. and Mrs. Graves had left. She said that she had a great fuss with the latter, and that they went away in a state of high wrath against her; besides this, she had had a quarrel with Charlie, the policeman, who had sided with Mrs. Graves during their quarrel. Mrs. Sanford said, further, that Charlie had acted very meanly in not making her any Christmas or New Year's present, and she didn't care whether he came there again or not. She said that Mrs. Graves had left her trunk to be called for, and that there was no doubt she had stolen some of Mrs. Sanford's towels and other things. She then went to the trunk, opened it, and took out a number of articles, which she said belonged to her. She took the articles into the kitchen, and secreted them in a hole in the floor, where she was able to take up a board. Ingham thought it rather strange that she should hide these things, if they were her own property, but he said nothing on the subject to Mrs. Sanford.

About five o'clock a young lady called to see Mrs. Sanford, and they seemed very intimate with each other. When they entered the sitting-room, Mrs. Sanford said:

"Ida, let me introduce to you Mr. Ingham; this is Miss Ida Musgrove, Mr. Ingham."

"Mrs. Sanford has spoken of you in such complimentary terms, Miss Ida," said Ingham, "that I have been very anxious to meet you."

"Now, how can you be so foolish, May," said Miss Ida, addressing Mrs. Sanford; "you always talk about me so extravagantly that people are very much disappointed when they meet me."

"Oh! that is quite impossible," chimed in Ingham. "I am sure that Mrs. Sanford hardly did you justice."

"I see, Mr. Ingham, that you are, like all the rest of your sex, a great flatterer," simpered Miss Ida, who was evidently greatly pleased with his compliments, but who wished to appear too modest to believe him to be in earnest.

Miss Ida was a brilliant brunette of fine features and figure. She was stylish and graceful in her appearance, and her dress showed remarkably good taste. She was very vivacious and merry, but a close observer would have noticed that she was not endowed with much sentiment, and a physiognomist would have said that she was more interested in the size of a man's fortune than in his looks or powers to please. The three chatted together very pleasantly for some time, and when Miss Ida rose to go, she said that she hoped to have the pleasure of seeing Mr. Ingham again; but she did not inform him where she lived, and was apparently rather indifferent with regard to him.

The next day Mrs. Sanford refurnished the back room where Mr. Trafton had died, and Ingham took the room vacated by the Graveses. On the same day, Mrs. Sanford missed her watch, and, after searching for it everywhere, she came to the conclusion that it had been stolen. She was greatly distressed about it, but she could not imagine who could have taken it.

A few days after this, Ingham came hurriedly into the sitting-room looking as if he had been running hard. He found Mrs. Sanford and Miss Ida in the kitchen, but when the former came into the sitting-room, he gave her a significant look, and said that he had "made a raise." Mrs. Sanford was highly pleased, but she had no time to make inquiries, as Miss Ida came in from the kitchen a moment later. They took supper together, and had a very gay time, as both Ingham and Mrs. Sanford were quite excited over the former's adventure. After Miss Ida had gone home, Ingham gave Mrs. Sanford ten dollars, and told her that he and another man had followed a stranger into the "Burnt District" just at dusk, and while the other man choked the stranger, Ingham had "gone through" his pockets. Owing to the fact that there were very few persons and no gas-lamps in their vicinity, they had not been observed in their work of robbery until they let the man go, when his shouts had attracted attention. He said that some men had chased them, and that he had escaped by running into a lumber-yard, where he had hidden the greater part of the plunder. He said that he had obtained a roll of bills, but that he could not tell how much money there was in all, as he had not had time to count it. He said that he did not expect to get much out of it, as he would be obliged to divide with his partner. The day following, Ingham, on his return to the house in the evening, found Mrs. Sanford standing in her room fixing her hair, while a man stood beside her with his arm around her waist. The door of her room was open, so that Ingham could not help seeing them, and he did not stop, but went straight to his own room. Mrs. Sanford soon afterward came to his door and told him that the man he had seen was Mr. Taylor G. Pratt, the real estate agent, who occupied the back parlor; that he was one of her best friends, and that he wanted to marry her. He had been away for the holidays, and had only just returned. She had told him that Ingham was her brother from Detroit, and that he was going to remain with her for some time. Ingham was then introduced to Mr. Pratt, and they talked with each other until supper-time. Pratt was a middle-aged man, with a mean-looking face and suspicious manner. They went to a restaurant for supper, and the gentlemen paid the bill equally. Pratt seemed to expect Mrs. Sanford to pay her share, and this made her angry, though she said nothing about the matter at the time. When alone with Ingham, however, she said that Pratt was a miserly cub, with no generosity whatever. She borrowed five dollars from him, nevertheless, and then invented a story about having lost the money to escape paying it back.

The next evening, when Ingham returned to his lodgings, he found Mrs. Sanford in a sad plight; one eye was wholly closed and discolored, while her whole face was bruised and inflamed to such an extent as to make her an unpleasant object to look at. Charlie Stokes, the policeman, was sitting by the stove, and Mrs. Sanford, with her head done up in wet towels, was moaning on the sofa. She explained that Mrs. Graves had been there, and had seized her by the throat, beaten, scratched, and kicked her until she was perfectly helpless from her injuries. Charlie, the policeman, was trying to condole with her, but he was evidently out of favor, for she finally told him to go out and not bother her any longer.

Ingham told her that she certainly ought to have Mrs. Graves arrested and punished severely, and he petted her so nicely that she said he was her best friend, and that she would do anything for him. He prepared a dressing for her black eye, and got some supper for her, telling her that on Monday—that day being Saturday—she ought to get out a warrant for the arrest of Mrs. Graves.

"Why didn't you hit her with the poker?" he asked.

"I did pick it up," she replied, "but I was afraid to hit her for fear I should kill her."

"Well, it would have served her just right, for she had no business to attack you first."

"I know that; but if I had killed her, just think how awful it would be! Why, her ghost would haunt me forever after. I don't want to be haunted. I'm afraid now to go into the room where Trafton died, and I wouldn't go in there alone after dark for fifty dollars."

Ingham comforted her all he could, but finally he said that he must go out for a time, and he did not return until about ten o'clock. He then went upstairs quietly, and went to bed. Two or three hours later, a heavy, groaning sound was heard in the house. It was difficult to tell exactly whence it came, but Ingham heard Mrs. Sanford spring up and open her door. He did the same, and saw her listening at the half-open door. The groans were not exactly like those of a person in distress, but they resembled the efforts of some stage ghost in a blood-and-thunder drama. Suddenly Mrs. Sanford stepped out, with her revolver in her hand, and began to walk toward the hall. He instantly overtook her, and asked her, in a whisper, what she was going to do. She made a significant motion with her revolver, and again stopped to listen. He then took the pistol away from her, saying that the noise was probably due to some drunken man who had got into the hall. He told her to go back to bed, and he would investigate. Accordingly, he went into the hall, and soon Mrs. Sanford heard him dragging a maudlin drunken fellow downstairs. This affair had been arranged by me, in the hope of frightening Mrs. Sanford into making some kind of a confession, but she was not so easily alarmed as I had hoped. The door had been left open by Ingham on his return to the house, and another detective had been sent to the top of the stairs to make the groans. From the determined way in which she walked out, with her pistol in readiness, it was evident that she would not have hesitated to shoot the unfortunate ghost on sight.

The next day Ingham showed her a fine gold watch, which he said he had snatched out of a man's pocket in a crowd. She wanted him to steal one for her, and he promised to do so, if possible, though it was more difficult to get a lady's watch. She then advised him to be careful to see that there was no private mark on the watch, lest he should be detected thereby. Then she asked whether the numbers on government bonds were all different. He said that there were different series, which were exactly alike except the letter, and he tried to explain the matter to her, but she could not understand it. She also wanted to know whether the bonds could be sold in a foreign country, and he told her yes; that that was the best way to sell them, if there was anything wrong about them. After some further conversation, she said she thought of going to Canada soon, and perhaps she would like him to take charge of her rooms while she was away.

---

## CHAPTER III.

*The Dangerous Side of the Woman's Character.—Mr. Pinkerton makes a new Move. — Robert A. Pinkerton as Adamson, the drunken, but wealthy, Stranger. — A "funny" Game of Cards. — The drunken Stranger has a violent Struggle to escape from Mrs. Sanford, and is afterwards robbed—according to the Papers.—Detective Ingham arrested, but very shortly liberated.*

IT has already been observed by the reader that, while Ingham had learned nothing new about the fate of poor Trafton, he had obtained a very excellent understanding of Mrs. Sanford's character. Her most prominent characteristic was the love of money, and this passion seemed to overpower all others. Her language and manners at times showed that she had once been a member of good society, while her reading and declamations from Shakespeare and other poets gave evidence of great natural talents. Combined with her greed for money was a strong element of sensuality, and though she usually granted her favors only where she expected a large pecuniary reward, still, at times, she was apparently as prodigal in that regard as if she had no care whatever for money.

Her mind was naturally powerful, and I had little hope of breaking down her will; she would evidently show fight to the last, and all that I could hope would be to learn enough secretly to insure her conviction without her confession. She was as shrewd as if all her life had been passed in evading the toils of the law; even in her sleep, or when pretending to sleep, she would talk with great freedom; but, as she never gave any intelligence of importance on such occasions, I put little faith in the soundness of her sleep. In her readiness to assist Ingham to hide his plunder, I saw the dangerous side of this woman's nature strongly revealed. If she were so willing to act as an accomplice in one crime, why not in another? As she had been so successful in her encounter with Trafton, might she not be glad to carry out the same scheme again? At least, there would be no harm in putting an opportunity before her, and her actions in one case might give some clue to those by which she had succeeded in the former affair.

"Yes, that will be a good plan," I soliloquized; "I will send a young fellow there with a large sum of money, and he will get drunk. Then, if she tries to rob him, I shall be certain that she did the same with young Trafton."

A "FUNNY" GAME OF CARDS. 321

I therefore arranged that Ingham should pretend that he had made the acquaintance of a stranger from the East, who had a large sum of money; he was to tell Mrs. Sanford that he would bring the stranger to her rooms to spend the evening; the stranger would be rather drunk when he arrived there, and they would give him more liquor, until he should be quite drunk; if she should then try to rob him, he would get away as well as possible, and Ingham would go after him. In a little while, Ingham would return and show her a package of bonds, stolen from the stranger, and tell her that he had knocked the man down with a brick bfore robbing him. The next morning a notice would appear in the papers to the effect that a stranger had been found in the burnt district, lying on the ground in an insensible condition, having been knocked down and robbed.

Ingham was instructed as to his part in the affair, and next day he told Mrs. Sanford that there was a young fellow down town whose acquaintance he had made, who had a large amount of money with him. Ingham said that the man's name was Adamson, and that he was a gambler in good luck. He wanted to bring Adamson to the house that evening, and she was very anxious that he should come.

I intrusted the stranger's part to my son, Robert A. Pinkerton, who assumed the name of Adamson for the occasion.

Accordingly, the two detectives met at my
14*

office, and Adamson was given five hundred dollars in fifty dollar bonds. They then went to Mrs. Sanford's house, and, on arriving there, Mr. Adamson was quite unsteady on his legs. Mrs. Sanford was nicely dressed to receive the stranger, and she made herself very agreeable to him, in spite of his apparent drunkenness. They played cards together for a time, and then Adamson proposed to play euchre with Ingham seven points for five dollars a game. While they were playing, Adamson became quite reckless, and he threw down his cards with such a look of drunken gravity as to be quite amusing. He lost almost every game, and, at length, he wanted to go out for a drink. Mrs. Sanford told him to go on with his game, and she would get what he wished.

"What do you want to drink?" she asked.

"Anything excep' warrer," he replied.

"What do you know about water?" asked Ingham; "I don't believe you can tell how it looks."

"Tha's a lie. I know how to tell warrer 's well's you. I (hic) can allus tell warrer—it looks jus' like gin. Get us some gin."

While Mrs. Sanford was gone, Ingham and Adamson arranged that the latter should pretend to have lost all his money to the former, and that he should insist upon playing one game for fifty dollars. This he was to lose, and he was to become angry and go away. Adamson then gave Ingham about fifty dollars to show as his winnings, and presently Mrs. Sanford came in. She

"All right," said Ingham; "I'll play you just one game for fifty dollars, and then we'll stop, no matter who wins. Just wait a minute, until I go to my room for a handkerchief."

While he was gone, Adamson pulled out a package of ten United States bonds, of the denomination of fifty dollars each, and said that he would put up one of them against Ingham's fifty dollars, and that he should send the rest to his mother. When Ingham returned, he counted out fifty dollars, and Adamson laid down one of his bonds.

"What's that?" asked Ingham. "Is that worth fifty dollars?" and picking it up, he examined it carefully.

"Yes'r; tha's worth more'n fiffy doll'rs; tha's worth fiffy doll'rs in gold."

"Will you guarantee that it is good and all right?" asked Ingham.

"Course I will; didn't you ever see a (hic) bond b'fore?"

"Oh! I know that's all right," said Mrs. Sanford, who was beginning to show the effect of the gin very strongly; "I've had bon's like that, too. Th' young man who died here had eighteen thousan' bonds like this."

"Well, all right," said Ingham; "let us cut for deal."

As the game progressed, Mrs. Sanford felt the strength of the gin more and more, and she soon became quite sick. Ingham got her some warm water, and she went into her own room to vomit.

She soon returned, feeling much better, and the game went on, Ingham winning by one point. Adamson then became very angry, and said he was going out; and, although the others begged him to stay, he put on his overcoat and insisted on going away. Ingham finally said that he didn't care whether Adamson went or stayed, and, so saying, he walked off to his own room. Mrs. Sanford used every argument to induce Adamson to stay all night, but, with a drunken man's obstinacy, he refused to remain any longer. He walked downstairs, with Mrs. Sanford clinging to him and coaxing him all the way, until they reached the lower landing, when she put her back against the door and refused to let him out. They then had a violent struggle, in the course of which she tore open his coat and vest in the endeavor to get at the bonds in his breast pocket. Finally, he was obliged to use all his force to get away, as she was like a tigress in her anger, and was evidently determined to rob him. Indeed, had he not been an active, muscular young man, she would, undoubtedly, have finished him then and there; as it was, he barely succeeded in making his escape, by forcing her back upon the stairs, and then springing out of the door before she could seize him again.

Meantime, Ingham was a silent spectator of this scene from the top of the stairs, where he stood holding the lamp. As soon as Adamson was out, Ingham rushed down and told Mrs. Sanford that he intended to have those bonds anyhow.

"All right," said Ingham; "I'll play you just one game for fifty dollars, and then we'll stop, no matter who wins. Just wait a minute, until I go to my room for a handkerchief."

While he was gone, Adamson pulled out a package of ten United States bonds, of the denomination of fifty dollars each, and said that he would put up one of them against Ingham's fifty dollars, and that he should send the rest to his mother. When Ingham returned, he counted out fifty dollars, and Adamson laid down one of his bonds.

"What's that?" asked Ingham. "Is that worth fifty dollars?" and picking it up, he examined it carefully.

"Yes'r; tha's worth more'n fiffy doll'rs; tha's worth fiffy doll'rs in gold."

"Will you guarantee that it is good and all right?" asked Ingham.

"Course I will; didn't you ever see a (hic) bond b'fore?"

"Oh! I know that's all right," said Mrs. Sanford, who was beginning to show the effect of the gin very strongly; "I've had bon's like that, too. Th' young man who died here had eighteen thousan' bonds like this."

"Well, all right," said Ingham; "let us cut for deal."

As the game progressed, Mrs. Sanford felt the strength of the gin more and more, and she soon became quite sick. Ingham got her some warm water, and she went into her own room to vomit.

She soon returned, feeling much better, and the game went on, Ingham winning by one point. Adamson then became very angry, and said he was going out; and, although the others begged him to stay, he put on his overcoat and insisted on going away. Ingham finally said that he didn't care whether Adamson went or stayed, and, so saying, he walked off to his own room. Mrs. Sanford used every argument to induce Adamson to stay all night, but, with a drunken man's obstinacy, he refused to remain any longer. He walked downstairs, with Mrs. Sanford clinging to him and coaxing him all the way, until they reached the lower landing, when she put her back against the door and refused to let him out. They then had a violent struggle, in the course of which she tore open his coat and vest in the endeavor to get at the bonds in his breast pocket. Finally, he was obliged to use all his force to get away, as she was like a tigress in her anger, and was evidently determined to rob him. Indeed, had he not been an active, muscular young man, she would, undoubtedly, have finished him then and there; as it was, he barely succeeded in making his escape, by forcing her back upon the stairs, and then springing out of the door before she could seize him again.

Meantime, Ingham was a silent spectator of this scene from the top of the stairs, where he stood holding the lamp. As soon as Adamson was out, Ingham rushed down and told Mrs. Sanford that he intended to have those bonds anyhow.

He told her to sit up for him, and then ran out after Adamson. In less than an hour, he returned and saw Mrs. Sanford watching for him from a front window. When he went upstairs, she was still somewhat under the influence of the liquor she had drank, but she asked him where he had been.

"That's all right," he replied, flipping over the ends of the package of bonds; "I guess I've made a good enough haul this time."

"Oh! you are a splendid fellow," she said, leaning on his shoulder. "I didn't think you would dare to do it."

"I dare to do anything where there is any money to be made. You won't go back on me, will you?"

"What do you mean?" she asked.

"I mean, that you won't give me away to the police?" he asked, anxiously.

"Why, of course I won't," she replied. "I never yet went back on any one who did the fair thing by me; and I know you will do that, won't you?"

"Oh! certainly I will; I will make you a nice present to-morrow."

"I don't want a present to-morrow," she said, sullenly; "I want my share now."

"But I shall have to cash these bonds first," he said. "They would be of no use to you in their present shape."

"I can get them cashed as well as you can," she replied. "Come, hand over; I don't want half, but I want my share now."

"What is your hurry?" he demanded. "Can't you wait until to-morrow?"

"No, I can't; I want my share, and if you are going to be mean, I will be mean too. You can't keep those bonds unless I say so, and if I choose to report you, I can have them all taken from you, besides sending you to Joliet."

"Oh! if that's the way you talk," replied Ingham, "I shall know what to do. If you can't trust me until to-morrow, I can't trust you at all. You can't scare me by threats, and if you want to get any of this money, you must deal fairly with me; I'm not afraid of being arrested."

"All right, then," she answered, with a wicked look in her eye; "we'll see whether you will 'come down' or not. If you want to keep it all, I shall take care that you don't keep any of it. I'm going to the police station at once."

She was, evidently, just ugly enough to do as she said; and, as Ingham had the bonds in his possession, he did not fancy the idea of letting her go for the officers just then; so he replied:

"You can go right along, if you want to, but, in that case, I shall go somewhere else."

He then quickly brought his hat and overcoat into the sitting-room; and, seeing that she was still making preparations to go out, he took a hurried departure, taking a room at a small hotel for the night.

In the Chicago *Tribune* of January 14, 1872, the following item appeared:

"HIGHWAY ROBBERY.

"At about twelve o'clock last night, an officer of Pinkerton's Preventive Police stumbled over the body of a man near the corner of State and Washington streets. Stooping down, he discovered that the man was half drunk, half insensible, bruised and bleeding. On being restored to his senses, he gave his name as Robert Adamson, stating that he had come from Troy, New York, having with him several hundred dollars in currency and bonds. The time between drinks was very shor~ yesterday afternoon, and he has no clear ˙ what happened after dark, up to the ˌ ˙ ͜er found him minus his money and ͜ ͜ ͜ ͜ ˳. He remembers drinking frequently ˌ a stranger, who made himself very agreeable, but cannot state the time when they parted company. He describes the stranger as a tall, slender man, with black side-whiskers, giving a sufficiently minute description of him to afford the police a valuable clue, and it is likely that the highwayman will soon be overhauled."

About noon of the day that the above was published, Ingham went to call upon Mrs. Sanford, and she received him very coolly.

"How do you feel this morning?" he asked. "Does your head ache?"

"No, I feel all right," she replied. "Have you seen that fellow that was here last night?"

"No, I have not seen him," he replied. "Why do you ask? Has he been here looking for me?"

"Yes, he came here this morning, and asked me all kinds of questions about you; and now, if you are arrested, it will be your own fault. I would have shielded you, if you had done the fair thing by me; but now you must look out for yourself."

"You are very unreasonable, Mrs. Sanford," he replied; "it would have been very dangerous to have left any of those bonds with you, for if the man had brought the police here, they would have searched the house, and would have found the bonds. Then you would have been arrested, and you would have been obliged to tell where you got the bonds. Now, as soon as I get the bonds cashed, I will treat you handsomely, but I do not intend to run any risks."

"There would have been no danger of their finding the bonds, if you had left them with me; and, even if they had found them, I never would have told where I got them. You might have been fair enough to give me one hundred dollars at least."

"He did not have any money besides what I won from him, except the bonds; and, as I said before, I did not dare to leave those in the house."

"I am sorry I ever let you into my house," she said, presently. "I thought a great deal of you, and I expected to assist you when I received my money; but now I have lost confidence in you. I suppose, if you got a chance at my money, you would take that too. I begin to think I know where my watch went; the detective wanted to search you for it two or three times, but I wouldn't let him, and this is the way you reward my confidence."

"Mrs. Sanford, you are talking wild," he answered, angrily. "I have always treated you well, and when I made a raise the other day, I gave you a part of it. I intended to do the same this time, but you acted so suspiciously that I thought best to wait awhile. Now, as soon as I get these bonds cashed, I will give you some more money, but not till then."

"You can keep your old money," she retorted; "I don't want any of it. You think you were very smart, yesterday, but you don't know what danger you are in. I could have you arrested this very day if I chose."

"I know you could; but what good would it do you? I should be punished, to be sure, but you would not get a cent; while, if you keep quiet, I will make you a fine present."

"I don't want your present, nor you either," she replied. "I don't want you in my house any longer." Then, as Ingham started toward his room, she said: "Keep out of there; you can't go into that room, for I've let it to a young couple, who are in there now."

"All right, then," replied Ingham; "I will call again to-morrow."

"You needn't take things so mighty cool," she replied, perfectly white with anger. "You may find yourself in jail before you know it."

"I know it," he answered, carelessly; "but it's my nature to take things cool, and so, if you want to put me in jail, you can; but you can't scare me a bit, and you may as well understand it first as last."

The following morning, I received from Mr. Trafton, who was then in Philadelphia, the numbers of the bonds which were missing. They were five-twenty bonds of the issue of 1865, numbers 57,109 and 87,656, series A, and number 37,515, series B. Information of the robbery had been sent to the Treasury Department at Washington, and to all the sub-treasurers in the United States, in order that, in case any of the interest coupons should be presented for payment, they might be traced back, possibly, to the hands of the thief.

In *The Tribune* of Monday appeared the following item:

### "BEATEN AND ROBBED.

"A MAN TAKES A WALK WITH A COMPARATIVE STRANGER, AND IS KNOCKED DOWN AND ROBBED OF NEARLY $1,000 IN GREENBACKS.

"Mention was made in yesterday's TRIBUNE of the finding of a man, named Robert Adamson, on the corner of State and Washington streets, he having been beaten and robbed of several hundred dollars in greenbacks. The police were looking for him yesterday, but failed to find him. It was ascertained that he had been boarding at No.

92 West Madison street, and that, on Saturday night, he indulged in several games of euchre with a man who also boarded at the place. While the game was in progress, and Adamson was under the influence of liquor, he displayed an express company's envelope full of money. At the conclusion of the game, the two men went out to 'take a walk.' Yesterday morning, Adamson's companion returned to the house, and, it is said, offered the landlady $500 if she would say nothing about his having played cards with Adamson. She refused, and would not allow the fellow to take his trunk away, which he wanted to do very badly. The landlady sent her little daughter to police headquarters for an officer, and one was sent over to arrest the man; but he had left previous to the officer's arrival. It is not known how much money Adamson had, but it must have been in the neighborhood of $1,000, or the man who took it would not have made such a munificent offer to have the fact of the theft kept secret."

In accordance with my instructions, Ingham went to Mrs. Sanford's house about noon on Monday. He told her that he had read in the paper that she had reported him to the police as being the assailant of Robert Adamson. She denied ever having done so, and offered to swear that she had never betrayed him. He replied that he felt sure there must be a mistake, as he could not believe it possible that she would betray him. He felt perfect confidence in her, and had no fears that she would try to have him arrested.

"Besides," he continued, "I don't care now whether they arrest me or not. I'm not afraid of being held, for I am generally shrewd enough to cover my tracks pretty thoroughly, if I have a start of two or three days."

"You can't prove that you didn't rob that man," she replied.

"I don't need to; all the proof must come from the other side, and they haven't any witnesses who can swear that I did the robbery."

"I could prove it, if I choose to go against you," she said.

"No, you couldn't," he replied. "You didn't see me; and, while your testimony would, perhaps, be circumstantial evidence, your oath would be no better than mine, as you have no one to swear to the same thing."

"Oh! I have great credit up at the station," she said, in a boasting manner. "They recollect the finding of eighteen thousand dollars under the pillow of the young man who died here, and they have all confidence in me, for they know I might have easily stolen all he had. But I think it is best never to do anything wrong, and then there is no fear of getting into trouble."

"That's all right, if you can do it," he replied; "but I must have a living, and if I can't get it one way, I will another."

Just then some one knocked at the door, and

presently Charlie Stokes, the policeman, walked in. They talked together a few minutes, and then Stokes said:

"Step this way a moment, Mr. Ingham, I wish to speak to you alone."

They walked to the head of the stairs, and Ingham then asked what he wished to talk about.

"Well, there seems to be some kind of a misunderstanding at the police station," said Stokes, keeping his eyes on the ground, "and they have sent me to ask you to walk around to the office."

"A misunderstanding about what?" asked Ingham. "What do you mean?"

"Well, you know all about it," continued Stokes, in the same mysterious way.

"I beg your pardon; I don't know what you have reference to; please explain."

"Oh! you know well enough. You are wanted on account of that man you robbed last Saturday night."

"I did not rob any man Saturday night, and I am surprised that you should make such a charge against me, knowing me as well as you do," said Ingham, in an injured tone.

"I have nothing to do with it," replied Stokes. "I am simply obeying the captain's order, and I have no personal feeling against you whatever; but I have been sent to take you down to the station, and I must obey orders."

"Then you arrest me?" inquired Ingham.

"Well, you must go to the station with me to see the captain."

"Not unless you arrest me," replied Ingham. "I want to know whether I am to consider myself under arrest."

"Yes, you can consider yourself arrested, if you want to," replied Stokes, who did not seem to like to take the responsibility of making the arrest under the circumstances.

"I don't want to, and I shan't, unless you say so," persisted Ingham.

"Well, then, I *do* say so, and we will go now. We can walk along together like two friends, however, and no one need know that you are my prisoner."

"I don't care who knows it," said Ingham; "but I think there is something strange in the way of arresting me."

"Well, I hope you will come out all right," Stokes replied, adding significantly, "and perhaps you will, if certain folks don't appear against you."

"I'm not afraid," replied Ingham; "there is no one who can say anything against me."

On arriving at the station, the same consideration was shown to him, and the station-keeper asked him to make himself comfortable in the main sitting-room.

"Am I under arrest?" he asked again.

"No, not exactly; you can take it easy for a time, and you will have an examination soon."

"If I am not under arrest," Ingham replied, "I shall not stay here."

"Why not?" asked the station-keeper.

"Because I have no business here unless I am a prisoner," was Ingham's reply.

"We can lock you up in a cell, if we want to," said the station-keeper; "but we thought you would prefer to be comfortable up here."

"Then I *am* a prisoner?" again inquired Ingham, who seemed anxious to have his status satisfactorily explained.

"Yes, confound it; if you are determined to have it so, you are."

About five o'clock the sergeant of police came in, and asked Ingham his name.

"Ingham," was the reply.

"Jack Ingham?"

"No; John Ingham."

"What is your business?" asked the sergeant.

"I'm not employed at all, just now.

"Have you ever had any work to do in this city?" again queried the sergeant.

"No; not yet."

"Who was that man you were playing cards with the other night?"

"What night?" asked Ingham.

"Well, Saturday night."

"Whereabouts?"

"At your boarding place."

"Oh! I play cards with a great many fellows," Ingham replied. "I don't know which one you mean."

"Well, we know who he was," said the sergeant.

"Then what are you asking me for?" said Ingham. "Am I under arrest?"

"I guess you will have to stay here awhile," was the sergeant's reply.

Presently a number of persons came into the room, and Ingham thought he saw among them one of the bindery girls who had formerly lodged with Mrs. Sanford. She looked at him very hard, and then went out into the hall, where he could hear her talking with the station-keeper and Stokes. He also heard the sergeant call a policeman and give him some instructions, in which Ingham caught the words, "Pinkerton's office." The man then put on his coat and went out. Presently the sergeant approached him again, and, looking at him significantly, said:

"Now we know all about your playing cards with that man, and afterward robbing him."

"I don't know what you mean," Ingham replied; "I don't know what man you are talking about."

"Didn't you see that piece in the paper yesterday?" asked the sergeant.

"I saw a number of pieces in the paper yesterday, but I can't tell which one you are referring to."

The sergeant then showed him the item headed "Highway Robbery," and said:

"Now, we can prove that you came back to your landlady with a large package of money, and offered her five hundred dollars to keep quiet about the fact of your having played cards with this young fellow, and then having followed him out."

"Well, if you can prove that, you had better do it," said Ingham; then, changing his tone, and looking straight in the sergeant's face, he added: "Now, look here, sergeant, if you have any charges against me, just state them."

The sergeant muttered something about locking him up, and started to go out.

"If you lock me up," replied Ingham, coolly, "I hope you are prepared to take the consequences."

"Who the devil are you, anyhow?" asked the sergeant.

"No relation of yours, I assure you," was the reply, and the sergeant went away.

At this time, a tall, dignified man came in and asked the station-keeper a question. The policeman replied that there was no such man there.

"I know better than that," said the stranger, "and I must see him."

The station-keeper declared positively that they had no such man, and the stranger then went upstairs. In a few minutes the sergeant came in and told Ingham to follow him. As they were going upstairs, they met the tall stranger coming down. Ingham felt confident that this man was looking for him, and, in passing, he pinched the stranger's leg. The pinch was returned, and the tall man stopped; but Ingham and the sergeant went up to the captain's room. After asking Ingham his name, the captain said:

"Where were you last Saturday night?"

"That is none of your business," said Ingham.

"Come, now, you needn't put on any airs," said the captain; "I want to know all about this."

"Captain," Ingham replied, "if you have any charges against me, I should like to hear them. I don't put on any airs, but I want to know what I am under arrest for."

Turning to the sergeant, the captain said:

"How long would it take you to bring that man on here, sergeant?"

"Three or four days, at least," was the answer.

Just then the tall stranger entered, and the captain took him into a private room, where they remained some time. When they came out, the sergeant joined the captain for a few minutes, while the tall gentleman introduced himself to Ingham as Judge B——, and said that the captain would let him go. This proved true, for the captain very soon came out, and told Ingham that he was at liberty.

## CHAPTER IV.

*Connecting Links.—Mrs. Sanford's Ability as an Imitator of Actors.— One Detective tears himself away from her, and another takes his Place.—Mrs. Sanford's mind frequently burdened with the Subject of Murder.—New Evidence appearing.—A Peep at the stolen Bonds.—The Shrewdness of the Murderess.*

INGHAM did not return to Mrs. Sanford's until late in the evening of the day of his arrest. On arriving there, he was admitted by Charlie Stokes, the policeman, who seemed very much surprised to see him. Mrs. Sanford was also quite astonished, and turned very pale on seeing him. However, they soon began talking in a very friendly way, expressing their regret at his arrest and their pleasure at his release. Charlie did not remain long, and after he was gone Mrs. Sanford made all kinds of inquiries as to the manner of his escape.

"Why, Mrs. Sanford," he replied, "I told you they couldn't hold me. There was absolutely no evidence against me, and they were afraid to even lock me up. I have been ten years in this business, in New Orleans and elsewhere, and I have never been caught yet. The only thing which puzzles me, is to account for my being arrested at all!"

"You don't suspect that I had any hand in it, I hope?" asked Mrs. Sanford.

"Oh, no indeed! I trust you perfectly; but I think that one of those bindery girls may have seen me with Adamson on the street. One of them came into the station while I was there, and looked at me very hard, as if trying to identify me. Still, I don't see how she could have suspected anything, unless some one put her up to it."

"Perhaps some bartender may have seen you drinking with him during the afternoon," she suggested, "and he may have described you to the police."

"Well, I should like to know who it was," he said, savagely, "for I would shoot him like a dog."

As Mrs. Sanford had rented Ingham's room, there was no place for him to stay, and he went away about midnight, telling her that he would return next day. He did not go there, however, until after dark, as he felt confident that the police would try to "shadow" him. He found Mrs. Sanford quite uneasy about him, as she thought he had been arrested again. He invited her to go to the theatre, and, on their way home, they stopped at a restaurant to get a late supper. As there were no accommodations for him, he was obliged to go to a hotel for the night, but Mrs. Sanford promised to have a bed put into the unfurnished room for him the next day. The next afternoon he called again, and Mrs. Sanford said that Charlie had been there, and had told her all about their visit to the theatre the night before. She said that he knew exactly where they had been, what they had had for supper, and what they had paid. Ingham was thus made aware that he was being watched, and his position, therefore, became very embarrassing.

"Oh! by the way," she exclaimed, suddenly, "did I tell you that I got back my watch?"

"No; how did you recover it?" he asked.

"Well, that man Graves had it, and I had to pay one hundred dollars to get it back."

"That was a great shame," said Ingham, sympathetically, as if he fully believed her.

"Yes, I got my watch and several other trinkets, which I had all together in one box. See, here they are," she said, producing a box.

Ingham looked at them with great interest, and, among the old sleeve-buttons, odd earrings, and other broken pieces of jewelry, he saw two gold shirt studs, one diamond-shaped, and the other star-shaped. This was a small matter, but it was one of the connecting links, nevertheless, in the chain of evidence against her; for, from the description, I felt sure that these were young Trafton's missing studs.

Ingham spent the evening with her, and she was very friendly indeed, seeming anxious to remove any suspicion he might have that she was responsible for his arrest. She had made no arrangements for him to sleep there, however, and so he went to a small hotel for the night. When he reported at my office the following day, I gave him four hundred dollars in money, and told him to show it to Mrs. Sanford as the proceeds of the sale of the stolen bonds. Accordingly, when he went there in the afternoon, he counted over a large pile of bills before her astonished eyes, and asked her if he didn't know how to make things pay well.

"Why, where did you get all that money?" she asked.

"I sold those bonds which I showed you the other night," he replied. "I tell you, it isn't every man who knows how to dispose of property when it falls into his hands."

"Now you will be flush for a long time, won't you?" she said, in her most amiable manner. "What are you going to do with all that?"

"Oh! I shall have to divide with my partner first," he replied.

"Did you have a partner in this affair?" she asked. "You did not tell me about him."

"Oh! yes; I had the same partner as in the other case," Ingham replied. "He held Adamson, and I struck him with a brick. However, here is a present before I go, May," he continued, tossing two ten-dollar notes into her lap. "I will give you some more in a day or two."

Mrs. Sanford was very much gratified, and said that she cared more for him than for any one else, and he could depend upon her for anything. Ingham then left her, and came to my office to return the money. In the evening he took Mrs. Sanford and Miss Ida Musgrove to the theatre, and the latter, evidently having heard of his improved fortunes, treated him with great cordiality. They returned to the rooms of Miss Ida after the theatre was out, and Mrs. Sanford gave some fine imitations of different actors and actresses, in a way which showed great powers of mimicry, as well as considerable dramatic force. It was very late when Ingham and Mrs. Sanford got home, and they immediately went to bed.

The next day, Ingham went away as usual, and stayed until nearly dark. When he saw Mrs. Sanford, he professed to be in a very sulky mood, and said that he had been gambling all day.

"At first I won right along, and I was nearly two thousand dollars ahead at one time; but the cursed luck changed, and I began to lose every bet; so that, when I left, I had only ten dollars in my pocket out of all that money I got for the bonds."

Ingham could not control his feelings as he thought of his loss, and he swore and raved like a crazy man. Mrs. Sanford was very much disappointed, also, but she did not say much, except that he ought to have known better than to gamble. There were two or three new lodgers coming in and out while he was there, so that he did not have much time to talk to her, and he went away early in the evening.

Owing to the arrest of Ingham, and his quarrel with Mrs. Sanford, I had decided to relieve him from this operation, and to put another man in his place. His story about gambling was a part of my plan; and the next day, when he called upon her, he was under instructions to announce his intended departure from the city. Accordingly, he did so, giving as a reason the fact that he had lost all his money, and that the police were watching him so closely that he was afraid to attempt another robbery in Chicago. He told her that he was going to St. Louis, and that he should come to see her immediately, if he ever should return.

She appeared very much distressed at the thought of losing him, and told him that when she got her money, she would let him have as much as he wanted. She made him promise to write to her, and when he went away, she cried with seemingly genuine sorrow.

Three days later Mrs. Sanford received a visit from a gentleman who said he wished to rent a furnished room. Mrs. Sanford seemed to like his appearance, and she offered him the small back room at a low rent. Having decided to take it, he told her that his name was Henry C. Morton, recently from England.

"Oh! I am so glad you are from the old country," said Mrs. Sanford, "as I am from Edinboro' myself, and my father is Lord Chief Justice of the courts there. He is very rich, and has treated me very liberally since I left my husband; why, only last week, he sent me three thousand dollars."

Just then a Mr. Bruce, the owner of the furniture store below, came in, looking rather tipsy. Mrs. Sanford introduced the two men, and Mr. Bruce said something about being an Irishman.

"Why, what a strange coincidence," said Mr. Morton. "Here are three persons, each representing one of the three kingdoms of Great Britain. If I had some one to send for some ale, we would drink a toast to Britannia, God bless her!"

After talking together for some time, Mrs. Sanford and Mr. Morton went into the sitting-room, and Mr. Bruce went down to his store. Then Morton said that he had left his valise at the Stock Yards, and that he would go for it at once. On his return, he found two rough-looking men at the door trying to get in, but the bell would not ring, and so Morton went away for half an hour, leaving the men knocking and kicking on the door. About eight o'clock, he came back and found the door open. He went upstairs and entered the sitting-room. Mrs. Sanford was full of apologies for having locked him out, but she said that she had had trouble with one of her boarders, and she had resolved to keep him out of the house. While they were talking, the two men whom Morton had seen at the door came in, and a quarrel immediately sprang up between Mrs. Sanford and the younger of the two. In a short time, they both became furiously angry, and they used the most bitterly opprobrious language toward each other. Finally, Mrs. Sanford, who was ironing, rushed at the young man with a flatiron in her hand, and she would undoubtedly have seriously injured him if he had not escaped into his own room at the head of the stairs. She then laid a heavy poker on the table beside her, and said that she would mash his skull if he came near her again. In a short time, he again reëntered the room, when, seizing the poker, she rushed at him like a fury. He succeeded in avoiding her until Morton and the other man induced her to give up the poker; and both the strangers then went away, saying that they should be back at eleven o'clock.

After their departure, Mrs. Sanford dropped into a chair and cried for a time, saying that she never had acted so before in her life, as no one had ever treated her so shamefully. Then she became loquacious and confidential, telling Morton the old story of her father being Lord Chief Justice of Scotland, and her husband a wealthy man in Buffalo. She recited the reasons she had for leaving her husband, and said that her father first sent her one hundred and fifty dollars after the separation, but that she thought so small a sum was an insult, and so she sent it back. She added that he had promised her three thousand dollars very soon, and that she expected to receive it in a week or two. From this subject, she drifted to the story of young Trafton's death, which she told with great minuteness. She said that when she found he was dead, she fainted away, and did not recover for nearly two hours.

While she was running on in her story, a loud noise was heard, and she explained to Morton that Mr. Bruce had been drinking all day, until he was afraid to go home, and that now he was quite drunk in her room. She said that he had been very kind to her in letting her have furniture on credit, and so she wanted to make him comfortable until he was sobered off. During the evening she recited a number of selections from Byron, Scott, and Longfellow, and even gave several parts from Shakespeare's plays with great force and beauty of elocution. She also talked a great deal about Jack Ingham, a former lodger in her rooms, and she seemed to have a very high opinion of him. She said that he was obliged to leave town because the police were after him about something he had done, adding, that she didn't care for that, however, and she would never go back on a friend, but would shield him for anything except murder. It was after two o'clock in the morning before they retired, and as she had not fitted up Morton's room properly, she made a bed for him on the lounge in the sitting-room. As Mr. Bruce was lying dead-drunk on her bed, she was obliged to sleep on the floor of her room.

About four o'clock Morton was awakened by Mrs. Sanford, who said that she could not sleep in her room, as Bruce snored so loudly, just as Stanley Trafton did the night he died.

"Oh! it is horrible to think of," she said, shuddering. "I shall go crazy if I stay in there any longer."

She then lay down on the table and covered herself with a bedspread she had brought from her own room. About six o'clock they were awakened by a loud noise at the outer door, and Mrs. Sanford said that those drunken loafers had come back again. She immediately got up, took a revolver from her room, and went down to the door, where she told the men to go away, as she would not admit them at that time of night. While she was talking Bruce began moving around, and he found his way into the hall. Then Morton heard a great crash, as if some one had fallen downstairs, followed by a call from Mrs. Sanford, in tragic tones, for him to come and help her. Morton went out and found that Bruce had fallen from the top to the foot of the stairs, and on going down he discovered the unfortunate representative of the Emerald Isle lying in a heap against the front door. The two men outside had evidently been scared away by the noise, and they did not return until eight o'clock. Bruce was not hurt, except a cut on his hand, which Morton bound up, and then quiet reigned again until after daylight. About nine o'clock Morton went in to see Bruce, whom he found sitting up in bed. Bruce said that his money was gone, and that Mrs. Sanford had drugged him the night before to enable her to steal it. Morton called Mrs. Sanford, and asked where Bruce's money was. She said she had put it away for safe keeping, and, lifting the mattress, she took out two pocket-books and a box containing her watch, trinkets, etc. Having given Bruce his pocket-book, she went out, and he then counted his money. He said he ought to have eighty-one dollars, but that she had helped herself to ten dollars; it was not worth while making a fuss about it, but he said that he knew she had drugged him.

After awhile, Mr. Graves came in, and had a private interview with Mrs. Sanford. She seemed afraid of him, while he acted as if he had some hold upon her. When they came into the sitting-room, where Bruce and Morton were talking together, Mrs. Sanford asked Graves to lend her a dollar, but he refused.

"Pshaw! I don't want it," she replied. "I only asked to see whether you'd lend it, as I have quite enough of my own;" and, so saying, she took out her pocket-book.

Morton saw her count out nine ten-dollar bills and nine one-dollar bills. From the fact that she showed just ninety-nine dollars, it was probable that she had only recently changed one of the one-hundred-dollar bills taken from young Trafton. She then opened another compartment, and took out two pieces of folded paper, of a creamy tint, apparently about the size of two sheets of foolscap. They were folded several times, and were crammed in pretty tight.

"Do you know what those are?" she asked.

"No, I do not," he replied; "what are they?"

She merely laughed, and closed the pocket-book, whispering that she didn't want Graves and Bruce to see her money. She said she did not wish to be left alone with Graves, for fear he should rob her; so Morton asked him to go out and play a game of billiards. Bruce was in a great state of anxiety, lest his wife should have come down to the store to see where he had spent the night, and he remained with Mrs. Sanford.

Morton did not return to Mrs. Sanford's until late in the evening, and he found her dressing to go to a ball. She insisted that he should go, offering to pay all the expenses. He pretended to be very much hurt at her suggestion, saying that he never would permit any lady to pay anything when he took her out. She was dressed very tastefully, and presented a very stylish appearance, so that she attracted a good deal of attention at the ball. Before going, she sent Morton to a drug store for a drachm of morphine, saying that she must have it, as she used it constantly.

The next morning, they did not get up until a late hour, and Mrs. Sanford said that she did not feel very well. While talking together, they drifted into a discussion about money. Morton, like a genuine John Bull, maintaining there was no safety except in gold, or Bank of England notes.

" But we don't have either in this country," said Mrs. Sanford; "and now, suppose you had a large sum of money, what would you do with it?"

" That's just what I would like to know," he replied. " I expect to receive one hundred pounds from England very soon, and I don't know where to keep it."

"Well, I shall put my three thousand dollars into bonds," she said. "They can be registered, so that no one can use them except the rightful owner, and the interest is payable in gold."

"I don't know anything about bonds," said Morton, "especially these American bonds, which sometimes depreciate very fast."

"Oh! the bonds of the United States are good anywhere," she replied, "and they will sell for their face in England or Canada just as well as here. They are the best securities there are. I have some now, and I intend to get some more."

While talking, Morton picked up a card which was in her work-basket, and saw that it was an advertisement of a gift concert or lottery. She noticed it, and said that it had been left there by a man named Druen, who used to come to see her. She said that he had stolen a five-hundred-dollar bond from her, however, and he had never been there since. Soon afterward she went to sleep again, and did not awake until evening, as she was very tired from the effects of the ball. Morton remained in the house all day; and, when she woke up, he got supper for her. She seemed very much pleased at his thoughtfulness, and said that she never had had any one so kind to her since she left her husband.

"I want you to go to the bank with me some day," she said, "as I want to draw the interest on some of my coupons, and then you will see what good securities American bonds are."

"I shall be very glad to go with you," said

Morton; "for, if they are really good securities, I will invest some money in them."

"Oh! there is nothing better," she replied, "and I will show you mine."

She then took out the pocket-book she had shown him before, and unfolded one of the pieces of paper. Morton saw that it was a five-hundred-dollar bond, of the issue of 1865, payable in 1885, with about twenty or thirty coupons attached. He was so surprised and excited at seeing the bond, that he could hardly tell what to do, and so he failed to notice the most important point—the number. By the time she had opened the other bond, however, he had his wits a little more under command, and he was able to remember that the figures of the number were five, seven, one, zero, and some other figure; but he could not recollect positively the order in which they came.

"You can go to the bank to-morrow and get the coupons cashed for me, can't you?" she asked, after putting away the bonds.

"Oh! certainly, if you wish me to do so," he replied.

Then she laughed, and said:

"You would be arrested if you should take these bonds to the bank."

"How so?" he asked, apparently in great surprise. "Why should I be arrested?"

"Because the bonds belong to me, and you would have to give an account of the way in which you obtained them."

"Oh! well," he replied, "you could give me an order, and that would make it all right."

"Yes, I suppose so," she said, carelessly.

Her object, evidently, was to make Morton believe that it would not do for him to attempt to steal the bonds; for, though she trusted him to the extent of showing him her money and valuables, she was eternally suspicious and careful.

Of course, on receiving Morton's report, I felt quite confident that the two bonds he had seen were a part of those taken from young Trafton. Still, I had no positive proof of their identity, and, in accordance with my invariable custom, I took no hasty step, being confident that my detective would soon elicit all the facts. I wrote to Mr. Richard S. Trafton, however, suggesting that he have himself appointed administrator of his son's estate, so that he could begin proceedings instantly, the moment I was ready.

Several days passed, during which Morton gained Mrs. Sanford's confidence more and more. She was anxious one evening that he should rob Mr. Bruce, who came in half drunk; but Morton told her that he never worked that way.

"Why, Jack Ingham would have killed a man to get money out of him," said Mrs. Sanford. "Jack wasn't afraid to do anything for money."

"Well, that isn't my style," said Morton, contemptuously. "Do you suppose I am going to have a scuffle and struggle, ending perhaps in murder, when I can make ten times as much by a little skillful work with my pen? I don't want the police to be snuffing 'round my heels on account of highway robbery and such small game ; when *I* do anything to set them after me, it will be for a big stake, and even if they catch me, they will be mighty glad to compromise. Oh! no ; not any little jobs for me ; it is only the big rascals who can work safely."

Morton succeeded in inducing her to leave Bruce alone, though she had evidently meant to drug him, for she took a glass of beer, which she had poured out for him, and threw it into the sink. They all drank considerable beer, however, during the evening, and Mrs. Sanford, having taken also a large dose of morphine, became nearly insensible. On seeing her condition, Morton and another lodger thought they had better put her to bed ; but as Bruce was in a drunken stupor in her room, Morton determined to try the effect of putting her into the room where young Trafton had died. No sooner had they laid her on the bed, however, before she sprang up, gazed around an instant, and then rushed shrieking from the room, saying that she dare not lie there, and that she had seen "him" lying beside her. She was then placed on the lounge in the sitting-room, where she became quite hysterical. Morton sat beside her, and soothed her until she became quiet, and about midnight she fell asleep.

Morton said to me, on making one of his reports, that she would often determine to give up morphine and liquor, and live more respectably. Then she would become excited from the craving for the drug, and would take a dose, which would soothe her, make her amiable, and give her energy enough to do anything; gradually she would become wild again, and would be almost unbearable, while the maddening effect lasted, especially if she took any liquor to add to her temper; finally, the influence would pass off, leaving her weak, despondent, and stupidly affectionate. I saw that she was not likely to confess anything to any one, and I therefore decided to bring the affair to a crisis without delay.

## CHAPTER V.

*A moneyed young Texan becomes one of Mrs. Sanford's Lodgers.—The Bonds are seen, and their Numbers taken by the Detectives.—Mrs. Sanford Arrested.—Sudden and Shrewd Defense by the Prisoner.—She is found guilty of "Involuntary Manslaughter," and sentenced to the Illinois Penitentiary for five years.—Misdirected Philanthropy, and its Reward.—Mr. Pinkerton's Theory of the Manner in which Trafton was Murdered.*

HAVING discussed my plan with my superintendent, Mr. F. Warner, I sent for one of my youngest men, named Thomas Barlow, and gave him explicit instructions as to the course which he was to pursue in connection with Mrs. Sanford.

On the first day of February, therefore, a young fellow called at Mrs. Sanford's about five o'clock in the afternoon, and asked if she had any rooms to rent. She was very civil to him, and offered him the room at the head of the stairs, for three dollars a week. While she was showing him the rooms, she asked him a number of questions about himself; and as he was a smooth-faced, innocent-looking young man, he told her all about his affairs. He said that his name was Thomas Barlow, from Texas, where his father was a great cattle-raiser; he had brought several hundred head of cattle to the city, and had sold them at a high price; he intended staying in Chicago for a short time, and then he should go up the Red River of the North, in the early spring, to do some fur trading, as he believed there was a good deal of money to be made up there, by any one with sufficient capital; he intended to have a good time in Chicago first, however.

As soon as Mrs. Sanford learned that he had money with him, she became very affectionate indeed, telling him that she would make him more comfortable than he could be anywhere else, and that she would treat him like a prince. She introduced Morton as her brother, and said that they would all go to the theatre together. At first, Barlow refused, but she insisted so urgently, that he finally consented to go. He went away for an hour to get his valise, and when he returned, Mrs. Sanford was dressed in her most stylish clothes, as if determined to make the best possible impression upon him. He was very good-natured and boyish, apparently believing all she told him, and laughing at all her attempts to be funny. After leaving the theatre, she learned that one of her old acquaintances was to have a "grand opening" in a new saloon, and she was obstinately determined to find the place. After walking about for an hour, she called a hackman, and offered him five dollars to find this new saloon, where she was anxious to take a drink, as she said, "for good luck and old acquaintance' sake." After driving about until midnight, she learned that the opening was postponed, and they then went to a restaurant near her house to get supper. It was two o'clock before they went to bed, but before going, Mrs. Sanford learned that Barlow was to receive his pay for the cattle in a check for over four thousand dollars. She talked with him about the risk of carrying money around on the person, and told him that he ought to buy bonds, as then they would not be lost even if they should be stolen. He agreed with her, and said that he would try to buy some bonds when he got his check cashed.

The next morning they took breakfast with Mrs. Sanford, as she seemed anxious to keep Barlow with her as much as possible. It was noticeable that she did not, as she had usually done in all previous instances, tell him anything about young Trafton, who had died in her house, "with eighteen thousand dollars in bonds in his boots." She told Barlow that she had some bonds, and he would do well to get the same kind.

"I don't know much about them," he replied, "but if *you* think they are good, I guess they are good enough for me. What are they like? I never saw any."

"I will show you mine," said Mrs. Sanford. "I am going to sell one of them soon, as my lease is up at the end of the month, and I want to buy a house."

She then went into her bedroom, closed the door, and remained several minutes. When she came out, she had a fat pocket-book in her hand, and she took from it the two pieces of folded paper which she had shown to Morton. On opening them, she spread them out, and both Barlow and Morton saw the numbers plainly, as they looked over her shoulder.

"There, these little tickets are coupons," she explained to Barlow; "and every six months I can get fifteen dollars in gold by cutting off one from each bond."

"Did you say you wanted to sell one?" asked Morton. "If you do, perhaps you might sell it to Mr. Barlow, as a sample of the kind he wants to get."

"Yes, that would be a good idea," said Barlow; "then they can't fool me with any other kind, when I go to buy."

"Well, I guess I will do it," said Mrs. Sanford; "at any rate, you can see me about it before you go to buy yours."

She then put the bonds into the pocket-book again and went into her bedroom. On her return, Barlow told her that he must go down town to get paid for his cattle, and he asked Morton to go with him. Accordingly, the two men went out about noon, but Mrs. Sanford called Morton back a moment to tell him to stay with Barlow all day.

"Don't you lose sight of him for a minute," she said; "and bring him back here with all his money."

They did not return until after four o'clock, and Barlow told her that he had been obliged to go to the stockyards to get paid. He then went to his room for a few minutes, and Mrs. Sanford asked Morton whether Barlow had his money with him.

"Yes, they gave him a check for the amount, but it was too late to get it cashed, and he will have to wait until to-morrow."

"Couldn't we get it away from him and forge his name to it?" she asked. "We could get it cashed the first thing in the morning."

"It would be too risky," he replied, "as they probably know him at the bank, and we should be arrested at once. But you can offer to go with him to the bank in the morning, and he is so soft that you will not have much trouble in getting a large sum out of him."

During the evening, Mrs. Sanford was very affectionate toward Barlow, and she learned all about him. He told his story in such a way, that she believed him to be an innocent country boy from Texas, whose most dangerous experiences had hitherto consisted of hairbreadth 'scapes from steer and bull. He showed her a check on the First National Bank for about four thousand dollars, and told her that when he got it cashed in the morning, he would give her a nice present. It was then agreed that she should go to the bank with him next day. The evening was spent in reading aloud and singing, and they all retired much earlier than usual.

When Morton and Barlow left Mrs. Sanford at noon, they had, of course, come to my office to report their discovery of the stolen bonds. There was now no possibility of a mistake, as they had seen the two bonds of the series A, numbered 57,109 and 87,656. I therefore instructed Mr. Warner to obtain a warrant for her arrest, and a search warrant for her house, both to be served the next morning before the hour appointed for going to the bank with Barlow. Everything was prepared in advance, a trustworthy constable was obtained to make the arrest, and a telegram was sent to Mr. R. S. Trafton in Cleveland, asking him to come to Chicago immediately. A reply was received the next morning, stating that he had left by the evening train.

About eleven o'clock on Saturday, February 3, Mr. Warner and the constable arrived at Mrs. Sanford's rooms. On knocking at the door of the sitting-room, they were admitted by Morton, who asked what they wanted.

"I would like to engage rooms, if there are any to rent," said Mr. Warner.

"I will speak to the landlady," said Morton, going to the door of her room.

"Tell the gentleman to call again," said Mrs. Sanford; "I am not dressed, and can't see him."

"I only wish to see her a few minutes," Mr. Warner replied, addressing Morton in a tone loud enough to be heard by Mrs. Sanford, whose door was slightly ajar.

"Well, I can't see the gentleman until this afternoon," she replied.

"I have some important business, and I must attend to it now," answered Mr. Warner, putting his foot in the opening and pushing the door in with his shoulder; then he continued, addressing the constable, "This is Mrs. Sanford, and you can arrest her now."

The constable immediately took charge of her, and she was allowed to complete her toilet, though Mr. Warner first searched her dress, before letting her put it on. He then made a careful search of the bedroom, during the progress of which Mrs. Sanford was very noisy and troublesome, crying, and pretending to go into hysterics several times. Once, when Mr. Warner was looking very carefully through her trunk, she said to him, in very tragic tones:

"By the way you act, one would think you were looking for a murdered man."

"Well, perhaps if we had come a little sooner, we might have found one," he replied, quickly, giving her a sharp glance.

As nothing had been said to her or to any one

else about any charge except that of larceny, this remark was highly significant; and, on her trial, it undoubtedly had great weight with the jury.

Mr. Warner soon found the pocket-book containing the bonds under the mattress of her bed, and after examining them sufficiently to identify them, he gave them to the constable. Mrs. Sanford was then taken to my office, and, as Mr. Trafton had arrived from Cleveland, we tried to have an interview with her relative to young Trafton's death. She was too crafty, however, and she pretended to go into hysterics whenever we began to question her.

Meantime, Morton and Barlow had accompanied her, and Morton offered to get her a lawyer to advise her. She was very grateful to him, and said he was her only friend. He soon brought in a lawyer well versed in defending criminals, and the whole party then went to the justice's courtroom. At the close of the examination, she was held to await the action of the Grand Jury, and, in default of two thousand dollars bail, she was sent to the county jail. She told Morton that her lawyer could not half lie, and that she should not pay him a cent. She stood up, when the justice's decision was announced, and made quite a speech; and the native cunning of the woman was never more clearly shown than in this plea, which was undoubtedly invented on the spur of the moment. She claimed that young Trafton had given her the bonds to support her child, whose father he was, and she spoke with so much vigor and cunning that many persons believed her statement to be true. Thus, without consultation or legal advice, she invented in a moment the strongest possible defense against the charge of larceny,—the charge of murder had not then been brought.

When she was removed to the jail, she gave Morton the keys to her rooms, telling him to take charge of everything there, and to find a purchaser for her furniture. He therefore informed two young men who were lodging there that Mrs. Sanford had been arrested, and that they must find other rooms, as he intended to sell out the furniture. After they had gone he cleaned up the house, packed Mrs. Sanford's trunks, and made everything look as well as possible. While she was awaiting trial, he visited her every day and gave her various delicacies to improve the prison fare. One day he pretended to have pawned his overcoat for five dollars, in order to get her some lemons, tea, and sugar. She was very much touched, and she gave him five dollars to get back his coat; but this action was due to a momentary impulse. She had plenty of money, and was able to get anything she wanted; but her desire to hold fast to her money was greater than her wish for good food. Indeed, she came near jeopardizing her cause by refusing to pay the lawyer she had engaged, but finally she gave him a retaining fee of fifty dollars.

She was very anxious to learn who were the detectives employed in working up the case, and she said that she believed Barlow had had something to do with her arrest. Morton agreed with her, and, as the papers had said that there were three engaged in the case, he suggested that perhaps the two men whom she had turned out of doors were also detectives. She never suspected either Ingham or Morton for a moment; and when Ingham called upon her in jail, she was delighted to see him. She tried to get bail from the two brothers, named Pratt, who had occupied one of her rooms, as one of them had been very intimate with her; but they were afraid of getting mixed up in her difficulties, and so refused to help her obtain bail. She also asked Ingham to swear to a number of falsehoods about her intimacy with Trafton, and when he refused to do so, for fear of being tried for perjury, she said that she could get "her Billy" to swear to anything. This "Billy" proved to be one William Simpson, a barkeeper, and her former paramour. He was tracked for some time by my detectives, but he suddenly disappeared, and was not seen again until her trial for larceny, when, just as she said, he was willing to swear to anything. He then disappeared again, but I did not take much interest in following him up, as I knew that he would not dare to repeat his perjury when the murder trial should take place. His testimony was to the effect that he had overheard a conversation between Mrs. Sanford and young Trafton, in which the latter acknowledged that he was the father of Mrs. Sanford's child, having been intimate with her in Buffalo about eighteen months before. The question of a support for the child was discussed between them, and Trafton said that he would give her fifteen hundred or two thousand dollars in bonds, to enable her to bring up his child in comfort. The witness also testified that Trafton and Mrs. Sanford were very intimate with each other, often occupying the same room together; that Mrs. Sanford often spoke of her former intimacy with him; and that he inferred from their conversation that Trafton had been the cause of her separation from her husband. This testimony was very skillfully manufactured and artistically developed, so as to make Trafton appear in the light of a libertine and profligate, and Mrs. Sanford as a confiding wife, led astray by the wiles of a treacherous man. In spite of the bad character and appearance of this fellow Simpson, his testimony had enough weight with some of the jury to cause a disagreement, and Mrs. Sanford was remanded to jail.

Mr. Robert S. Trafton was anxious to bring her to punishment, as he felt confident that she had caused the death of his son. The circumstances of the case caused considerable delay, and it was not until January 27, 1873, nearly a year after her arrest, that the trial on the charge of murder took place.

The testimony in this trial was highly interesting on many accounts. The County Physician, who had made the first post-mortem examination of the remains, and who had given congestion of the lungs as the cause of death, stated that he found the deceased lying dead in Mrs. Sanford's rooms, and that he took charge of the property found in his possession. He stated that he should have made a closer examination if he had not found the bonds and money; but he did not suspect foul play, and therefore made only a hasty investigation.

By the testimony of two or three witnesses it was shown that on the night of Trafton's death Mrs. Sanford went into two saloons about midnight, asking for "her Billy," meaning the man Simpson, by whose testimony she escaped conviction on the larceny charge, he being then living on her bounty. While looking for him she was very wild and excited, her clothes being disordered, and her watchchain broken. To one witness she said that she wished Billy to come to her house to look at the "prettiest corpse she ever saw." One witness testified that she returned to his saloon about five or six o'clock in the morning, and induced him to go up to her rooms to look at the body; he did so, and found the body of a man lying in bed, partly covered up. She had a large roll of money and papers in her pocket-book.

A surgeon of the highest reputation in Cleveland was called, and gave his testimony in the most direct and convincing manner, like a man who knew perfectly well what he was talking about, and who was not guessing at any of the facts as stated by him. He declared that death resulted from the blow on the right side, aided by the violence on the throat and neck. There was very slight congestion of the brain and of the lungs, but he was positive that death was not the result of either of these; indeed, leaving out of consideration the marks of external violence, he said that he should not have been able to account for Mr. Trafton's death. At the conclusion of his re-direct examination he said that death could be caused by a heavy blow of the fist, followed by choking, and he would swear positively that Trafton's death was produced by violence. The testimony of this witness was corroborated by that of several other surgeons of high reputation, and then a sensation was created by the calling of John Ingham for the prosecution.

As Mrs. Sanford saw her well-beloved friend, Jack, take the stand and acknowledge himself to be one of Pinkerton's dreaded detectives, she broke down and cried bitterly. Ingham related the history of his connection with the affair, stating the different stories which Mrs. Sanford had told about Trafton's death, and also her fear of going in the room where he died. He then gave the inside history of his arrest for the alleged robbery of Adamson, showing that it had been planned in advance by me to induce Mrs. Sanford to give him her confidence. After her arrest for larceny, he had visited her in jail, and she had tried to get him to swear that he had heard Trafton promise to give her the bonds to support her child. When he objected, on the ground that he might be arrested for perjury, she had told him that "her Billy," meaning William Simpson, would swear to it anyhow.

The testimony of Mr. Warner relative to finding the bonds in Mrs. Sanford's possession was corroborated by that of the constable; they also repeated Mrs. Sanford's remark made during the search, before any charge of murder had even been suggested: "By the way you act, I should think you were looking for a murdered man."

When the testimony for the prosecution was all in, the defense had a turn, and they produced as many medical experts to prove that Trafton did not die of violence, as the other side had to prove that he did not die a natural death; indeed, from the medical testimony given, there might have been grave doubts raised as to whether he had any business to die at all, for, according to both sides, no adequate cause of death had been discovered. Several witnesses testified that they believed him to have been on a long spree just before his death, but these were soon rebutted by equally trustworthy witnesses for the prosecution.

In summing up, the counsel for the people presented a highly plausible theory of the manner in which the murder was committed, and asked a verdict on the following grounds:

Young Trafton, as shown by the testimony of his father and others, visited Chicago to buy grain, and he was, therefore, under the necessity of carrying with him a large amount of money.

Being unable to get a room at any hotel convenient to business, he probably entered the first place where he saw the sign, "Rooms to Rent," and engaged a sleeping-room, taking his meals at a hotel near by. While lodging with Mrs. Sanford, he was trying to buy grain at a paying figure, and he was daily in consultation with Captain Dalton, who commanded one of his father's schooners. Finding that he could not buy to any advantage in the existing condition of the grain market, he sent the schooner back to Cleveland on the last day of November, in order that she should not be caught in the ice in the straits at the close of navigation. He was then ready to return himself, and, doubtless, on going to his lodgings, he so informed Mrs. Sanford. As he had made no secret of his reason for visiting Chicago, she was, probably, well aware of his object, and also of the fact that he had a large amount of money with him. Seeing his careless ways, the idea occurred to her to rob him, and, having his expected departure in view, she knew that she would have only one more opportunity to carry out her scheme.

On his return that evening, therefore, having just parted from Captain Dalton in perfect health and sobriety, he was invited to eat supper with her. Suspecting no harm, he sat down and ate a hearty supper. In some way, either in his food or drink, a dose of morphine was given to him, and he soon fell fast asleep. The woman's opportunity was before her, and all the natural thirst for money which characterized her came upon her with full force, urging her on and inciting her to any lengths necessary to accomplish her object. Having laid him on his bed, she began to search his pockets with the stealthy touch of a practiced hand. Finding nothing at first to reward her search, she pulled off one of his boots and discovered the United States bonds, which he had concealed there. But the violence necessary to remove the boot caused him to partly waken from his drugged sleep, and he became vaguely aware that some one was trying to rob him. Still in a drowsy, confused state, however, he was unable to do more than to sit up and clutch wildly at his assailant; having caught one of the bonds, he clung to it until it was torn in two pieces, the fragments plainly showing how they had been wrenched asunder in the clasp of two determined hands—those of the murderess and her victim. But she soon found that he was gaining his senses too rapidly, and that she would be foiled in her attempted robbery; hence, with every blinding passion aroused, her greed and her fear equally inciting her to action, she struck him a heavy blow on the thigh and another more powerful one on the side. Partly stunned by the concussion, he fell back, and she then seized him by the throat. Her round, plump hands, though powerful enough to strangle him, left only slight marks of abrasion on the skin, and in a few minutes all was over. His property was at her mercy, and she gave no thought to the body of her victim until she had seized every piece of valuable paper in his possession.

But her position was a dangerous one, and, on cooling off somewhat, she saw that something must be done to remove any appearance of foul play. How could it be done most effectually? Manifestly by giving no apparent ground for suspecting that she had any object in his death; and no course would be more effectual than to leave such an amount of property in his possession as to make strangers believe that none of it had been taken. It may well be imagined that this was her hardest task; for to give up money was probably a greater hardship for her than for some people to give up life. Still, it would never do to run the risk of being accused of murder; so, reluctantly, she placed one bond in his pocket, and, by accident, included with it one-half of the torn bond, the other half being placed under his head, in the boot from which it was taken. She then undressed the body, placed it naturally in bed, and went out to look for "her Billy," her paramour and panderer in vice.

This was the history of the crime, as pictured by the prosecution; and all her actions since that fatal night had been in harmony with such a theory. Her allegations of intimacy with young Trafton were unsupported, save by the testimony of this William Simpson, her paramour. It was noticeable that, while this man had testified in the trial for larceny that he had overheard Mr. Trafton's acknowledgment of being the father of Mrs. Sanford's child, in the murder trial he was not asked to give any such testimony, nor was the existence of such a child even hinted at by the defense. The counsel for Mrs. Sanford were well aware that she had never had a child, and that this fact could be proven if necessary. On discovering, too, that Jack Ingham was a Pinkerton detective, instead of Mrs. Sanford's best friend, they saw other reasons why it would not be advisable to cause Mr. William Simpson to perjure himself again.

The defense contented themselves with claiming that there was no sufficient evidence to prove that Mr. Trafton had died a violent death at all, and that there was no evidence whatever to show that, even if foul play had occurred, Mrs. Sanford had been the guilty person. This plea was ably presented by the counsel, and the judge then briefly charged the jury as to the law, and the form of their verdict. During the early part of the trial, Mrs. Sanford behaved very badly, often contradicting witnesses aloud, and making many audible remarks to the jury and the Court; after the testimony for the defense began, however, she paid very little attention to the proceedings, often dozing and sleeping in her chair. This habit was, undoubtedly, due to the use of morphine, of which she consumed large quantities.

The jury retired at three o'clock, and, on the first ballot, they stood nine for conviction and three for acquittal. After discussing the testimony for more than four hours, a compromise was reached, and the judge having been informed that the jury had agreed upon a verdict, the prisoner was brought in to hear the finding.

All being in readiness, the clerk read the verdict as follows:

"We, the jury, find the defendant guilty of involuntary manslaughter, and fix her time of imprisonment at five years in the penitentiary."

At the word "guilty," Mrs. Sanford gave a violent start; but, as the remainder of the finding was read, she seemed to feel agreeably surprised. She asked for a glass of water in a low tone, turned very white, and then fainted away before the water could be handed to her.

She was then removed to the jail to await the argument on a motion for a new trial. While there, she gave one of the most effectual evidences of her ruling passion—greed. She was the object of considerable sympathy among a certain class of sentimentalists, and the amount of compassion wasted upon her was remarkable to those who knew her real character and habits; but there is no accounting for tastes, and so Mrs. Sanford was treated with great consideration by a number of well-meaning but unsophisticated people. Among the Good Samaritans who took the most interest in her was a lady named Mrs. Jones, and this lady visited her quite frequently in her cell, bringing her books and papers.

One morning, Mrs. Jones complained of feeling unwell, and Mrs. Sanford immediately gave her a glass of water. Soon after drinking it, Mrs. Jones became very sleepy, and in a few minutes, she was in a sound slumber. This effect had been produced, of course, by a dose of morphine in the water, and Mrs. Sanford then proceeded to rob Mrs. Jones of all her valuables. Mrs. Jones was in moderate circumstances, and her purse was not sufficiently well filled to satisfy Mrs. Sanford's avaricious demon; hence, she made a thorough search for other plunder. It happened that Mrs. Jones, having lost all of her upper teeth, had supplied their place by an artificial set, mounted on a plate of solid gold. Not content, therefore, with plundering her benefactress in other respects, Mrs. Sanford actually took the set of teeth from Mrs. Jones's mouth, and hid them in her own trunk.

Of course, on awakening, Mrs. Jones missed her teeth and charged Mrs. Sanford with having taken them. The latter denied having done so, railed and swore at Mrs. Jones, and tried to prevent the officers from searching the cell. The teeth and other articles stolen from Mrs. Jones were found at the bottom of Mrs. Sanford's trunk, and Mrs. Jones retired from the jail strongly impressed with the conviction that philanthropy had its hardships as well as rewards.

The motion for a new trial being overruled, sentence was pronounced in accordance with the verdict of the jury, and Mrs. Sanford was consigned to the Illinois State Penitentiary at Joliet.

In regard to the manner in which young Trafton was murdered, I have always had a theory of my own; and, while of course I do not pretend to any surgical learning, I give it for what it is worth, prefacing it, however, with the remark that several eminent physicians concur in my opinion, or, at least, admit its strong probability.

It will be remembered that Mrs. Sanford used morphine continually, and that she boasted of her ability to administer it in just the proper proportion to cause her victims to fall into a heavy sleep. In all probability, as suggested by the State's Attorney, she gave young Trafton a dose at supper; but it is also possible the effect was not sufficient, and that when she tried to rob him, he slightly revived, struggled, and, seizing one of the bonds in a convulsive grasp, tore it in two.

So far, the theories are identical, but I failed to see a sufficient cause of death in the slight blow and mild choking, especially as the lungs did not present the conditions which would have appeared had death resulted from strangulation or asphyxia. On searching Mrs. Sanford's rooms, Mr. Warner found two or three small syringes, intended for making hypodermic injections, and these led me to believe she caused Trafton's death by morphine alone. My idea was as follows:

When she found that Trafton was not sufficiently drugged to enable her to rob him in safety, she probably let him alone, and the drug again took effect to the extent of putting him to sleep. She then resorted to a subcutaneous injection of morphine, knowing that the soporific influence of the drug would thus be made more rapid and powerful. This operation was performed on the side, and then near the large veins of the leg, and thus were caused the apparent bruises filled with extravasated blood. Now, the effect of morphine varies largely, according to the constitution, temperament, and habits of the persons to whom it is given; but the combined result of internal and external doses almost invariably is death.

It seems altogether probable to me, therefore, that Trafton came to his death in that manner, and that the traces of morphine in the wounds, as in the stomach, had wholly evaporated before the Cleveland surgeons made their examination, twelve days after death.

Whatever may have been the means, however, there can be no doubt that murder most foul was committed, and that Mrs. Sanford richly deserved a greater punishment than was awarded to her. Whether she had any accomplice will never be known, but it is probable that she had some one in the house who was aware of the murder after it had been committed, if not before. This would account for the absence of the fifth bond, which was never recovered, but which was afterward traced back from the Treasury Department, when it was presented there, to some unknown woman, who had sold it in Milwaukee. This woman was evidently not Mrs. Sanford, but her identity could not be discovered, and, therefore, all trace was lost.

THE END.

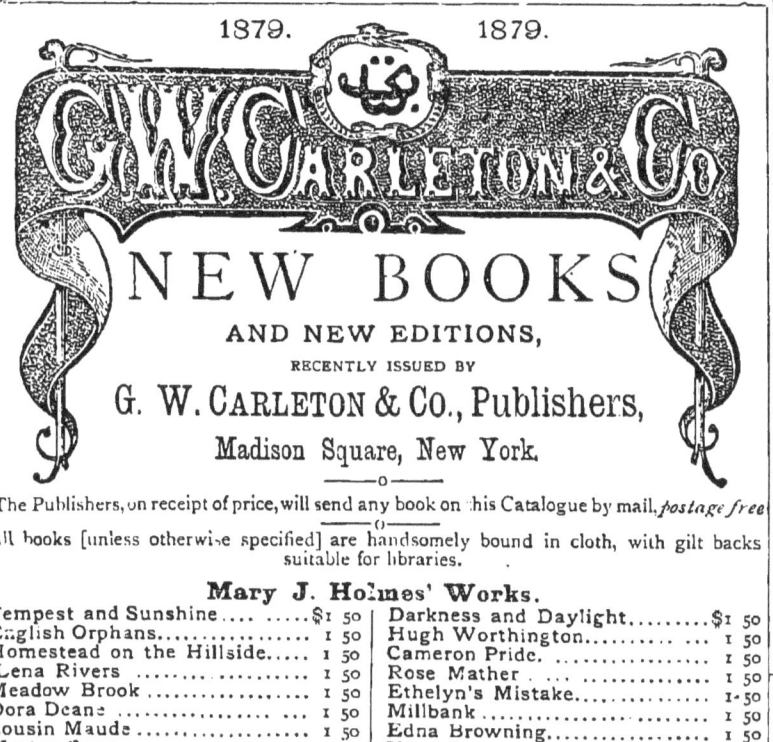

# 1879.
# 1879.

# NEW BOOKS
## AND NEW EDITIONS,
RECENTLY ISSUED BY

## G. W. CARLETON & Co., Publishers,
Madison Square, New York.

The Publishers, on receipt of price, will send any book on this Catalogue by mail, *postage free*

All books [unless otherwise specified] are handsomely bound in cloth, with gilt backs suitable for libraries.

### Mary J. Holmes' Works.
| | | | |
|---|---|---|---|
| Tempest and Sunshine | $1 50 | Darkness and Daylight | $1 50 |
| English Orphans | 1 50 | Hugh Worthington | 1 50 |
| Homestead on the Hillside | 1 50 | Cameron Pride | 1 50 |
| 'Lena Rivers | 1 50 | Rose Mather | 1 50 |
| Meadow Brook | 1 50 | Ethelyn's Mistake | 1 50 |
| Dora Deane | 1 50 | Millbank | 1 50 |
| Cousin Maude | 1 50 | Edna Browning | 1 50 |
| Marian Grey | 1 50 | West Lawn | 1 50 |
| Edith Lyle | 1 50 | Mildred ........(New) | 1 50 |
| Daisy Thornton....(New) | 1 50 | | |

### Marion Harland's Works
| | | | |
|---|---|---|---|
| Alone | $1 50 | Sunnybank | $1 50 |
| Hidden Path | 1 50 | Husbands and Homes | 1 50 |
| Moss Side | 1 50 | Ruby's Husband | 1 50 |
| Nemesis | 1 50 | Phemie's Temptation | 1 50 |
| Miriam | 1 50 | The Empty Heart | 1 50 |
| At Last | 1 50 | Jessamine | 1 50 |
| Helen Gardner | 1 50 | From My Youth Up | 1 50 |
| True as Steel....(New) | 1 50 | My Little Love | 1 50 |

### Charles Dickens—15 Vols.—"Carleton's Edition."
| | | | |
|---|---|---|---|
| Pickwick, and Catalogue | $1 50 | David Copperfield | $1 50 |
| Dombey and Son | 1 50 | Nicholas Nickleby | 1 50 |
| Bleak House | 1 50 | Little Dorrit | 1 50 |
| Martin Chuzzlewit | 1 50 | Our Mutual Friend | 1 50 |
| Barnaby Rudge—Edwin Drood | 1 50 | Curiosity Shop—Miscellaneous | 1 50 |
| Child's England—Miscellaneous | 1 50 | Sketches by Boz—Hard Times | 1 50 |
| Christmas Books—Two Cities | 1 50 | Great Expectations—Italy | 1 50 |
| Oliver Twist—Uncommercial | 1 50 | | |
| Sets of Dickens' Complete Works, in 15 vols.—[elegant half calf bindings] | | | 50 00 |

### Augusta J. Evans' Novels.
| | | | |
|---|---|---|---|
| Beulah | $1 75 | St. Elmo | $2 00 |
| Macaria | 1 75 | Vashti | 2 00 |
| Inez | 1 75 | Infelice ......(New) | 2 00 |

# G. W. CARLETON & CO.'S PUBLICATIONS.

## May Agnes Fleming's Novels.
Guy Earlscourt's Wife.........$1 50 | A Wonderful Woman........$1 50
A Terrible Secret ............. 1 50 | A Mad Marriage............ 1 50
Norine's Revenge ............. 1 50 | One Night's Mystery........ 1 50
Silent and True................ 1 50 | Kate Danton................ 1 50
Heir of Charlton—(New)....... 1 50

## The Game of Whist.
Pole on Whist—The English standard work. With the "Portland Rules."....$1 00

## Miriam Coles Harris.
Rutledge.....................$1 50 | The Sutherlands............$1 50
Frank Warrington............. 1 50 | St. Philips................ 1 50
Louie's Last Term, St. Mary's. 1 50 | Round Hearts for Children.. 1 50
Richard Vandermarck.......... 1 50 | A Perfect Adonis—(New).... 1 50

## Mrs. Hill's Cook Book.
Mrs. A. P. Hill's New Southern Cookery Book, and domestic receipts....$2 00

## Julie P. Smith's Novels.
Widow Goldsmith's Daughter.$1 50 | The Widower ...............$1 50
Chris and Otho................ 1 50 | The Married Belle.......... 1 50
Ten Old Maids................ 1 50 | Courting and Farming...... 1 50
His Young Wife............... 1 50 | Kiss and be Friends—(New). 1 50

## Victor Hugo.
Les Miserables—From the French. The only complete unabridged edition....$1 50

## Captain Mayne Reid.
The Scalp Hunters............$1 50 | The White Chief...........$1 50
The Rifle Rangers............. 1 50 | The Tiger Hunter.......... 1 50
The War Trail................ 1 50 | The Hunter's Feast........ 1 50
The Wood Rangers............ 1 50 | Wild Life................. 1 50
The Wild Huntress............ 1 50 | Osceola, the Seminole..... 1 50

## Artemus Ward.
Complete Comic Writings—with Biography, Portrait, and 50 Illustrations....$1 50

## A. S. Roe's Select Stories.
True to the Last.............$1 50 | A Long Look Ahead........$1 50
The Star and the Cloud....... 1 50 | I've Been Thinking........ 1 50
How Could He Help it?....... 1 50 | To Love and to be Loved... 1 50

## Charles Dickens.
Child's History of England—Carleton's New "School Edition," Illustrated..$1 25

## Hand-Books of Society.
The Habits of Good Society—The nice points of taste and good manners...$1 50
The Art of Conversation—for those who wish to be agreeable talkers......... 1 50
The Arts of Writing, Reading, and Speaking—For self-improvement...... 1 50
New Diamond Edition—Small size, elegantly bound, 3 volumes in a box...... 3 00

## Carleton's Popular Quotations.
Carleton's New Hand-Book—Familiar Quotations, with their authorship....$1 50

## Famous Books—"Carleton's Edition."
Arabian Nights—Illustrations....$1 00 | Don Quixote—Dore Illustrations..$1 00
Robinson Crusoe—Griset. do... 1 00 | Swiss Family Robinson. do... 1 00

## Josh Billings.
His Complete Writings—With Biography, Steel Portrait, and 100 Illustrations.$2 00
Old Probability—Ten Comic Almanax, 1870 to 1879. Bound in one volume. ... 1 50

## Allan Pinkerton.
Model Town and Detectives...$1 50 | Spiritualists and Detectives....$1 50
Strikers, Communists, etc...... 1 50 | Mollie Maguires and Detectives 1 50
Criminal Reminiscences, etc.... 1 50 | The Mississippi Outlaws, etc.. 1 50

## Celia E Gardner's Novels.
Stolen Waters. (In verse)......$1 50 | Tested....................$1 50
Broken Dreams. (Do.) ....... 1 50 | Rich Medway's Two Loves.... 1 50
Terrace Roses................. 1 50 | A Woman's Wiles............ 1 50
A New Novel.................. 1 50

## Carleton's Popular Readings.
Selected Prose and Poetry—Edited by Mrs. Anna Randall-Diehl............$1 50

# G. W. CARLETON & CO.'S PUBLICATIONS.    3

## "New York Weekly" Series.

| | | | |
|---|---|---|---|
| Thrown on the World......... | $1 50 | Nick Whiffles................. | $1 50 |
| A Bitter Atonement.... ...... | 1 50 | Lady Leonora ................ | 1 50 |
| Love Works Wonders. ....... | 1 50 | The Grinder Papers.......... | 1 50 |
| Evelyn's Folly... ............. | 1 50 | Faithful Margaret ......... | 1 50 |
| Lady Damer's Secret.......... | 1 50 | Curse of Everleigh............ | 1 50 |
| Peerless Cathleen.............. | 1 50 | | |

## Violet Fane's Poems.

Constance's Fate; or, Denzil Place.$1 50 | From Dawn to Noon..........$1 50

## M. M. Pomeroy ("Brick.")

| | | | |
|---|---|---|---|
| Sense. A serious book.......... | $1 50 | Nonsense. (A comic book)...... | $1 50 |
| Gold Dust. Do. ........... | 1 50 | Brick-dust. Do. ....... | 1 50 |
| Our Saturday Nights.......... | 1 50 | Home Harmonies. ............ | 1 50 |

## Mrs. E. P. Miller.

Mother Truth's Melodies—A new Children's picture Kindergarten...........$1 00

## Ernest Renan's French Works.

| | | | |
|---|---|---|---|
| The Life of Jesus....Translated.$1 75 | | The Life of St. Paul. Translated.$1 75 |
| Lives of the Apostles. Do. 1 75 | | The Bible in India—By Jacolliot. 2 00 |

## G. W. Carleton.

Our Artist in Cuba, Peru, Spain, and Algiers—150 Caricatures of travel.......$1 00

## Miscellaneous Publications.

Gervaise [L'Assommoir]—English translation from Emile Zola's French novel.$1 00
The Gospels in Poetry—Newly translated by Elijah H. Kimball............... 1 00
The Two Brides—A new novel by Rev. Bernard O'Reilly, L.D................ 1 50
A Southern Woman's Story—By Mrs. Phoebe Yates Pember................ 75
Parlor Amusements—Games, Tricks, and Home Amusements, by F. Bellew.. 75
Love [L'Amour]—Translation from Michelet's famous French work.......... 1 50
Woman [La Femme]— Do. Do. Do. 1 50
Verdant Green—A racy English college Story. With 200 comic illustrations.... 1 00
Ladies and Gentleman's Etiquette Book, of the Best Fashionable Society.. 1 00
Stratagems and Conspiracies—Attempts to defraud Life Insurance Companies. 2 00
Beatrice Cenci—Translated from the Italian novel, with portrait, by Guido...... 1 50
Morning Glories—A charming child's book of stories, by Louisa Alcott....... 1 50
The Culprit Fay—Joseph Rodman Drake's Poem. With 100 Illustrations..... 2 00
The Parlor Musical Album—Vocal and instrumental. Beautifully bound .... 1 50
Birds of a Feather Flock Together—By Edward A. Sothern, the actor...... 1 50
Trip from New York to San Francisco—Mrs. Frank Leslie. Illustrated... 2 00

## Recent Novels.

| | | | |
|---|---|---|---|
| Spell-Bound—By Alex. Dumas...$0 75 | | Widow Cherry—B. L. Farjeon..$0 25 |
| Heart's Delight—Mrs. Alderdice. 1 50 | | Solomon Isaacs— Do. Do. .. 50 |
| Wired Love—By E. C. Thayer... 50 | | Fallen Among Thieves—Rayne... 1 50 |
| Doctor Antonio—By Ruffini...... 1 50 | | The Baroness—Joaquin Miller... 1 50 |
| Once and Forever—Miss Grant.. 1 00 | | One Fair Woman— Do. Do. .. 1 50 |
| Under the Rose—Mrs. Wood.... 1 00 | | San Miniato—Mrs. Hamilton. ... 1 00 |
| Madame—By Frank Lee Benedict. 1 00 | | Another Man's Wife—Mrs. Hartt 1 50 |
| Hammer and Anvil— Do. 1 00 | | He and I—By Sarah B. Stebbins.. 50 |
| Little Guzzy—By Habberton. ... 1 00 | | Annals of a Baby— Do. Do. .. 50 |
| Doctor Mortimer—Fannie Bean.. 1 50 | | Me—By Mrs. Spencer W. Coe..... 50 |
| Lady Huckleberry's Opinions.. 25 | | Comic Primer—By Frank Bellew.. 25 |
| Edith Murray—Joanna Mathews. 1 50 | | That Awful Boy............... 50 |
| Outwitted at Last—S. A. Gardner 1 50 | | That Bridget of Ours.......... 50 |
| Vesta Vane—By L. King R...... 1 50 | | Bitterwood—By M. A. Green.... 1 50 |
| Louise and I—Charles R. Dodge. 1 50 | | Peccavi—By Emma Wendler...... 1 50 |
| My Queen—By Sandette.......... 1 50 | | Conquered—By a new author...... 1 50 |
| All For Her—A tale of New York. 1 00 | | St. Peter's Bride—Mrs. S. Harper 1 50 |
| All For Him—By All For Her,... 1 00 | | Fizzlebury's Girl—De Cordova... 50 |
| For Each Other— Do. Do. .. 1 00 | | Eros—A tale of love and soda water. 50 |
| Janet—An English novel.......... 1 50 | | Mr. Ghim's Dream.............. 1 00 |
| Innocents from Abroad. ...... 1 50 | | Parlor Table Companion........ 1 50 |
| Flirtation—A West Point novel.... 1 50 | | Trump Kards—Josh Billings..... 10 |
| H. M. S. Pinafore—The Play ... 10 | | What d'ye Say— do. .... 10 |

# G. W. CARLETON & CO.'S PUBLICATIONS.

## Miscellaneous Works.

| | |
|---|---|
| A Harvest of Wild Oats—A Novel, by Florence Marryatt | $1 50 |
| Milly Darrell—A Novel, by Miss M. E. Braddon, author of "Aurora Floyd" | 1 50 |
| Why Wife and I Quarreled—By the author of "Betsey and I are Out" | 1 00 |
| True Love Rewarded—A new Novel, by the author "True to the Last" | 1 50 |
| Threading My Way—The Autobiography of Robert Dale Owen | 1 50 |
| The Debatable Land—By Robert Dale Owen | 2 00 |
| Lights and Shadows of Spiritualism—By D. D. Home | 2 00 |
| Glimpses of the Supernatural—Facts, Records, and Traditions | 2 00 |
| Lion Jack—A New Illustrated Menagerie Book for Boys.—P. T. Barnum | 1 50 |
| West India Pickles—Journal of a Tropical Yacht Cruise. by W. P. Talboys | . 50 |
| G. A. Crofutt's Trans-Continental Tourist—New York to San Francisco | 1 50 |
| Laus Veneris and other Poems—By Algernon Charles Swinburne | 1 50 |
| Parodies and Poems and My Vacation—By C. H. Webb (John Paul) | 1 50 |
| Comic History of the United States—Livingston Hopkins. Illustrated | 1 50 |
| Mother Goose Melodies Set to Music—with comic illustrations | 1 00 |
| Jacques Offenbach's Experiences in America—From the Paris edition | 1 50 |
| How to Make Money; and How to Keep It—By Thomas A. Davies | 1 50 |
| Our Children—Teaching Parents how to keep them in Health.—Dr. Gardner | 1 00 |
| Watchman; What of the Night ?—By Dr. John Cumming, of London | 1 50 |
| Fanny Fern Memorials—With a Biography, by James Parton | 2 00 |
| Tales from the Operas—A Collection of Stories based upon the Opera Plots | 1 50 |
| New Nonsense Rhymes—By W. H. Beckett, with illustrations by C. G. Bush | 1 00 |
| Progressive Petticoats—A Satirical Tale, by Robert B. Roosevelt | 1 50 |
| Souvenirs of Travel—By Madame Octavia Walton Le Vert, of Mobile, Ala | 2 00 |
| Woman, Love, and Marriage—A spicy little Work, by Fred Saunders | 1 50 |
| The Fall of Man—A Darwinian Satire, by author of "New Gospel of Peace" | 50 |
| The Chronicles of Gotham—A Modern Satire, . Do. . Do. | 25 |
| Ballad of Lord Bateman—With illustrations by Cruikshank (paper covers) | 25 |
| The Yachtman's Primer—For amateur Sailors. T. R. Warren (paper covers) | 50 |
| Rural Architecture—By M. Field. With plans and illustrations | 2 00 |
| Transformation Scenes in the United States—By Hiram Fuller | 1 50 |
| Kingsbury Sketches—Pine Grove Doings, by John H. Kingsbury. Illustrated | 1 50 |

## Miscellaneous Novels.

| | | | |
|---|---|---|---|
| Led Astray—By Octave Feuillet | $1 50 | A Woman in the Case—Turner | $1 50 |
| She Loved Him Madly—Borys | 1 50 | Johnny Ludlow. From London ed. | 1 50 |
| Through Thick and Thin—Mery | 1 50 | Shiftless Folks—Fannie Smith | 1 75 |
| So Fair yet False—Chavette | 1 50 | A Woman in Armor—Hartwell | 1 50 |
| A Fatal Passion—C. Bernard | 1 50 | Phemie Frost—Ann S. Stephens | 1 50 |
| Seen and Unseen | 1 50 | Marguerite's Journal. For girls | 1 50 |
| Purple and Fine Linen—Fawcett | 1 75 | Romance of Railroad—Smith | 1 50 |
| Pauline's Trial—L. D. Courtney | 1 50 | Charette—An American novel | 1 50 |
| A Charming Widow—Macquoid | 1 75 | Fairfax—John Esten Cooke | 1 50 |
| The Forgiving Kiss—By M. Loth | 1 75 | Hilt to Hilt. Do. | 1 50 |
| Kenneth, My King—S. A. Brock | 1 75 | Out of the Foam. Do. | 1 50 |
| Heart Hungry—M. J. Westmoreland | 1 75 | Hammer and Rapier. Do. | 1 50 |
| Clifford Troupe. Do. | 1 75 | Warwick—By M. T. Walworth | 1 75 |
| Silcott Mill—Maria D. Deslonde | 1 75 | Lulu. Do. | 1 75 |
| John Maribel. Do. | 1 75 | Hotspur. Do. | 1 75 |
| Passing the Portal—Mrs. Victor | 1 50 | Stormcliff. Do. | 1 75 |
| Out of the Cage—G. W. Owen | 1 50 | Delaplaine. Do. | 1 75 |
| Saint Leger—Richard B. Kimball | 1 75 | Beverly. Do. | 1 75 |
| Was He Successful ? . . Do. | 1 75 | Beldazzle's Bachelor Studies | 1 00 |
| Undercurrents of Wall St. . Do. | 1 75 | Northern Ballads—E. L. Anderson | 1 00 |
| Romance of Student Life. . Do. | 1 75 | O. C. Kerr Papers. 4 vols. in one | 2 00 |
| To-Day. . . . . . . Do. | 1 75 | Victor Hugo—His autobiography | 2 00 |
| Life in San Domingo. . . Do. | 1 50 | Sandwiches—By Artemus Ward | 25 |
| Henry Powers, Banker. . Do. | 1 75 | Widow Spriggins—Widow Bedott | 1 75 |
| A Book about Doctors | 2 00 | Wood's Guide to N. Y. City | 1 00 |
| A Book about Lawyers | 2 00 | Loyal unto Death | 1 75 |
| Manfred—By Guerrazzi | 1 75 | Bessie Wilmerton—Westcott | 1 75 |